# Beyond Neutrality

# Beyond Neutrality

## Confronting the Crisis in Conflict Resolution

### Bernard S. Mayer

JOSSEY-BASS
A Wiley Imprint
www.josseybass.com

Published by Jossey-Bass
A Wiley Imprint
989 Market Street, San Francisco, CA 94103-1741   www.josseybass.com

Jossey-Bass books and products are available through most bookstores. To contact Jossey-Bass directly call our Customer Care Department within the U.S. at 800-956-7739, outside the U.S. at 317-572-3986, or fax 317-572-4002.

Jossey-Bass also publishes its books in a variety of electronic formats. Some content that appears in print may not be available in electronic books.

**Library of Congress Cataloging-in-Publication Data**

Mayer, Bernard S., date.
   Beyond neutrality : confronting the crisis in conflict resolution /
Bernard S. Mayer.
        p. cm.
Includes bibliographical references and index.
     ISBN 0-7879-6806-4 (alk. paper)
   1. Conflict management.   2. Mediation.   I. Title.
     HM1126.M39 2004
     303.6'9—dc22                                                    2003024184

Printed in the United States of America
FIRST EDITION
*HB Printing*                    10  9  8  7  6  5  4  3

# Contents

Preface      ix

## Part One: The Crisis

1. Conflict Resolution: A Field in Crisis      3

2. The Resistance to Conflict Resolution      41

3. The Use (and Misuse) of Mediation      82

4. Ten Beliefs That Get in Our Way      115

5. Conflict Resolution and Society      149

## Part Two: From Resolution to Engagement

6. The Power of Engagement      181

7. The Conflict Specialist      215

8. Embracing Advocacy      248

9. Redefining Conflict Resolution      280

References      297

About the Author      305

Index      307

To Ethan and Mark

# Preface

When we have the courage to face conflict, take on problems, learn from crisis, and work on our weaknesses, we grow. This is an outlook embedded in the values of most conflict resolution practitioners. I believe this applies to our field, as well as to each of us as individuals.

The practice and profession of conflict resolution has reached a comfortable, and therefore dangerous, point in its development. We are accepted, established, and routinely used in many areas. But we are also encountering some serious warning signs that we ought not be afraid to look at and learn from. These signs include the limitations on how we are used, the continuing skepticism about what we have to offer, the mixed results of research and evaluation, the struggles of our professional organizations, and the oversupply of conflict resolution practitioners.

The challenges we face now are both helpful and exciting. By facing them courageously and with an open mind, we can grow as a field and as practitioners. These challenges give us an opportunity to consider again who we are—what is at the heart of what we do, how we think, what we believe in, and what we have to offer others. In this effort, we can overcome the limits we have put on ourselves by how we have defined our purpose and role, and in the process, we will become a more powerful, respected, and ultimately useful field of practice.

If we are afraid to confront these challenges—to face our problems, look at our limits, or listen to what others are telling us, either directly or through their actions—we risk becoming less influential, respected, and useful. In fact, we risk losing our independent identity.

That is why I have written this book. This is the right time to take a few steps back and challenge some of our most cherished assumptions—for example, about cooperation, neutrality, respect, competition, social change, and the purpose of conflict resolution. And it is time to take seriously those who have criticized or dismissed our work—not necessarily agreeing with their conclusions but listening very carefully to their concerns. It's hard to do this, but it is also stimulating and energizing.

---

This effort is a loving critique of our field. Loving because I deeply respect the work of conflict resolution practitioners and the contribution that our field has made. Loving because I love the work that I have been privileged to do during my twenty-five years as a mediator, trainer, and conflict resolution practitioner. I believe conflict resolution practitioners offer something more than valuable—in fact, something essential—to our conflicted world. We have had the courage to take on difficult and important problems, challenge established approaches and institutions, and risk entering a new and unproven field that has had neither an established career path nor a secure source of revenue. This makes me optimistic that we can be creative and courageous in rethinking our field.

But this is also a critique—because we have fallen too easily into a limited set of roles and purposes. Moreover, we have not challenged ourselves to take a hard and unflinching look at the reasons for the limits we've encountered, the questionable nature of some of our most common assumptions, or the mixed results of our efforts. I think we should always be our own most knowledgeable and powerful critics. If we are not skeptics, then we will be more vulnerable to the criticisms of those who do not share our values and aspirations.

Some readers will disagree with parts of this book, and even with its basic premise. But whether or not you agree that we face a crisis, or with my characterization of the nature of this crisis, or with my sense of what we have to do to contend with it, I hope you'll be encouraged to think through—and discuss—your own assumptions about conflict and our field. I hope this is a book that provokes a reexamination of who we are, what we do, why we do it, and how we think about it. This book is not just a critique, however, but a proposal for how we can build on our values, skills, knowledge, and experience to overcome the barriers we face.

I suggest two broad changes in how we think of ourselves and the services we offer that, if adopted, can profoundly change how we present ourselves to the public and how we will be perceived by them. First, I propose that we grow beyond a focus on conflict resolution and consider how we can help people engage in all stages of a conflict process, even when resolution is neither their goal nor their option. Second, I argue that we need to get past our primary identification with the third-party role and consider a broader range of roles, in many of which we will not be acting as either neutrals or third parties.

---

This book begins with two basic beliefs. First, we need effective approaches to conflict more than ever before. During my career as a practicing mediator, we have not seen a significant reduction in the pernicious impact of conflict in our world, our communities, our organizations, or our society. If anything, the world is a more dangerous place to engage in conflict than ever before. Second, the field of conflict resolution has not reached its potential to have an impact on how conflict is conducted. The profession of conflict resolution is not making significant progress in having the impact we can and ought to have.

As I wrote this book, world events of course had an impact on me. I started thinking about how our field can play a more significant role in dealing with conflict in the months after September 11. During the actual writing, the United States marched down what seemed like an inexorable path toward war with Iraq, then fought that war, and is currently dealing with its aftermath. At the same time, the conflict in the Middle East rages on, and the alienation between the United States and the Islamic world seems to be deepening and creating the conditions for more violent interchanges in the future. Our limited role in carving out a response to these and other current events has underscored the need to consider how we can increase our reach as a field.

My colleagues and I at CDR Associates have had the opportunity to travel and work in many different parts of the world. We have also had the privilege of working in many different arenas of conflict, from family to community to organizational to public policy. Leaders and managers from many government agencies, corporations, international organizations, and nongovernmental organizations have used our services or attended our training programs. I am proud of the work we have done, but I cannot escape the feeling that we have usually worked at the periphery of the essential issues that these organizations or communities face rather than at the heart. I believe this is a feeling that many other conflict resolution professionals experience. But rather than examining what this is all about, we tend to avoid facing the roots of this dilemma. We can do better than this.

Another source of my thinking comes from my background as a social activist and a social worker. In both of these roles, albeit in very different ways, it has been essential for me to look at the root issues, the core problems, and the hidden strengths of a person, a group, or a social system. This is what we now need to do as a field. To do this, we need to listen to the feedback from others, even when it is given in an unbalanced or even unkind way.

I have always been attracted to conflict resolution in part because it draws on the values and skills of my social activist background and my psychotherapeutic training. It is a way in which I can help people grow, deal with the issues they are facing as individuals and as groups, and try to build a more peaceful, just, and democratic world. At CDR, we have often discussed our underlying purpose as promoting "deep peace" and "deep democracy" in our communities and our world. Deep peace and democracy go beyond forms and rules and are more than the absence of war or dictatorship. They reside in the values and attitudes of individuals and groups who compose a social structure. Systems that have embraced peace and democracy on this level are characterized by a peaceful approach to all conflicts, no matter how serious, and a meaningful involvement of everyone in the decisions that affect our lives. Achieving deep peace and democracy has been both a motivating and a comforting way of understanding our mission.

This kind of peace and democracy is not based on finding shallow solutions to big problems or on suppressing or dissipating strong feelings and serious conflicts. And it is not based on denying genuine problems, even if they are difficult to fix. But our field has often been criticized by social activists as doing just that. That's why we need to take a new look at our role in society. In particular, we need to face the elements of our work that may in fact contribute to the maintenance of social control. This is sometimes painful, because an important motivation for me has been the belief that the work I have been doing is clearly supportive of progressive social change. Certainly this is part of what we do, but the picture is more complicated. Consequently, we need the courage to reevaluate the real impact of our work if we are to reach our potential to promote deep peace and deep democracy.

---

The most important source of my thinking has been my own practice. I have had the opportunity to work on some incredibly challenging conflicts and with some amazing people, many of whom have appreciated my assistance. I have also encountered people who have wondered what difference the effort made, questioned the resources it took, or, worse, thought my intervention made things worse.

I used to joke that as a therapist, and later as a mediator, the way to feel successful is to take credit for everything that goes well and blame all the failures on circumstances or people beyond our control. In fact, I think we should err in the opposite direction. That is, we should appreciate that almost all of our successes are due to fortunate circumstances and to the underlying wisdom and courage of the disputants with whom we are working. We should also acknowledge that an important reason that we are sometimes less successful are the limitations of our own thinking, creativity, and skills.

I too have had doubts about what impact I might have made. Or maybe it is more accurate to say that I have occasionally swung between overvaluing my contribution and doubting whether anything I did made much of a difference at all. I do not know of any social worker, psychotherapist, teacher, mediator, counselor, or organizer who has not felt similar doubts. But these misgivings or questions can be healthy (when they are not taken to an extreme). Of course, learning from our successes is important, but facing our doubts may be even more valuable. I have tried to think through which of my beliefs and assumptions have been valuable, which have gotten in the way, and which are too simplistic to stand up to the complexity of conflict and time. My conclusions are reflected in this book.

---

In my previous book, *The Dynamics of Conflict Resolution: A Practitioner's Guide*, I examined the underlying concepts that are valuable to practitioners and are the foundation for conflict resolution practice across many different arenas. I wrote that book in the belief that these concepts are what really make us a field and that, along with our personal skills, they are what give us the potential to assist people in conflict.

In a sense, this book is a follow-up. Here, I ask us to think more deeply about our role, our impact, our assumptions, and our purposes—so we can break through the considerable limitations we have faced in using our potential to help people and systems in conflict. In doing so, we do not have to give up the basic values, concepts, or tools of our field; instead, we can build on them and consider how to apply them more broadly and more powerfully.

My intention has been to write a book that would be relevant and thought provoking to anyone interested in conflict. Inevitably, I have written from my own middle-class, Caucasian, male, North American perspective. Some of the assumptions that I have ascribed to the conflict field and some of the approaches to engagement and avoidance of conflict that I outline may reflect this perspective, despite the fact that I have worked in many different cultural settings and in many parts of the world. When I discuss, for example, our attitudes toward neutrality and our procedural focus, there is no question that I am taking a North American perspective. Nevertheless, I think the key issues raised here are relevant to the entire field.

This book is organized into two parts: the first on the crisis in our field, the second on the concept of conflict engagement. Chapter One is a summary of the nature of the crisis and the possible response we can make to it. Chapter Two summarizes the critiques of conflict resolution and the results of research on conflict resolution practice. Chapter Three looks specifically at mediation, which I view as the current signature service of conflict resolvers. Chapter Four examines and challenges some of our most cherished beliefs and assumptions. Chapter Five looks at the role that conflict resolution plays in society. Chapter Six starts the second part of the book by arguing for a refocus from conflict resolution to conflict engagement. Chapter Seven puts forward a concept of our role as a conflict specialist (or conflict engagement specialist). Chapter Eight looks specifically at the advocate's role as an important part of what we can offer as conflict specialists. The final chapter considers the future of our field.

## Acknowledgments

My most important teachers have always been the clients I've worked with and the students I've taught, and they continue to be. Their courage, enthusiasm, insights, and critiques are my most significant sources of understanding and professional growth. My wonderful colleagues and partners at CDR Associates have been my supporters, my guides, my co-learners, and my friends. I particularly thank Jonathan Bartsch, Dan Dozier, Suzanne Ghais, Mary Margaret Golten, J. Michael Harty, Judy Mares-Dixon, Julie McKay, Christopher Moore, Louise Smart, Susan Wildau, and Peter Woodrow for their support, insights, and review of my ideas and writing. Working with a team as talented, dedicated, and wise as this one has been one of the anchors that has allowed me to make this effort.

Many other friends and colleagues have supported me in various ways in developing this book. John Paul Lederach, William Ury, Carl Schneider, David Hart, Jay Rothman, Peter Adler, Wendell Jones, Zell Steever, Nina Meierding, Kathy Hale, John Lande, Guy and Heidi Burgess, Gail Bingham, Chip Hauss, Christopher Honeyman, and Margaret Shaw provided sounding boards and checks and balances for the development of my ideas. Arnie Shienvold copresented a workshop at the 2002 Association for Conflict Resolution conference in which some of the ideas in this book were first tested in public. All of these colleagues have pointed me in some valuable directions and helped me avoid some pitfalls; of course, I managed to find others to fall into despite their best efforts. Many people provided support and encouragement at different stages of this effort. Tom and Sara Mayer, Reggie Gray, Michael Covey, Allan Guitar, Bill Kramer, Judy Duffield-Kramer, Paul Osterman, Don Selcer, Howard Cohen, Chet Tchozewski, and Michele Bourgeois provided personal support as this book was conceptualized and written. Jennifer Mathers helped me with the literature search. Ellen and Hope Moon and Sibyl Macfarlane were wonderfully tolerant of my preoccupation with my computer and my tendency to cocoon myself during this past year.

There are two people whom I want to especially acknowledge. Alan Rinzler, my editor, first pressed me to develop my thinking more sharply before allowing me to plunge into this writing project. Throughout the process (a word he dislikes) of writing, he helped me find my voice, focus on my theme, keep my audience in mind, and write boldly and consistently. Alan did not hold back in either his criticisms or his praise—always honest and direct, always constructive. My biggest supporter, sounding board, reviewer, reference checker, and emotional keel is my partner, Julie Macfarlane. Her help has been constant, steady, and essential.

Finally, this book is dedicated to my most important teachers— the two people who constantly remind me why our work is important: my sons, Mark Mayer and Ethan Greene. They have always supported me in my work, even when it took me away from home way too often. Ethan and Mark have been my most honest critics and most unabashed supporters. They have always practiced what I have preached about conflict engagement. They are an inspiration, and I thank them from the bottom of my heart, now and always.

Boulder, Colorado                                     *Bernie Mayer*

# Beyond Neutrality

# PART ONE

# The Crisis

# 1
## Conflict Resolution: A Field in Crisis

Conflict resolution as a field is facing a serious crisis, and the way in which this crisis is approached will determine the future shape of the field—indeed, its very existence. The root of the crisis lies in the failure of the field to engage in its purpose seriously. That is, the conflict resolution field has too often failed to address conflict in a profound or powerful way. As a result, the public has not genuinely embraced the field. We are at a point where we can either face the nature of this crisis and grow as a result, or we can fail to adapt and, in that case, very likely cease to exist as an independent field of practice.

As is usually the case with crises, we face a significant opportunity as well as a major challenge. We can realize that opportunity if we are willing to grow beyond our dependence, indeed, our fixation, on neutrality as a defining characteristic of what we do and if we can see our role in conflict as far broader than that of dispute resolvers. Our challenge is to change our focus from conflict resolution to constructive conflict engagement and, accordingly, change our view of ourselves from neutral conflict resolvers to conflict engagement specialists. If we do this, we can become a more powerful and accepted force for changing the way conflict is conducted.

This does not mean abandoning old roles; rather, it means building on them and dramatically expanding what we offer to people in conflict. To achieve this transformation, we first have to face the nature of the crisis clearly and courageously, and then we have to open up our thinking about how we can broaden and deepen our roles in conflict. If we do this, we can rescue our field, but the challenges we face are great and the crisis serious.

## The Nature of the Crisis

We often congratulate ourselves about the growth of conflict resolution and its increasing recognition by the general public. We are no longer a marginal group of innovators presenting to an unaware public a completely new way of looking at and approaching conflict. But the field's growth has obscured the fact that it is facing a major crisis in achieving broad acceptance, profound impact, or mainstream use. As a result, the conflict resolution field has not yet lived up to its potential for changing the way conflict is handled in our organizations, communities, or societies. Signs of this crisis are plentiful.

### Symptoms of the Crisis

Conflict resolution professionals are not significantly involved in the major conflicts of our times. Many conflict resolution practitioners play useful but essentially marginal roles in large-scale public conflicts (examples are the Middle East, Iraq or Korea, and major environmental or social policy), but we are not involved at the center of the conflict or decision-making processes. This is not to say that conflict resolution professionals have never been involved at the center of major conflicts. Practitioners such as William Ury, Harold Saunders, and Roger Fisher have worked with governmental leaders on major conflicts. Organizations such as the Carter Center, the Consensus Building Institute, and CDR Associates have played an important role in a number of major conflicts. But their efforts, though important, are still the exception.

People involved in conflict do not readily or naturally turn to conflict resolvers. In many arenas, if mediators had to rely on people voluntarily asking for their services, they would have almost no business. Instead, people must be persuaded, cajoled, or mandated to use mediation and related services.

Advocates, activists, and governmental officials generally look on conflict resolution processes with great suspicion. After years of efforts at winning their support and trust and despite many experiences with conflict resolution efforts, activists and advocates still express a great deal of suspicion and skepticism about conflict resolution. People fear that collaborative problem-solving processes will prove expensive, time-consuming, compromising, and ineffective. As a result, there is ongoing resistance to participation in consensus-building dialogues and related conflict resolution processes.

Government agencies such as the Environmental Protection Agency and the Department of the Interior that in the past have used conflict resolution processes to fulfill aspects of their mission are questioning this approach and withdrawing resources from consensus-building efforts. Although they may continue to see mediation as valuable for solving internal personnel disputes, increasingly they are questioning conflict resolution forums as a means for dealing with the policymaking process. Some of this may reflect the particular beliefs of the current political leadership, but this trend also reflects questions that have arisen about the expense and effectiveness of consensus-building forums.

Many more people want to act as conflict resolvers than to use conflict resolution services. The interest people have shown in becoming mediators, facilitators, or dispute system designers has continued to outpace the interest of the public in using these services. Many conflict resolution organizations would have a hard time surviving were it not for the interest that people continue to show in conflict resolution training. But if the interest in becoming conflict resolution practitioners continues to outstrip the interest in using the services of these practitioners, people will become increasingly disinterested and perhaps resistant to training as well.

The culture of how conflict is handled on a societal, communal, organizational, and interpersonal level (at least in North America) may be slowly evolving. Participatory and interest-based approaches are gradually inserting themselves alongside more traditional hierarchical and positional models of decision making and conflict management. But it is not clear that this is related to the impact of the conflict resolution field.

Despite many efforts to achieve a genuine diversity of practice and practitioners, most conflict resolution organizations continue to be primarily middle class in orientation and overwhelmingly white. This may in part reflect problems in reaching out to people from diverse backgrounds and maintaining a consciousness about issues of diversity in all elements of our activities. However, we should also consider the possibility that the nature of the services offered and the concept of the field currently being articulated may speak to a narrow range of people. The underlying assumptions current in our field about what people want in conflict may reflect the class, ethnicity, and privileged status of the dominant groups in our field. For example, the concepts of neutrality and impartiality that we commonly rely on to describe our role and establish our credibility are grounded in a particular cultural context.

When people do turn to conflict resolvers, they often want approaches that are out of sync with the articulated values of the field. People often want advice, recommendations, and evaluations of their case; assistance in persuading others; or vindication of their actions and positions. Often disputants more readily look to people with power or a history of power to assist them, even if these people are neither trained in conflict resolution nor credible as neutrals. In this respect, the needs of people or institutions in conflict may be contradictory to or at least very different from the values and ideologies of conflict resolution practitioners.

At professional conferences, the ratio of practitioners who have succeeded in making conflict resolution their sustaining source of work to those aspiring to do so is abysmally low. Panels of successful mediators discussing their business development practices are plentiful, popular, and well attended, and probably not particularly helpful.

The field's very identity and independence as a field of practice is under attack. In fact, the conflict resolution field is facing the prospect of being entirely absorbed into existing professional disciplines, particularly law. Independent practitioner organizations such as the Association for Conflict Resolution, the Association of Family Conciliation Courts, the National Association for Community Mediation, and the National Conference of Peacemaking and Conflict Resolution (now PeaceWeb) struggle to achieve their place and to grow; some struggle for their survival; while the Alternative Dispute Resolution Section of the American Bar Association flourishes. Many practitioners question whether they can get the public acceptance, credentials, or professional standing through conflict resolution organizations that they can get through other professional identities.

Evaluations of conflict resolutions efforts are mixed. In many arenas, the promised savings in time, money, and energy are hard to document, and the research into consumer attitudes and satisfaction is mixed. Even where there are high levels of individual satisfaction with a conflict resolution program, there is little evidence that overall changes in the way decisions are made and conflicts are resolved have been engendered by conflict resolution efforts.

These are not isolated symptoms but part of a trend that should concern us greatly. The way we have constructed our field and our practice is being questioned in many quarters. Our services continue to be underused. The hopes we have had about transforming the culture of conflict and its resolution have not materialized. We need to face this crisis rather than avoid, deny it, or explain it away.

## Responding to the Crisis

None of this is news to conflict resolution practitioners. Since the beginning of our emergence as a field of practice in the late 1970s, we have talked about the disparity between the need for conflict resolution services and the market for them. We have had to engage in vigorous marketing efforts to become noticed, get referrals, and begin to overcome resistance to our approach. While some of this resistance may have been rooted in the professional protectionism of other fields or in adversarial institutional structures, this has hardly been the whole story. We have often had to resort to approaches that might violate our natural inclinations or beliefs to overcome this resistance—for example, mandatory referral systems, evaluative practices, and ongoing institutional contracts that threaten our stance of impartiality.

For years we have faced skeptics who have viewed us as naive at best and more likely as dangerously disempowering to people embroiled in conflict. In recent years, conflict resolution practitioners have often felt less like innovators of an important and creative new approach to major social issues and more like defenders of an established practice that is under attack from a variety of directions.

We have answered these criticisms, attempted to modify our practices, and tried to engage the skeptics in constructive dialogue— that is, after all, what we do. But have we genuinely listened to the doubts and criticisms? Have we really faced the nature of what we do that feeds this skepticism, this reticence to use our services? Have we looked deeply enough at our own interests, needs, assumptions, and concepts? Have we practiced what we preach to others in conflict or in crisis? I don't think so.

If we are to survive this crisis, learn from it, thrive as a field, and, most important, make a significant and positive difference in the way we approach conflict in our communities and in our world, then we must face the challenge. We must do so clearly, courageously, and wisely. We must be willing to question our assumptions and our habits of thinking and acting. And we can do this. We have the experience and skills to take a hard look at ourselves, build on our strengths, learn from our failures, and emerge stronger and better able to help transform the way conflict is conducted.

The story is certainly not all bleak. Conflict resolution has made an impact in many ways. Mediation, arbitration, policy dialogues, facilitated consensus-building processes, school-based conflict resolution programs, restorative justice efforts, collaborative law projects, shared neutrals programs, and the like are an accepted and still growing feature of the decision-making and dispute resolution landscape. A growing pool of trained and talented conflict resolvers exists. Our understanding of conflict and conflict resolution continues to grow, and people are far less likely to have a blank stare when we identify ourselves as conflict resolvers or mediators. Many organizations and institutions have come to rely on our services— the courts, labor unions, human resource departments, planning agencies, schools. More than individuals in conflict, these agencies are our most important constituents: they keep us in business and appreciate our services. This is a source of great hope, because it is evidence that we have something important to offer to people and organizations in conflict. We can build on the successes we have achieved, the track record we have established, and the credibility that we have developed.

In facing the crisis, we should not lose sight of what we have accomplished and what we have to offer. But we should not hide behind these either. By having the courage to look deeply at the limits of our practice and our thinking, we can emerge as a much more powerful field of practice with a far greater capacity to address the significant conflicts of our time. Let's consider some of the signs of the crisis more fully.

## Where Is Conflict Resolution in Major Conflicts?

The significance of a conflict depends on people's relationship to the issues involved. To someone who is seriously affected, any conflict can seem major. Mediators have helped many people through divorce, grievances, neighborhood disputes, and environmental conflicts, and for the people involved, these conflicts are likely to be seen as major disputes— conflicts that really count. As a field, we can look with satisfaction at our role in helping people work on these issues. But we must also face the limits implied by this success.

Consider how where we are as a profession is mainly remarkable for where we are absent. After September 11th, did we have a role to play? Were we part of the process of understanding the underlying conflict that led to the terrorist attacks? Were we involved in developing a strategy to respond to it? In considering how to build better relations with the Islamic world, are we seen as important resources by government leaders, international organizations, involved nongovernmental groups, the media, or the general public? If we had an opportunity to advise policymakers about how to deal with concerns about weapons of mass destruction, would we have anything to say? When our professional organizations have made policy statements about these issues, has anybody noticed, our own members included? In fact, the Association for Conflict Resolution issued a policy statement on weapons of mass destruction suggesting a variety of alternative approaches to dealing with Iraq and other countries in November 2002. No media coverage or even membership interest ensued.

While I was writing this book, war was impending with Iraq, a crisis was brewing concerning nuclear weapons development in North Korea, the situation in the Middle East continued to deteriorate, and India and Pakistan seemed close to war. Perhaps these situations have always been the domain of diplomats, politicians, and area experts, and we should not expect to be part of the policy formation process. However, what is striking is the almost total absence of members of our profession from any public discussion of these issues. There seems to be a nonstop series of discussions, commentaries, panels, interviews, and debates in the media about these topics. Diplomats, politicians, journalists, military experts, area experts, political analysts, pollsters, legal experts, and an assortment of other media favorites are repeatedly consulted, but not a conflict resolution practitioner is in sight in these discussions—including some who are quite well known (Roger Fisher, William Ury, and even Jimmy Carter come to mind). We might be able to identify a couple of instances in which conflict resolution practitioners have been interviewed or had commentaries published about alternative approaches to dealing with these escalating conflicts, mostly in local media outlets, but that has been the extent of our involvement.

In November 2002, as a spokesperson for the Association for Conflict Resolution on Iraq, I was interviewed by a large midwestern radio station about alternative approaches to dealing with Iraq. I discussed the importance of understanding the underlying interests of all parties, of considering how to approach a negotiation in an integrative manner, and how there was no necessary contradiction between doing so and adopting a tough stance on weapons of mass destruction. Two things were interesting to me about this interview. One was that the interviewer, whose views favored negotiation, was interested not in how to resolve this conflict but rather how to engage me in the political conflict as a participant. More than anything else, he wanted me to judge the administration's performance. The other was that despite thinking about this issue a great deal, I did not feel that as a conflict resolution practitioner, I had much to say that would be particularly interesting to the public or of value to policymakers. To me, this is symptomatic of a basic problem we face as conflict resolvers—and is a result of an overly narrow way of thinking about conflict and its resolution.

To blame our minimal involvement in major conflicts on the perversity of the media or the indifference of the public would be to draw exactly the wrong conclusion. Conflict resolution practitioners have to face the fact that people have not seen our relevance to these issues, and if we are honest with ourselves, we as conflict resolvers probably don't feel that we have much to offer either. We can talk about looking at underlying interests, separating the people from the problem, convening dialogues, engaging in citizen-to-citizen diplomacy, and addressing the emotional dimension of the conflict. These might be worthwhile observations, but they do not resonate with people concerned with or embroiled in such situations. On some level, the public knows something we have to face. What we have to offer in major conflicts is quite limited, even if the powers that be were to listen to us.

We can ask the same question about the role of conflict resolution professionals in major conflicts in almost any arena. What role are we playing on major environmental issues such as drilling in the Arctic National Wilderness Reserve, global warming, revising rules about logging in national forests, or energy policy? Or in the social policy arena: affordable housing, health care, immigration policy, welfare, day care, drug abuse, capital punishment, incarceration practices, or abortion.

Significant conflicts exist in all these arenas, but the role of our field in helping address them has been minimal. Some colleagues have participated in dialogues about these issues or have helped to deal with specific manifestations of these conflicts, mostly at a local level. Others are trying to build organizational frameworks to bring our skills to bear on a larger scale. But so far these efforts have been fairly peripheral—certainly in their impact on policy.

This raises four important questions: What is a conflict resolution practitioner? What role do we currently play in major conflicts? Why don't we play a more expanded role? Should we care?

## What Is a Conflict Resolution Practitioner?

If we think of conflict resolution practitioners primarily as third-party neutrals, that is, as mediators, arbitrators, facilitators, or fact finders, then our relevance will be limited by the degree that those roles are considered useful in any particular conflict. Since that is how we have primarily thought of ourselves and presented ourselves to the public, it is not surprising that our relevance has been limited accordingly. Instead, I suggest we view conflict resolution practitioners (or, as I shall propose we consider ourselves, specialists in conflict engagement) as people who have special knowledge of the dynamics of conflict, conceptual tools that assist people in developing constructive approaches to conflict, and a range of roles they can play and intervention strategies they can use in assisting people who are involved in conflict. In this sense, conflict resolution practitioners are not defined simply by a role they play or their neutral stance. Instead, they are defined by their knowledge of conflict and the variety of ways in which it can be approached.

As in other fields, people may specialize in providing particular types of services on which they make particular efforts to become adept, such as mediation or facilitation. But these practices should be seen as manifestations of a larger field out of which they arise and which provides the intellectual and institutional framework for our work.

Everyone at one time or another is a conflict resolver, from presidents to school teachers, from generals to parents. In that sense, conflict resolvers are involved in all conflicts. But there is a difference between conflict resolution as a basic human skill and conflict resolution as a field of practice. The temptation is to define that difference in terms of the neutral role, but that is a limiting self-concept. As important as the neutral can be, it is only one role, and often a very limiting one in conflict. Instead, our field should seek to define itself more by its understanding of conflict and its ability to translate that understanding into practical ways of intervening in conflict— or helping other individuals or groups to intervene—from a number of different roles or stances.

## What Role Do Practitioners Play in Major Conflicts?

When major conflicts erupt, the role of conflict resolution practitioners has been very circumscribed. We are only occasionally involved in attempting to resolve these conflicts, and we seldom have a presence in the core arenas in which these issues are worked through. The role of conflict resolvers in addressing major conflicts tends to have the following characteristics:

- *Localized.* The more local the conflict is, the more significant a role we are likely to be asked to play, although even with local conflicts, once they erupt beyond a certain level of intensity, conflict resolution practitioners are less likely to be viewed as an important resource. For example, we are much more likely to be asked to assist with a dispute involving a complaint about racial discrimination in a hiring process than with affirmative action as a national policy.

- *Peripheral*. Conflict resolvers are seldom asked to involve themselves in the core issue of major conflicts, but they are sometimes used to work on peripheral aspects. We may not be involved in working on a major peace initiative in the Middle East, but we have been involved in helping to develop an approach to sharing water resources in that part of the world. We have been asked to conduct public meetings and facilitate advisory groups on significant environmental or social policy issues, but we are less frequently involved at the heart of the decision-making process. Some of these initiatives have been extremely useful, particularly some of the "Track II" (that is, nongovernmental) efforts to bring citizens from warring countries together in various formats, but nevertheless, these tend to be one step off from the central efforts to resolve the conflict.

- *Advisory*. We are often asked to assist with facilitating advisory processes, but we are less frequently involved with actual decision-making negotiations. In many school districts, difficult decisions are being made about closing older neighborhood schools for reasons of demographics and efficiency. Conflict resolvers are often involved in facilitating an advisory panel or public involvement process to provide input to decision makers about this, but we are less likely to be involved in negotiations where actual decisions about closures and trade-offs related to them are made.

- *Short term*. Conflict resolvers tend to be brought in on a short-term and specific basis to deal with a particular manifestation of a dispute, even when the issue itself is of long-term duration. Sometimes this is an asset, since it allows for a different perspective and less involvement in the conflict dynamics. But the short-term nature of our involvement can also breed distance, distrust, and superficiality in our approach. In many locations in the West, there have been decades of dispute about how to allocate water among farmers, urban interests, wildlife preserves, and recreational interests. Conflict resolvers are more likely to be brought in to deal with a specific manifestation of this issue, perhaps during a particularly dry season, than to be involved on a long-term basis dealing with the ongoing nature of the problem.

- *Narrow.* When we do involve ourselves in major disputes, we tend to focus on a narrow approach to the issues, not on the broader or deeper aspects that ultimately fuel the conflict. We work on narrow agreements about land use, emissions, forest plans, individual grievances, or contracts, but we seldom have access to or get involved in the broader policy or systemic issues that these represent.

The role that conflict resolvers have played in major conflicts has often been helpful, sometimes healing, and frequently appreciated. In consort with other resolution efforts, we have occasionally had a profound impact, such as in the cumulative effect of years of citizen dialogues and lower-level peacemaking efforts in Northern Ireland. A number of conflict resolution organizations, such as Search for Common Ground, Partners for Democratic Change, and the Mennonite Central Committee, have committed themselves to long-term involvement in societies experiencing serious conflict, and their contributions have been significant. My point is not to negate the value of what these and other efforts have accomplished. Nor do I mean to bemoan the limits of our role, but to understand it and learn what it means for who we are and how we are seen, and the implications of this for the conflict resolution field.

## Why Don't We Play a More Expanded Role?

Answering this question is key to understanding who we are and where we are going as a field. A major purpose of this book is to offer an analysis of and prescription for how to be more useful and accepted as resources in conflict. Five factors seem paramount in why we are not more involved in resolving major public conflicts:

- *Disputants do not necessarily want resolution.* People want to win, to build a movement, to carry on an important struggle, to achieve meaning, to address basic issues, to gain political advantage, or other similar goals. Resolution implies too shallow an outcome or goal to many. When we were asked to facilitate the Alaska Wolf Summit in the 1990s to discuss wolf control policy in Alaska, it was clear that most of the participants on all sides of the issue saw this as a long-term struggle to which no resolution was likely. Furthermore, for many, waging the struggle was more important than achieving a consensus on wolf management policy.

• *Disputants do not think of themselves as in a conflict.* They think of themselves as involved in a cause, a popular movement, a political effort, or a policy debate, and our role is not seen as relevant to these. Conflict implies more of a relationship, an interactive process, with a potential outcome—resolution—than many people will accept. Often, accepting that a conflict exists implies that others involved have either a certain amount of power or standing that requires that they be dealt with in some way. In the wolf summit, many Alaskans did not view themselves in a conflict with national animal rights groups. They might have viewed those groups as creating a problem, but they would not have granted them the status of being participants in a conflict.

• *No one, including ourselves, is very clear about what we have to offer.* Seldom do people embroiled in major conflict think that what they need are professional neutrals or dispute system designers. We neither promote ourselves nor are normally hired because of our technical expertise, political power, or organizing skills. In fact, people are often confused about exactly what it is that we do offer. Process is a subtle concept for most people, and what those in conflict are most aware of is their need for power, protection, and good solutions. When people understand what it is we offer, they often either feel no need for this or are very suspicious, perhaps viewing our services as potential vehicles for manipulation. We are often unclear ourselves about what our real value is to people stuck in conflict, and we often define our potential contribution in limiting terms.

• *Our approach to resolution often seems superficial.* We often seem too eager for resolution, and as a result, it sometimes seems that we are seeking solutions that do not match the level of depth at which participants experience a conflict. Too often, people feel we are promoting a lowest-common-denominator approach or a facile or short-term solution that does not address the underlying seriousness of a conflict. Focusing on communication, mutual interests, or creative exchanges may be important and helpful, but deeply engaged disputants often do not see this as addressing their deepest concerns and values. In the Alaskan situation, we might have been able to make progress on a wolf control or habitat management plan, but no one felt that we would be able to take on the deeper issues about Alaskan identity, the value (and definition) of wilderness, local control versus national interests, and other basic issues that were close to the heart of what most people really cared about.

• *People are suspicious about neutrality*. People often do not trust our neutrality. They are suspicious of the concept and question, often correctly, whether we can genuinely be as neutral, impartial, and unbiased as we say we are. More important perhaps, neutrality is not what people embroiled in deep conflict are usually looking for. They want assistance, advocacy, advice, power, resources, connections, or wisdom. We tend to rely heavily on a neutral stance to obtain trust and credibility, whereas disputants are more inclined to accept the procedural help of a nonneutral who brings other resources to bear and to doubt the practical usefulness of someone who is genuinely neutral. There are times when neutrality is essential, but conflict resolvers place too much reliance on it as a defining feature of the role we play. In many situations, if we emphasized this less, we might actually be trusted more.

This raises the question about who we are if we are not neutrals. How are we different from lawyers, advocates, activists, decision makers, or substantive consultants? The answer to this will grow from a deeper understanding of and belief in what we have to offer, in the value of our understanding about conflict dynamics, and in our clarity about the multiple roles we can play and the skills we can offer to people in conflict.

## Should We Care?

If we continue to be used as mediators, arbitrators, facilitators, and dispute system designers and if the results of our efforts are positive, why should we care if we are not seen as players in major conflicts?

Perhaps as individual practitioners or organizations, we should not, but as a field, we most definitely should. Conflict resolution as a field of practice is relatively new (although not as a human endeavor), and our survival as an independent discipline is far from assured. We are still more a collection of roles, practice approaches, and overlapping values than a well-integrated field with common intellectual frameworks, independent educational structures, and a clear and publicly understood role. To a large extent, these are provided to us by our other fields of origin (for example, law, mental health, labor relations, human resources, or planning).

Historically, we have been more of a movement than a profession (see Chapter Five). As a movement, we have been committed to altering the way decisions are made, disputes resolved, policy debated, and contracts negotiated. To do so, we have proposed new professional roles that have challenged the existing practices of other fields. These fields have responded by trying to subsume conflict resolution roles within their own activities. Lawyers now embrace mediation as one of their areas of expertise. So do many mental health practitioners, planners, and organizational development specialists.

We should be pleased to see our practices and ideas mainstreamed in this way. But unless there is also a strong independent field of conflict resolution, then the basic philosophy, values, and alternative ways of thinking that the field represents will get seriously diluted and perhaps lost. Currently, the image we have of ourselves as a social movement, which is significantly altering the way society handles its conflicts, is not matched by the reality of our impact. A clear and independent identity seems essential to realize the underlying goals and values of the field. That is why our lack of involvement in the broadest conflicts of our time is concerning.

If we viewed ourselves as divorce specialists, environmental consultants, or labor relations specialists, then we would want to be seen as having something relevant to say on major family, environmental, or labor issues. But that is not the primary way we have chosen to identify ourselves. Instead, we have identified ourselves as conflict resolvers. We have taken on this identity because of our concerns about how conflict is handled and our belief that we have something of importance to offer in this arena. Those concerns are well founded, and we do have something of importance to offer. But neither the general public nor policymakers seem to see us as experts in dealing with conflict. Instead, they view us as people who play a very specific and limited role of occasional usefulness.

If this continues to be how we are seen, we will eventually lose our precarious standing as an independent field of practice (although conflict resolution may continue to exist as a field of study). Mediation, for example, may come to be seen as a specific role that lawyers, social workers, or management consultants occasionally choose to play. The professional training and knowledge base that will be viewed as important will be the particular substantive knowledge of practitioners, not their broader or deeper understanding of conflict. In other words, conflict resolution as such will continue to be viewed as a secondary area of knowledge—more as a set of specific skills and a particular cluster of roles than as a freestanding and rich field. We may well head down this road, but if we do, our ability to shape the way conflicts and decisions are handled in our society will be curtailed, and our potential to help people embroiled in serious conflict will continue to be limited.

Our field has been able to maintain a certain élan as a new and creative endeavor, and we have received attention from other fields, and to some extent from the public, disproportionate to our actual numbers or involvement in conflicts. We have been able to establish ourselves as an innovative movement that has challenged the traditional way other fields and significant institutions, such as the courts and government agencies, conduct their business. But eventually, movements like ours have to become institutionalized and their value accepted by society if they are to have an important ongoing role. Fields such as psychology, social work, and education have made this transition. Others, such as organizational development and cross-cultural studies, have not yet succeeded in this and are facing many of the same challenges we are.

We cannot continue to fall back on our role as innovators as the source of our professional credibility or impact. We have probably reached the limit of our potential influence and impact on this basis alone. An innovative professional movement that does not achieve a level of institutionalization and is not broadly accepted by the public it intends to serve will begin to fade in influence and resources. Until the late 1960s, community organization and group work were considered to be two of the three major fields of social work education and practice. Graduate programs, field placements, accreditation procedures, and job classifications in social work were organized around this concept. But during the 1970s and 1980s, the viability of these approaches from the perspective of the public and the client base faded. The values and skills of organizing and group work are still relevant, but with few exceptions, these are no longer independent specialties within social work practice. The perspective and skill base that these disciplines promoted may not have been entirely lost, but they have a decidedly diminished presence and impact within social work and in the larger communities that they once served. New fields emerge; old ones disappear. Sometimes this is a sign of maturation and development. But I believe something important will be lost if the field of conflict resolution cannot find a permanent and meaningful place in helping address the most serious conflicts of our time and if instead it is absorbed into existing fields of practice. The best way to avoid this is to face the sources of resistance that we encounter and to learn from these.

So even if many mediators, facilitators, arbitrators, and other conflict resolution practitioners continue to have work, the field's lack of significant involvement in major conflicts is both a symptom of a larger problem and a warning sign that should not be ignored. Our continued existence as a field is related to how relevant we are seen to helping understand and deal with the major conflicts that we can read about every day or hear on the nightly news. Right now, we are not seen as very relevant. This is one major indicator of the crisis in our field. A second has to do with people's reluctance to use our services.

## What the Public Wants, and What Resolvers Deliver

Conflict resolvers should not be surprised that we have interests that do not exactly coincide with those of our clients or the public we serve. Anyone who has ever mediated a case involving advocates or agents, be they attorneys, union officials, or human resource personnel, knows that the interests of the advocate and those of the client are often very different and sometimes significantly out of sync with each other. Why should we be any different? We have a vision of who we are, what we have to contribute, and how we feel conflicts should be approached. This vision is hardly the same as the goals and aspirations of the client population we serve, though not in contradiction to it, and facing this can be uncomfortable for us. But what is harder to accept is the frequency with which people do not want what we have to offer at all—or at least not on the terms we offer it.

### What Conflict Resolution Practitioners Offer

Generally we feel that if we bring disputing parties together in a safe atmosphere using a thoughtful process, they will be able to communicate their concerns, listen to each other, identify alternatives, and make wise decisions. For many years, we have offered this service, these skills, and this vision to the public in one way or another. Along with this have come the values and rhetoric of empowerment, self-determination, participatory democracy, and nonviolence. We have deeply believed in these values, they reflect our sense of what must be cultivated and nurtured in our society, and very few of the disputants we work with would disagree with these in the abstract. Furthermore, conflict resolution practitioners have shown that their approaches can work in many different situations. People repeatedly report high levels of satisfaction from their experiences in mediation (for example, see Wissler, 2002) almost regardless of the mediator's approach. So what is the source of the resistance to our work that we so often encounter?

## How We Understand the Public Resistance to What We Offer

If the public seems to accept the value premise of our field and if there is a genuinely high level of satisfaction with the outcome of conflict resolution efforts, why is it that people are so often reluctant to use our services? Why must the public be cajoled, persuaded, and even forced into using mediators? Why do people so frequently approach collaborative dialogues with foreboding, resistance, suspicion, or fear? One common explanation is that they don't understand conflict resolution or mediation, that they need more education, that it is still too unfamiliar. A second is that advocates, particularly lawyers, are threatened by the encroachment of conflict resolvers into what has traditionally been their domain and are therefore throwing up roadblocks and steering their clients away from conflict resolution processes. These dynamics may be present, and probably often are, but they hardly explain the persistence of this dilemma. For well over twenty years, the public has been hearing about and experiencing conflict resolution, facilitation, and other consensus-building processes. Lawyers and union representatives have often (though not always) embraced it, and many are eager to become mediators.

Some at least rudimentary knowledge of conflict resolution is very widespread. William Ury (2000) tells of an experience he had in 1995 on a little island off Papua New Guinea. He was walking by a local bar when some people inside called out to him and asked what he was doing in New Guinea. "I've come to learn about clan war and how to stop it," he said. "Oh you mean 'conflict resolution,'" was the response of a man who, it turned out, had just attended a workshop at his church about mediation (p. 131). Though the education may not be perfect, though there are many institutional roadblocks to the integration of conflict resolution processes into traditional decision making, and though some in the legal and advocacy community continue to show resistance, we are no longer in a situation of being an unknown entity about which the public is little informed. Something more is going on in relationship to the public's reluctance to use our services—something that has to do with a lack of congruence between the values, assumptions, and interests of conflict resolvers and those of the public we seek to serve.

Two assumptions, both entirely in keeping with our values about conflict, will help us understand and react more productively to the issue of use and resistance. First, we should assume that the public knows exactly what it is doing and does not need some external authority to tell them how to proceed. Second, we should assume that if we dig deeply enough, we can find the level at which our interests and values and those of the wider public we serve are not in conflict—that an integrative solution is possible. If we assume the public knows what it is doing, then we have to go beyond the solution of more education and more mandatory referrals to conflict resolution processes. If we assume that we do have something to offer that is congruent with the public's interests, then we have to identify what it is and how we can offer it.

## What People Want in Conflict

What does the public, that is, people who are embroiled in conflict, want, and how is it different from what we offer? McEwen and others have pointed to an interesting paradox (McEwen and Milburn, 1993). When people participate in mediation, they report high levels of satisfaction, but nonetheless they resist participation. This pattern has endured for years. What is the source of the resistance? There are six needs that many feel will not be met by mediation or other consensus-building processes:

• *Voice*. People embroiled in conflict want to be heard, and heard in a powerful way by people whom they think count. These people are not necessarily those with whom they are in conflict, but instead are the people who represent social authority and cultural legitimacy. In traditional litigation, the judge represents that authority and legitimacy, although the actual experience of appearing before a judge does not always give people a sense of voice. The premise of confidentiality, while allowing for a more flexible and low-stakes approach to the resolution of conflict, may actually interfere with people's ability to have a voice. This is also true in collaborative dialogues, which seem to provide far less a sense of public voice than do lawsuits, media appearances, demonstrations, and other forms of more public expression (Silbey, 2002).

Moreover, people want their voice to be expressed and heard in a way that reinforces their sense of who they are and is congruent with their values. If people's self-image and belief system reinforce consensus-building approaches, then they may be drawn to those forums, but many disputants are looking for an approach that promotes their sense of themselves as powerful, decisive, and courageous. Consensus-building approaches may not offer this kind of reinforcement.

- *Procedural justice.* When people say they want their "day in court," it is not just about being heard. It's also about being given the same fair opportunity to resolve their conflicts or meet their needs that they feel everyone else is being given. In fact, this might be naive, because the courts do not treat everyone equally. But they purport to, and this is the underlying presumption of a rule of law. Also, people believe that they more or less know the basic rules of the litigation game, flawed though they may be, even though their vision of these may actually be extremely distorted by the romanticization of legal proceedings in the media and popular culture. Whether through the courts or some other forum involving a process that people believe is clear, predictable, consistent, and powerful, people are looking for a process to resolve conflict that they view as just and fair (Welsh, 2001a). The very fact that conflict resolution processes genuinely offer a more flexible, individualized, and often private process can interfere with their ability to fulfill people's desire for procedural justice.

I was once asked to arbitrate a case involving the eviction of a public housing tenant for behavior threatening to his neighbors. Although it seemed quite clear that he would be able to achieve a better housing deal through a negotiated agreement, he insisted on going through with the full panel hearing because he did not believe his case would have received a "fair hearing" otherwise. In particular, he wanted to make sure that the procedural rights the housing contract gave him were completely exercised before he would agree to leave the housing project, even though it was apparent that he would obtain a better outcome in private negotiations with the housing managers.

* *Vindication.* Disputants in traditional conflict resolution processes usually do not get the kind of vindication they desire, and mostly they know this, but there is always the chance that they might. Disputants do not usually see their conflict in purely utilitarian terms. Considerable normative aspects are generally involved. Disputants often believe that their conflict is not just about perceived incompatible interests, but about right and wrong, and that the needs of the different parties are not of equal worth. Vindication is therefore important—vindication in the sense that the outcome somehow furthers disputants' sense that they are right and that their cause is just. Seldom does this kind of vindication occur. The fantasy of a powerful representative of social norms looking down from the bench and indicating that one party to a dispute is just and righteous and the other shallow and evil may almost always be just that: a fantasy not likely to be realized. But it is at least conceivable. An analogous image is that of the righteous political forces sweeping the evil politicians or organizational leadership away and replacing them with people with virtuous approaches to public policy or corporate decision making. Such pure and simple solutions to serious conflicts seldom, if ever, take place, but they too are at least conceivable.

The premise of most conflict resolution practice is that the normative or value-based elements of conflict are not a productive focus and that people need to let go of their desire for total victory and accept an outcome that will meet their most essential interests. This is true whether we are talking about a medical malpractice suit, a divorce, a grievance, an environmental struggle, or the conflict in Northern Ireland. Thus, the very desire or need for vindication is negated in most conflict resolution processes. The problem is that vindication may in fact represent people's deepest needs. Legal, political, or public confrontation approaches, although they may make it more costly and difficult to meet other needs in a creative and effective manner, do not reject the need for vindication as a premise to participation in the process itself. Conflictants are often willing to give up on the hope for vindication, but they are able to do this only if they feel they have given their best shot at obtaining it. Seldom do people feel that collaborative processes are their best shot.

• *Validation*. Related to vindication, but not quite the same, is the need for validation—validation of feelings and point of view. Most people who feel hurt, unfairly attacked, or victimized do not want to give up their angry or outraged feelings too readily. Many of us can recall a time when we have been reluctant to give up our righteous anger about something even though we learned that we were mistaken about what had occurred. We may have been happy to learn that the situation was not as awful as we had assumed, but it is still sometimes hard to give up the emotions that have been stirred up. Sometimes people refuse to accept new information simply because of this.

Most conflict resolution techniques do not require people to sacrifice their feelings and may even offer an opportunity to express them that is not available in more traditional methods. Nonetheless, the goal of establishing an integrative, face-to-face problem-solving forum makes it hard to maintain these feelings with the intensity that they have been experienced. By emphasizing personal interaction and the need to understand each other's point of view, most conflict resolution processes almost inevitably require a softening of the expression and often the experience of the emotional side of conflict. They also call on people to begin reexamining their often polarized, stereotyped, and simplistic view of each other. This is both a primary value of conflict resolution procedures and a negative incentive for those who are so committed to their views about others that they do not want them challenged by face-to-face interchange. The validation many conflictants desire is to some extent contradicted by these typical approaches to conflict resolution.

- *Impact.* Disputants want to experience two types of impact: specific and broad. Specifically, people want to feel that they can have an impact on their own situation. In that sense, they want to feel empowered. The paradox here is that many forms of conflict resolution offer people the potential to have a more direct impact than traditional approaches, but to have confidence in their ability to have this impact, they have to have confidence in their own power—personal and structural. Often people engaged in serious conflict do not have such confidence. Effective conflict resolution processes can help them experience their power and apply it in a meaningful way. But they are often discouraged about engaging in these processes because they either do not sense that they can be powerful in these forums or they want to associate with the power of others, such as advocates. In many divorces, for example, parties are unwilling to give up the traditional use of lawyers as spokespeople or negotiators and to use them instead as advisers or consultants. This may account for some of the reservations that people express about divorce mediation or collaborative law. Even if people can be very powerful as direct parties to a negotiation, they often do not have confidence in or trust this personal exercise of power.

The desire to have a broad influence is a second dimension to people's desire for impact. This is related to their need for connectivity and meaning—to be part of a larger struggle or larger issue. In most conflict situations, disputants see their issue or grievance as part of a larger cause or drama. Each individual grievance in a workplace can readily be seen as a small battle in a larger struggle between labor and management. Each equal employment opportunity complaint can be viewed against a systematic background of institutional racism, homophobia, ageism, or sexism. Each environmental dispute can be seen as part of a larger struggle to preserve the environment or the economic viability of regulated organizations. While some conflict resolution processes address broader issues in ways that enable participants to experience the social impact of their efforts, these are the exception. In most situations, participants are asked to reach agreements about their individual conflict, and these agreements are often private, confidential, and non-precedent setting. As a result, people often have to disassociate, at least in part, the immediate agreement or conflict from the larger social issue. This can undercut the sense that people want to have that they are part of a larger struggle.

• *Safety.* Finally, people want to feel safe and protected. For most of us, engaging in conflict feels risky and scary. When people overcome their avoidance patterns and take on a conflict, whether by choice or involuntarily, they are often pulled in conflicting directions. They want to feel empowered and effective, but also safe and secure. Conflict resolution processes attempt to provide a safe environment in which people can discuss their concerns without fear of retaliation, but for many, safety is more likely to be found in a different way. For some, safety is more likely to be experienced in a formal process with very clear rules and procedures. For others, it is more likely to be achieved through the use of representatives who will engage the conflict on behalf of the disputants. Ironically, for many people, the use of advocates or formal systems offers the (usually false) hope that they can both engage in and avoid conflict at the same time. Therefore, conflict resolution processes can sometimes seem less safe than more adversarial or advocacy-based approaches.

None of these key needs are necessarily contradictory to the premises of conflict resolution, and the alternatives to which people may turn are often no better at meeting these needs. However, the ways in which we have structured our services and thought about what we have to offer have often implied to disputants that they were going to have to give up their deeper purposes or needs in order to accept our help. If this continues to be the case, and people continue believing that they have to sacrifice their aspirations to achieve voice, justice, vindication, validation, impact, or safety in order to engage in conflict resolution processes, then we can continue to expect resistance to our services from those who are deeply embroiled in conflict. Unless we address these concerns, conflict resolution as a field of practice will remain marginalized in impact and limited in scope. To address them, we have to challenge some of the most fundamental presumptions we have made about who we are and what we offer.

## Four Problematic Assumptions of the Conflict Resolution Field

The underlying nature of the problem we face lies in our own self-identity—how we view who we are as a field and what it is that we have to offer people. We are victims of our own overly narrow view of ourselves and what it is we bring to conflict. This view may have made it easier for us to identify what it is we do and to market our services, but it has also led to a constrained view on the part of the public about what they can get from us, and more important, it has constrained our own thinking. We need to challenge four key presumptions about who we are and what we do:

• *We overidentify our work with the third-party neutral role.* As professional conflict resolvers, we almost always see ourselves as third-party neutrals. We may be mediators, facilitators, arbitrators, designers, or trainers. But almost always we see ourselves as neutrals. An essential part of our self-definition is that we don't align ourselves with any one group and that we look at problems "objectively" (whatever that means). In my career, I am almost always hired as a neutral, and my credibility to some extent revolves on whether I can project and maintain that stance. This is a great source of strength, but also a significant limitation on both the services we offer and the readiness of people in conflict to use us. With neutrality comes one source of credibility, but also many sources of mistrust and doubt. Neutrals may offer one means for creating a safe, flexible, informal, and creative forum for interchange, but they do not offer sufficient opportunities for voice, justice, vindication, validation, or impact. Also, to accept the use of neutrals, people in conflict must buy into a certain presumption of moral, legal, and political equality. Therein lie the limits of neutrality and the suspicion many involved in conflict have about using our services.

Judges are perceived as neutral in some sense as well, but along with that neutrality comes the power of office, of social legitimacy. Judges carry with them the considerable weight of the social legitimacy that they convey. In the sense that they represent societal norms, judges are of course not neutral. In fact, they are expected to convey the potential of societal approbation or societal support through the decisions that they render. Mediators, facilitators, and other conflict resolution professionals do not offer that kind of social sanction. To the extent that people need this sanction, neutral conflict resolvers cannot avoid falling short.

Why is it that we have identified our role so strongly with the third-party neutral role? One answer is that the neutral stance appears to offer a clear message to the public about who we are or what we do. It simplifies our presentation of our values and our role. As neutrals, we purport to be clear about how we will think and behave. The values and ethical commitment that we bring to conflict are conveyed and defined by our commitment to being neutral. There are two problems here. One is that people in conflict often want or need something other than the intervention of third-party neutrals. When what they want is voice, vindication, or procedural justice, for example, neutrals offer very little. People intuitively understand this, but they don't typically articulate it in these terms. Instead, they resist, passively or aggressively, or simply avoid the use of third parties.

The second problem is that neutrality makes sense only as a statement of intention, not of behavior. We bring with us a set of beliefs, values, and interests to every conflict we enter, no matter how firmly we are committed to neutrality. Every action we take, or choose not to take, reflects this, and the disputants we work with are sensitive to this. So asserting ourselves as neutral may appear to clarify our role, but in reality it can easily serve to obfuscate or distort the real nature of what we have to contribute.

The role of a third-party neutral is an important and powerful one, but only one of many roles that people in conflict need. They need consultants, advisers, advocates, teachers, representatives, and substantive experts, as well as facilitators, conciliators, and mediators. As long as the field of conflict resolution is so closely identified with the third-party role, it will neither be used nor trusted when people's essential needs are for some other form of assistance. This is not to suggest abandoning the role or practice of neutrals, but rather to enlarge our definition of the field beyond this.

• *We are too focused on collaborative problem solving.* A second essential feature of our self-identity is that we see our role as necessarily connected to collaborative problem solving. Conflict resolution is repeatedly discussed in terms of bringing different parties together to air their concerns, discuss their differences, and seek out collaborative solutions through dialogue and creative problem solving. When collaborative or integrative problem solving is what is called for, we can provide expertise in designing and conducting processes for achieving this. But frequently disputants are neither interested nor ready to seek a collaborative outcome. Instead, they often want help with noncollaborative approaches—ones that they hope will further their cause, achieve victory, and give them the chance to be heard in a powerful and decisive way. In many parts of Europe (for instance, France and Norway), it is unacceptable to use the term *collaboration* to discuss a constructive approach to resolving conflict because that term has been associated with cooperation with evil. (During World War II, collaborators were those despised individuals who cooperated with occupying Nazi forces.) People in conflict are often worried that the collaborative processes in which they are urged to participate will require them to give up something of basic value or to cooperate with what they believe to be evil or malicious.

• *We think our job is to resolve conflicts.* We are in the conflict resolution business after all. Our major organizations and educational programs usually contain the term *conflict resolution* or *dispute resolution* (or *mediation* or *negotiation*). Resolving conflicts is a fine goal, but defining our field of practice in these terms poses some real problems. Medicine does not define itself in terms of making people healthy or curing illness. Law, engineering, psychology, and economics all shy away from narrow and instrumental self-definitions as well. We should too. The problem is that resolution is just one goal that we might have in relation to conflict, and a fairly poorly defined one at that.

We need to approach conflict in a much more diverse and complex way. Conflict is a process that is not always amenable to resolution, as we usually understand it. Often people experience and express a need for help in resolving conflict, although this can mean many different things (Mayer, 2000). But at other times, people in conflict want help understanding, surfacing, intensifying, or conducting a conflict, and then the goal of resolution can seem far off and almost irrelevant— especially if resolution means something other than victory. If we want to work with people enraged about racial profiling, government officials who feel that a citizens' group is completely unreasonable and inflexible, or individuals who believe their rights as an ethnic minority are being trampled on, then our offer to help them resolve their conflicts may seem totally irrelevant and may even provoke resentment. People in these circumstances believe that the only type of resolution that is currently available is shallow and temporary. Often resolutions or agreements can at best provide temporary resting places in an ongoing process of struggle. Those who offer resolution in such circumstances are therefore likely to be viewed as encouraging the abandonment of a deeply felt cause or belief and are going to be instinctively distrusted.

• *We don't view ourselves as having anything to offer people who want to continue and deepen a conflict.* The corollary problem to an exclusive focus on resolution is a failure to offer anything of value to people who want to remain in conflict, who feel that their purposes will best be served by continuing and deepening a conflict, and who feel that attempts at resolution are shortsighted at best, and possibly dangerous. The conflict resolution field has not given much more than lip-service (if that) to helping people engage in conflict effectively and constructively. We have viewed this as neither our purpose nor our strength. This significantly limits the role we can potentially play and the degree to which we can affect the way conflict is conducted.

Do we in fact have anything to offer people in conflict that they cannot get more readily and effectively from other sources? Won't people wanting to conduct a conflict always be better off working with a lawyer or some other "hired gun"? Our future ability to have an impact on conflict and to find a more powerful role for our field may well revolve around the answers to these questions.

I believe that the experience, skills, understanding, and concepts that we bring to our work as conflict resolvers can be used to assist people who are committed to continuing a conflict. But to do this, we have to embrace the value of conflict itself in a more committed way than is the norm in our field. And we have to believe that there is a reason for conflict resolution professionals to help people engage more deeply in conflict. This means becoming more comfortable with the roles of advocate, coach, trainer, adviser, and negotiator and accepting these roles as appropriate for conflict resolution professionals. And it means understanding that what we bring to them will be very different and distinct from what lawyers, agents, political organizers, or decision makers bring (see Chapter Seven). If we fail to accept these roles, they will still be filled, but they will be less likely to be filled by people with a commitment to taking an integrative view of conflict and more likely to be occupied by people with a rights- or power-based view of how to approach conflict.

None of this is to suggest that the role of the third-party neutral, committed to helping people resolve their conflicts in a constructive and collaborative manner, is not important and worthwhile. I have spent twenty-five years working as a third-party neutral and I am committed to the value of this work. The work of neutrals will continue to be a necessary and important part of the conflict resolution field. But at the same time, we have to understand the limits of this role and the problems with clinging to it as our sole approach to conflict. If we are going to overcome the resistance to our work, the criticisms of our efforts, and the limits in our ability to influence the way conflict is conducted, we are going to have to free ourselves from each of these four presumptions (which I consider further in Chapter Four) and develop a wider range of services and approaches that this implies.

## What Conflict Resolution Offers: The Essence of the Field

Challenging these assumptions will raise fundamental questions about our identity. What is our basis of unity, our reason for existence, and what connects those of us who identify ourselves as conflict resolvers? If the third-party neutral role is not at the heart of what we offer, what is? Should conflict resolution (or alternative dispute resolution) even be the descriptor we use to identify our work? Conflict resolution as a field consists of self-identified (as opposed to institutionally sanctioned) practitioners. For many, this is only a partial or secondary identification. Conflict resolution is not the field of origin of most practitioners. Most do not have a professional degree from a program in conflict resolution (although conflict resolution degree programs are proliferating), and relatively few make their living entirely from work that they identify as conflict resolution.

As a field, conflict resolution is loosely defined. Our attempts to strengthen this field have focused on institution building—developing credentials, standards for training, professional organizations, and certification procedures. However, whether conflict resolution prospers, grows, and becomes more widely accepted and more influential depends less on developing the infrastructure of a profession than on strengthening the clarity that practitioners share about the heart of what they have to offer and providing services accordingly.

Conflict resolution is more an idea, a vision, a set of values, or even a movement than a professional discipline. What is at the heart of this vision or values that can help us understand what our potential role can be in conflict? If we are clear about this, we will be able to be more flexible, creative, and influential. I believe six key characteristics are at the core of what brings conflict resolvers together and of what we have to offer to people in conflict:

- *A focus on the integrative potential of conflict.* Regardless of the conflict or of our role, we are oriented toward understanding and achieving the greatest integrative potential a conflict situation has to offer. That is, we are committed to identifying that aspect of a conflict that does not require one party to sacrifice its essential interests in order for another party to meet its (Lax and Sebenius, 1986; Thomas, 1983; Walton and McKersie, 1980). At the same time, to be effective, we must not be naive about this. We must also be willing to assist with the genuinely distributive elements of conflict when a limited amount of value must be apportioned. Nevertheless, we bring a set of values and tools to encourage that the integrative potential of conflict is not overlooked.

- *A needs-based approach.* Some refer to this as an interest-based approach (Fisher and Ury, 1981; Moore, 1991; Brett, Goldberg, and Ury, 1988). I believe the essence of our approach extends beyond interests to a broader range of human needs (Mayer, 2000). Whether we define this as interest or needs based, the essence of this approach is a commitment to understanding conflict and negotiation in terms of the needs people have that are motivating them and that must be addressed for them to be satisfied with the progress of a conflict process. The most skillful conflict practitioners are able to discern and help different parties understand the rich and complex range of interests at play in a conflict. This can be differentiated from a focus on power or on rights as a means of understanding and conducting conflict.

But more significant, it means understanding the complex and often subtle relationship between power, rights, and interests and making sure that a focus on power or rights does not overshadow an understanding of needs. The focus on needs is what helps people think wisely and in a mature manner about the nature of a conflict and the different possible roads through it. Related to this focus is a widely (although not universally) held commitment to carrying on conflict nonviolently—or at the very least to see violence and other coercive approaches to the application of power as a very dangerous tool to be applied with great caution.

• *A focus on communication*. Conflict intervenors must be communication experts, because communication is their central tool regardless of their role. What we have to offer people is assistance, advice, forums, and approaches for communication. This does not necessarily mean polite, friendly, direct, collaborative, or even tactful communication, but it does mean effective communication. Conflict can be understood as a means of communicating between people with different needs. Often the challenge for conflict resolvers is to find a way for conflict to be used to help people communicate with each other effectively, constructively, and with a minimum destructiveness.

In *Thirteen Days* (New Line Cinema, 2000), the popular film dramatization of the Cuban missile crisis, there is an interesting scene between Robert McNamara, the U.S. secretary of defense, and an admiral who was directing the fleet that was set to intercept Russian ships approaching Cuba. The admiral orders one of the ships to shoot star shells (harmless shells, fired as a warning) over the bow of a Russian ship, prompting an angry and tired McNamara to insist that no shots be fired without presidential authorization. The admiral says that these were not shots but just warning signals that were part of the U.S. Rules of Engagement that had been in place since the time of John Paul Jones. Frustrated, McNamara says: "You don't understand a thing, do you, Admiral? This is not a blockade. This is language, a new vocabulary, the likes of which the world has never seen. This is President Kennedy communicating with Secretary Khrushchev."

In a sense, all conflict is about sending clear and understandable messages, and even when people do not want to settle, they still have something important to communicate. Thus, communication is at the center of conflict.

- *A commitment to empowering disputants.* When people are in crisis, they often turn to others for assistance. The challenge for intervenors is how to help without disempowering. As a society and as helping professionals, we often respond to crisis by taking away power from the people in crisis. Conflict is often a form of crisis, and social institutions, such as the courts, often intervene by taking power away from disputants who are seeking help with the conflict. But to cope effectively with the crisis, people usually need to be assisted in becoming more empowered, better able to take control over their own lives. The best of intentions can often backfire and perpetuate a problem. This is true whether we are talking about psychological, familial, medical, economic, or community crisis. Across many different fields, an empowerment model of some sort is being advocated for people who are in crisis. Conflict intervenors face the challenge of helping people embroiled in conflict work their way through that conflict without further disempowering them.

- *Process focused.* While many conflict resolvers have entered into this work because of an interest in and knowledge about the substantive issues involved in conflict (for example, divorce, sustainable development, ethnic relations), what is special about a conflict resolver's role is this person's understanding and focus on process. Whatever the process may be—mediation, arbitration, collaborative decision making, negotiation, public agitation, or something else—one key role of the conflict professional is to help design, plan for, and conduct an appropriate process. While others may be more focused on the substance of the issues, conflict resolvers are particularly needed for their ability to anticipate and influence how the process unfolds.

- *System focused.* People embroiled in conflict tend to focus on their immediate needs, the particular relationships that they are feeling conflicted about, or the specific issue on which they are focused. But conflict is always about more than that. Conflict lies embedded in a system of relationships, needs, power exchanges, and historical dynamics. An action undertaken with a very immediate and particular purpose in mind can often have a far broader impact on a whole series of relations and interactions than the parties who are involved realize. Conflict can be thought of as a characteristic of complex adaptive systems (Jones and Hughes, 2003), and it is never completely predictable or analyzable. However, by becoming aware of the larger context within which conflict plays out, participants can extend their insights about the nature and dynamics of conflict. A key focus of conflict specialists is on the wider impact and implications of different actions undertaken in conflict and of the broader social, economic, political, cultural, and environmental forces interacting with each particular conflict.

How different conflict practitioners understand, appreciate, or act on these values and principles varies tremendously, and individual practitioners do not necessarily accept or embrace all of them. But as a group, particularly in the North American context, these seem to be the characteristics that broadly define conflict resolution as a field and distinguish it from other approaches to dealing with people in conflict.

The crisis that the field is facing will not be overcome by abandoning these principles, but by applying them in more creative, flexible, and realistic ways. As we consider the specific challenges to the field of conflict resolution, the underlying value and importance of these hallmarks should always be our guide. If there is a future for our field of practice, it will be in becoming wiser and more skillful in bringing these principles and perspectives to bear in all aspects of the work we do. But we will realize our potential only if we can face the shortcomings of our practice, the genuine problems that our approaches have encountered, and the limits we have put on ourselves by an overly constricted self-definition.

## The Limits of Resolution, the Power of Engagement

In view of the challenges to our field and the nature of the conflict process itself, the identification of our field with the resolution of conflict seems shortsighted and inaccurate. People involved in conflict need assistance during many other points in the conflict process—in preventing conflict, understanding that there is a potential conflict, raising that conflict to the level of awareness, escalating a conflict to the point where some response is provoked, conducting and carrying on a conflict until resolution may be possible, engaging in a resolution process, coming to resolution, and healing from conflict. If we are to flourish as a field, we have to become more involved in all aspects of this process. Right now, we are limiting ourselves to what may be the safest and most comfortable part of conflict, but this is a serious limit indeed.

We can be much more powerful intervenors if we expand our thinking about our role. On an intuitive level, we know this. It is often better to work with people on how to become more effective in pursuing the goals that have propelled them into conflict than it is to focus on how to find their way out of conflict. We are far more likely to achieve our potential as a field if our core focus is on how to help people engage in conflict effectively rather than on how to resolve conflict. By focusing on engagement, we can continue to bring to bear the key skills and outlooks that we have to contribute, the hallmarks of our practice, and we can address the legitimate concerns and criticisms that have been raised about what we do. Most important, we can become more effective in dealing with serious conflicts in a constructive way. We should think of ourselves as conflict engagement practitioners rather than conflict resolution professionals. Resolution is part of engagement, but only one part.

In this book, I explore more fully the criticisms and limitations of conflict resolution as a field, and I discuss what it means in practice to redefine ourselves as conflict engagement specialists. I do not suggest abandoning our important resolution roles, but of providing a broader context for our work. In particular, I will propose understanding advocacy to be an essential conflict role. Advocates should be embraced into our field. They have much to offer us, and we have considerable skills and experience to bring to this role. I will also suggest that coaching and organizing are essential roles for conflict practitioners. If these new roles are genuinely embraced into our work, they will redefine our field.

The challenge and the opportunity that this crisis offers is how to widen our self-perception, how to take what we have to offer even more seriously, how to accept and grow from the criticisms and even the indifference that the public has expressed. Only by doing this can we reach our potential as a field of practice and a social movement.

# 2

## The Resistance to Conflict Resolution

Conflict resolution works. We have experienced many successes in bringing together with productive results people who have diverse viewpoints, a history of conflict, and seemingly incompatible needs.

Why, then, has there been such a widespread avoidance or outright rejection of conflict resolution? Why are people so averse to using conflict resolution procedures except under exceptional circumstances or even duress?

In this chapter, I use a mediator's approach to understand this resistance. My intention is not to answer the critiques, to take issue with misconceptions that may be embedded in them, or to find solutions to this challenge. I will approach that later. First, I want to understand the fundamental nature of the resistance and criticism, look at some of the conclusions of research into conflict resolution, and consider the specific concerns or reactions of potential users of conflict services in different arenas.

I do not intend to provide a comprehensive review of the literature or research on conflict resolution (for this, see Wissler, 2002, and Kressel and Pruitt, 1989), but instead try to understand the essence of the concerns from the point of view of the people or organizations expressing them. Some of these take the form of well-articulated critiques, some appear as vaguer reservations or fears, and some are expressed through action or, more often, inaction.

Only by striving to understand what is at the root of these concerns will we be able to learn the appropriate lessons and adjust our practices accordingly. The twin obstacles to learning from these critiques are defensiveness—specifically, succumbing to the urge to dismiss the criticism as being ill informed or self-serving—and premature problem solving. In this chapter, I will attempt to avoid these tendencies in an effort to explore the nature of the challenges and barriers that the conflict resolution field faces.

## Critiques of Conflict Resolution

Conflict resolution processes have been criticized from many angles. Some of these critiques seem to contradict one another, but that is because they represent different values or concerns. For example, some emphasize the ineffectiveness of conflict resolution at reducing transactional costs, while others suggest that conflict resolution programs are too focused on providing cheap alternatives to adjudication, and therefore achieve inadequate or superficial outcomes. But the truth beneath many of these contradictions is that people often feel either unprotected or unserved by conflict resolution procedures.

Critiques of conflict resolution fall in three broad categories: political or policy, efficiency or effectiveness, and experiential or personal:

- Political or policy-based criticisms argue that conflict resolution processes do not further (in fact may hinder) some important social or institutional goals. Many of these criticisms relate to issues of power or concerns about how policy ought to be made and conflicts solved in a democracy.

- Efficiency or effectiveness critiques question conflict resolution processes from a more practical point of view: whether the time, money, and effort put into them are merited by the results achieved.

- Experiential- or personal-based critiques stem from the experience of participants in conflict resolution processes and the personal impact of these experiences.

These are by no means mutually exclusive critiques, but the essential arguments are very different in nature, and they should therefore be considered separately.

## Political and Policy Critiques

No approach can better serve the needs of trans-national corporations, waging a "take-no-prisoners/win-lose war on the world" than to have its only potential opposition, grassroots social and environmental change activists, adopt a win-win strategy. To adopt consensus-based solutions is a sure fire way to eventually turn all the forest activists into what, in Yiddish, are called "nudniks" (from nudge): people who are always trying to get you to do what they want by constantly pestering and annoying you [Jim Britell, environmental and community activist, 1997].

Business is willing to risk its chances with local stakeholders because it believes its odds are better in these forums. It is ready to train its experts in mastering these processes. It believes it can dominate them over time and relieve itself of the burden of tough national rules. It has ways to generate pressures in communities where it is strong that it doesn't have at the national level [Michael McCloskey, chairman, Sierra Club, 1996, p. 2].

In fact some might argue ADR [alternative dispute resolution] is oriented toward status quo by definition, for it does not address the inequality of power, thereby contributing to the maintenance of systems of inequality [Laura Nader, anthropologist and critic of mediation, 1988, p. 279].

"Conflict resolution" is itself a rather pompous, high-sounding theory with a very skimpy, simple-minded psychological basis. The axiom of this theory is that harmony among human beings is more natural than conflict—no original sin here!—and that if only we can get the parties in conflict to talk to one another, the level of "mistrust" will decline and mutual understanding increase, until at some point the conflict itself will subside. It is thinkable that such an approach to marriage counseling might in some cases be productive, but its extension to the level of statecraft, or to any conflict between collective entities, is an extreme case of academic hubris [Irving Kristol, political commentator and publisher, 1997].

Perhaps the last criticism is a little over the top, but otherwise the pattern of deep distrust and misgiving about conflict resolution and its impact on society is typical of many critiques. From a variety of political and professional perspectives, critics suggest that conflict resolution processes are not only ineffective but also dangerous, unfair, exploitative, naive, and disempowering.

Most of us who have worked as mediators or facilitators have experienced suspicion of this type from at least two different angles. Those who represent people or causes that are apparently in a less powerful societal position view conflict resolution as a means of preventing serious organizing, dissipating dissent through a show of dialogue, and focusing people on the potential for minor concessions rather than on the essence of exploitation. Those who are in positions of authority worry that collaborative processes require that compromises be made on issues even though there may be no legal requirement or policy imperative dictating compromise. They are worried that by simply participating in consensus-building efforts, they are undermining their authority and forcing lowest-common-denominator solutions to difficult problems.

The form and detail of these critiques are different when applied to large-scale consensus-building processes, interpersonal mediation, international peace building efforts, or organizational conflict resolution programs. But in all arenas, there are certain common features to the critique or the resistance. (In this discussion, I am not viewing resistance as negative, inappropriate, or hostile. Resistance is not about an unwillingness to accept a correct approach, insight, or reality. Rather, it refers to a reluctance to participate or to an active struggle to avoid taking part in conflict resolution procedures, but it is somewhat less than outright rejection or refusal. People may resist rather than refuse because they don't feel they have an option to refuse and are not clear about what they should do. They know a process will go forward with or without them, or they may think that through resisting, they can change the way in which a process will unfold. Resistance is often appropriate and sometimes provides the best option available.) One central theme is that a neutral nonadjudicative process leaves the strong stronger and the weak weaker. Rights and safeguards that have been achieved through hard-won battles over many years are thought to be too easily subverted or disregarded in conflict resolution processes. Limited resources that are more likely to achieve results in well-ordered adjudicative or regulatory procedures are feared squandered in the more uncertain and unregulated environment of conflict resolution.

Similarly, whether one is a CEO in a unionized organization, an elected official, or a chief of a regulatory agency, there is often a belief that collaborative programs are more for show than to make sound policies and decisions and that they require treating as equal people with less experience, wisdom, and perspective. Furthermore, many people in these positions feel that taking part in collaborative processes with community activists, union organizers, or advocacy groups places them in an awkward position. Simply by participating, they feel put in the position of having to act as equal players with people over whom they otherwise view themselves in a position of authority. They may also feel that in a negotiation, it will be hard for them to maintain parameters that they believe are quite reasonable without appearing rigid and uncompromising. This is analogous to the parent in a parent-adolescent mediation who is concerned that the very act of participating in such a process will undermine parental authority.

Several themes run through almost all policy-level criticisms across the different dimension of conflict resolution practice:

- Collaborative processes disempower the less powerful and systemically maintain the status quo. In conflict resolution terminology, the processes themselves prevent people from fully developing and using their best alternatives to negotiations.

- Traditional adjudicative, legislative, administrative, or regulatory processes are a more stable, orderly, certain, and intentional means for making public policy and resolving disputes. By privatizing dispute resolution, we essentially privatize policy formation and take it out of the public eye. This can occur through private negotiations about policy or issues or through the cumulative effect of private solutions to many individual or small group disputes (Fiss, 1984; Luban, 1995).

- The ideology underlying conflict resolution is incompatible with democratic ideals encouraging conflicts to be aired, vigorously pursued and contested, and then settled through legal or political means. By promoting a culture and value of harmony, we in effect suppress a discussion of major social issues that require a commitment to advocacy. This results in more real decisions being made in closed settings by people with access to power. We need more disputation, not less (Nader, 1993).

- Conflict resolution processes tend to suppress conflict and arrive at superficial and fragile solutions. Because the goal is harmony and resolution, there is a natural norm, embedded in both the process and the values of the conflict resolution professionals, to achieve resolution easily and with minimal angst. This leads to a search for easy solutions and superficial agreements.

- Conflict resolution tends to psychologize, personalize, and depoliticize conflicts that are rooted in social or institutional dynamics. This has the impact of diverting attention to individual attitudes, feelings, and behaviors instead of focusing on larger societal issues. If every conflict between management and labor, between environmentalists and corporations, or between divorcing spouses is framed in terms of relationships, communication, and individual behavior, then underlying social inequities or systemic problems can easily be lost or largely ignored. Individual grievances, for example, are often manifestations of significant differences about organizational priorities and decision-making processes.

• Conflict resolution is so thoroughly rooted in white, middle-class cultural norms that it is alien to people from different cultural or class backgrounds. Many of the basic concepts or values that underlie most approaches to conflict resolution are very specific to the culture of the majority of conflict resolution professionals. For example, our concepts of direct communication of concerns, of neutrality, of how to listen, of how to show respect, or of how to build rapport are culturally specific, and our processes therefore seem alien in many settings.

• Women in conflict are particularly vulnerable to the tendencies of conflict resolution activities to disempower the less powerful and psychologize social issues. Women are more likely to seek to focus on the psychological dimension of conflict and to try to preserve harmonious relationships; therefore, they are less likely to seek the assistance to which they might be entitled in order to address structural inequalities.

• Consensus-based processes fail to establish the body of case law, legal precedent, public record, and public reasoning that is the long-term basis of constructive public policy formation. Because consensus processes are individualistic, private, and interest based, they do not contribute in an orderly and effective way to building a legal or policy structure that can guide the way issues are handled over time.

There are other political and policy critiques about conflict resolution, but in one form or another, these are the themes that appear over and over again and seem to reflect major reservations from a variety of sources. Notably, all critiques have something to do with power.

In *Getting Disputes Resolved*, Brett, Goldberg, and Ury (1988) describe three major approaches to resolving disputes: power-, rights-, and interest-based approaches. They suggest that a healthy structure is one in which interest-based approaches predominate, backed up by low-cost rights-based alternatives; only in carefully controlled circumstances are power-based methods used. Once a secure rights-based method of dispute resolution (essentially the rule of law) is established to check unrestrained power-based alternatives, interest-based alternatives can and should flourish. Many of the critiques of conflict resolution suggest that the rush to embrace interest-based methodologies has weakened the structures that constrain undesirable power-based approaches. As a result, either the less powerful are placed at a disadvantage, or conflict is repressed. There is a parallel argument that any systemic effort to engage people in an interest-based approach will necessarily undermine the rights-based structure and thus expose people to the unbridled power of dominant or domineering individuals or organizations.

## Efficiency and Effectiveness Critiques

These forums are draining. I am the only environmental activist with scientific training in this region. If I participate in two of these dialogues, I won't have any time left to do anything else at all. And what do we have to show for it? We either will not arrive at any meaningful agreements or they will be ignored by those in power anyway [comment by a participant in a roundtable on ecosystem issues].

Another set of critiques of conflict resolution argues that mediation, facilitated dialogues, negotiated rule making, and consensus-building processes in general are cumbersome, slow, and resource consuming, and they do not lead to constructive results on a consistent basis. There are both process- and outcome-based aspects of these critiques.

Process-oriented comments focus on the demands and intensity of the process itself. Disputants are looking for a less stressful and more efficient approach to dealing with their conflicts. Even if they feel that the process was fair, the mediator unbiased, and the outcome just (which is certainly not how people always feel), participants often express a sense that the process was more arduous than it needed to be and that it took too much time, cost too much money, or was too emotionally draining.

In divorce mediations, for example, one source of resistance is the complexity that mediation appears to add to the process. Lawyers will at least fill out forms, file papers, finalize agreements, and appear in court for people. Mediation often seems to add a layer of complexity, another hurdle to cross, rather than a process of simplification and detoxification. Often people engage in mediation expecting a more evaluative approach and are disappointed (at least at first) if what they experience is an effort to help people engage in an interest-based negotiation. Lawyers often want mediators to take a firm hand in directing people toward settlement. They want mediators to cajole, persuade, urge, plead and push, and see that the alternative to this kind of approach is ineffective and directionless.

Conflict resolution is sometimes criticized for creating more delays in the process, for undercutting timetables established in regulations or contracts, providing an additional avenue for stalling or stonewalling, and compromising formal public notification and input processes. Often in an attempt to deal with the process concerns, conflict resolution programs are set up with unrealistic timetables, which can lead to overly pressured or evaluative approaches. For example, it is not that unusual for court-based mediation programs, as a consequence of case management timetables, to allow for minimal amounts of time to deal with some complex issues. The dilemma here is that too long a time frame can lead participants to fear that their disputes will never be resolved or that they will have to explore their issues, behavior, and needs more than they wish to. Too rapid a timetable can lead to a feeling of pressure, superficiality, and anxiety.

Some studies suggest that the amount of time saved in mediation or other consensual processes compared to more traditional or adjudicative procedures might be minimal. When agreements are reached, time is saved; when there is no agreement, time is lost. Certainly, when compared to full-blown court cases, mediated agreements can save considerable time, but most disputes do not go to a full trial; rather, they are settled out of court in some manner. Despite extensive research and evaluation, it is not clear that mediation is more efficient than advocate-negotiated settlements, at least in the sense of the time and effort involved.

Evaluating the efficiency of larger-scale processes is more complicated because it is harder to identify appropriate comparisons. For example, in the late 1990s, the U.S. Environmental Protection Agency initiated a series of dialogues under the rubric of the Common Sense Initiative. The idea was to bring regulators, community and environmental activists, workers, and the regulated community (primarily industry) together to look at regulatory processes and standards. Participants were asked to consider how to achieve "cleaner, cheaper, smarter" results by making voluntary agreements about processes and standards. For about two years, task groups met in a number of different industry areas (for example, chemical, electronic, metal), and some interesting and potentially valuable dialogues took place—but very little was achieved in the way of concrete results. Was this a good use of resources and time? This depends on how we view the long-term impact of such discussions.

Policy dialogues, regulatory negotiations, roundtable forums, and other similar processes tend to be intense and expensive. Some achieve tangible and measurable results, but perhaps the most important ones are more ambiguous in outcome. Inevitably, this leads to questions about the efficiency and the effectiveness of such processes.

Conflict resolution advocates sometimes argue that there are important intangible results of such dialogues; over time, they enable the development of consensus about important social issues and are cheaper and more efficient that the alternative legal, administrative, or political processes, which can involve a great deal of time, money and duress. But measuring these more intangible results is difficult and subjective.

Of course, there are many examples of facilitated dialogues that have led to concrete agreements and satisfaction on the part of participants. But the cumulative costs and benefits of these processes are more ambiguous. Furthermore, they have been particularly costly to those least able to provide the resources: the community and advocacy groups that represent important aspects of the public interest.

One of the problems that proponents of conflict resolution processes face in dealing with these critiques is self-inflicted. Many conflict resolution practitioners have claimed that our processes are more efficient, less time-consuming, less expensive, less likely to result in recurring conflicts, and more likely to lead to more satisfactory results for everyone. We have thereby put the burden of proof on ourselves, and it has proved difficult to back up these claims except anecdotally. For every story of a good result from conflict resolution efforts, there are less happy tales to tell as well.

If we look at the efficiency and effectiveness of conflict resolution efforts from the point of view of outcome, we encounter a further set of critiques. These deal more with the cumulative results—whether conflict resolution programs lead to better long-term agreements or to settlements that have effectively resolved long-term issues or difficult problems.

When we review the results of research below, we will see that they are at best ambiguous. In divorce mediation, for example, the evidence is mixed and inclusive as to whether there is any long-term difference in the level of conflict, the overall adjustment of parents or children, or the long-term satisfaction from those who have mediated their agreements versus those who have used other approaches to settling disputes (Pearson and Thoennes, 1989).

Similarly, although there are many studies showing positive results in terms of levels of agreement and satisfaction in small claims and employment mediation, it is not clear that the overall impact of these have led to better industrial relations, a greater sense of community cohesion, or a less alienated citizenry. This may be a lot to ask and hard to measure, but these are the kinds of results that we have promised either explicitly or implicitly over the years.

Taken together, the critiques of the effectiveness of conflict resolution from the perspective of process and outcome have led some critics to argue that the return may not merit the efforts (see the reaction to Kakalik and others, 1997—a Rand report—and the questions raised by Hensler, 2002).

This is not just an abstract concern. Since many conflict resolution programs depend on institutional funding, public, charitable, or corporate, the more widespread these critiques become, the more financially vulnerable and less sustainable our field will be. In tight economic times, an important and inevitable question will be whether mediation processes, public dialogues, or facilitated roundtables are saving or costing money. If the belief is that they are costing money, then many of these programs will be defunded— even if there is a great deal of satisfaction on the part of participants. Ironically, the more efficient the programs are in terms of saving money and resulting in efficient outcomes, the more likely they are also to be perceived by some critics as providing "poor people's justice" and being an inadequate alternative to more formal or adjudicative systems.

## Experiential and Personal Critiques

Another set of critiques looks at the experience of individuals who participate in conflict resolution procedures. Perhaps the best articulated of these critiques have been made from a feminist perspective (Grillo, 1991; Rifkin, 1984; Shaffer, 1998). There are many different angles on these, but as a group, they suggest that women are often victimized by conflict resolution processes themselves, that the impact of face-to-face negotiations on vulnerable women can be devastating, and that the personal experience of women in informal dispute resolution procedures has often been extremely distressful. The most intense of these criticisms have been directed toward family mediation, particularly when family violence has been involved (Wheeler, 2002). Great efforts have been made to try to address this critique, but this issue remains current in our field.

Some critiques challenge a basic value and presumption of the conflict resolution field: that people want control and involvement over the decisions affecting their lives and are more likely to have ownership over an outcome if they participate in crafting it. While people do want a sense of "procedural justice" (Welsh, 2001a; Macfarlane, 2001) and impact on the outcome, this does not necessarily translate into a need for direct participation. In fact, the reverse may sometimes be true: often people prefer not to be involved and have to endure the emotional and intellectual demands of actually engaging in a conflict and struggling with a negotiation process, particularly if the issues are very personal.

Conflict avoidance is a powerful urge, and many people find the direct participation required by most resolution processes to be painful and even traumatizing. Avoidance takes many forms, not all of them passive (Mayer, 2000). Some find it emotionally less demanding or traumatizing to stand up in a public meeting and give an impassioned two-minute speech about the unfairness of a proposed course of action than it is to sit in a room with people holding opposing points of view and work on a collaborative outcome. Similarly, some may find it less toxic to make an argument to a judge (or, better yet, let a lawyer make it for them) than to have to face their adversary in a problem-solving effort. As a result, participating in mediation can actually be more emotionally draining and even traumatizing than court action and certainly than lawyer-conducted negotiations.

When I practiced as a divorce mediator, I was aware that some people felt safer and less traumatized when their lawyers worked out the terms of an agreement, particularly early in the divorce process, than if they tried to work it through for themselves, especially in the immediate presence of their spouse. I tried to ascertain when this was the case (and why) and discuss this, but I am sure that I was not always aware of or sensitive to just how difficult this could be. Critics of mediation argue that this is far more often the situation than mediators realize or appreciate and that one of the real functions of advocates is to protect people from the "tyranny of participation" that conflict resolution processes can seem to impose. One symptom of this type of problem with conflict resolution is when people report that even if the outcomes were satisfactory, the process seemed incredibly wearing and demanding.

A related phenomenon is a more generalized resistance to the process of consensus (the "'c' word" is how it was referred to in several organizations I worked with). People often fear being forced to spend a great deal of time in a process that is neither effective nor enjoyable and that will put them under extraordinary amounts of stress in order to try to reach consensus. This is especially true if they also believe that a simple vote or authoritative decision would solve the problem. Those of us who work facilitating group consensus-building processes tend to be dismissive, even disdainful, of using parliamentary procedure or Roberts Rules of Order because we feel this is polarizing, stifles creativity, and is overly rigid. We might do well to consider why some people are attracted to it. In fact, formal procedure can occasionally be helpful and appropriate because it provides a mechanism for people to engage in a debate without having to deal with the ambiguity, uncertainty, and level of engagement that other approaches to conflict demand.

Other critiques reflect distrust of the supposed neutrality, objectivity, or fairness of conflict resolution. Sometimes this is about the skill of the mediator or facilitator; sometimes it is about the design of the process. Despite many standard-setting and training efforts, there is no way to ensure that all conflict resolution professionals will understand what it means to be fair and even-handed or to have the skills necessary to maintain this demeanor in very polarized conflicts.

There may be a more underlying conceptual problem as well. For many people, there is no such thing as neutrality or impartiality. If someone is not for them, then they are against them. The very concept of neutrality may be difficult, if not impossible, for some to accept, and the result is that conflict resolution processes may seem unfair, slanted, pressuring, and unsafe.

By presenting these criticisms, I am not necessarily endorsing them. I am asking that we take them seriously and not dismiss them, not attack the motives of those offering them, and not simply focus on what is wrong with the critiques. In order for our field to grow and to flourish, we have to listen to these concerns, learn from them, and incorporate their lessons. This does not, of course, mean that we have to accept or agree with all the underlying values or arguments inherent in them.

## The Lukewarm Results of Research

Research offers a particular prism, shaped by scope, methodology, and the eye of the researcher, on reality. No single piece of research can definitively tell us how well we are doing as individuals or as a field, but in the aggregate, it provides us with insight, feedback, perspective, and a disciplined look at what we do. If we look at the results of research into conflict resolution, we can draw both optimistic and pessimistic conclusions.

The cumulative results of research support neither the most assertive arguments for the use of conflict resolution processes nor the most negative critiques either. Instead, the weight of research suggests that conflict resolution generally leaves people feeling satisfied with the outcome, pleased with the process, and willing to buy into the results. The research does not document, however, that these efforts have had broad social impact, have led to much higher levels of satisfaction in comparison to all other approaches, have transformed the way in which conflict is being handled, or have resulted in better long-term agreements or postconflict adjustment.

Of course, every piece of research can be interpreted in multiple ways, and there is often a tendency in research to focus on what can be measured, which may be very different from what is important. As a result, a great deal of research looks at agreement rates, participant satisfaction, and compliance. These are easier to measure than changed relationships, communication patterns, or long-term adjustment.

The bulk of formal research has been in the area of mediation, particularly divorce, organizational, small claims, and court-connected programs. In these areas, enough cases can be identified and funding obtained to conduct effective program evaluation. In the public policy or environmental arena, a case study or, less often, a program evaluation approach has been more prevalent.

In this section, I do not intend to provide a comprehensive review of the considerable amount of research that has been undertaken. Instead, and in keeping with my purpose, I focus on some of the key concerns raised by research that conflict resolvers should take seriously. I could cite the ambiguous results of much research to question how strongly some of the concerns I have already discussed have been documented, but that would enable us to avoid the issues we should be facing. Instead, we should use the cumulative impact of research to focus on some potential issues in conflict resolution that demand attention:

• *Mediation is a supply-driven practice*. There is less of a demand for mediation and other conflict resolution processes than there is a supply of interested mediators and conflict resolution practitioners. If people are "voting with their feet," they are voting against mediation. Unless mediation is part of a mandatory system, it is generally underused.

Those who have participated in conflict resolution processes are generally satisfied with their experience, the role of the neutral, and the outcomes, and they would use mediation again. However, when comparing collaborative processes to other approaches (adjudication, arbitration, settlement conferences, lawyer-conducted negotiation), the results are mixed. When clients and lawyers are asked to rate their experience in mediation, for example, they are generally positive (for example, Wissler, 2002; Welsh, 2002; Bingham, 2002). However, when attempts have been made to compare satisfaction with mediation to satisfaction with other approaches, the results are more unpredictable and varied (Macfarlane, 1995; McEwen and Mainman; 1984; McEwen, 1999; and Wissler, 2002). Comparative studies are notoriously difficult to conduct in our field, and they are almost nonexistent in the public policy arena. This makes conclusions about the relative satisfaction people experience with different approaches to conflict difficult, if not impossible, to make. Statements by conflict resolution advocates about higher levels of satisfaction are therefore very hard to back up.

Mediation may be associated with a decreased likelihood of ongoing litigation or repeated filings, but it is hard to identify mediation as the major reason for this. One of the most encouraging findings of some research is that people who voluntarily settle their cases are less likely to return to court or initiate additional actions (Pearson and Thoennes, 1989; for impressive data on reduced recidivism for victim-offender programs, see Sherman, Strang, and Woods, 2003). In one of the most comprehensive studies of mediation in any sphere, Bingham, Chesmore, Moon, and Napoli (2000) reported on the impact of facilitative and transformative approaches to the mediation of equal employment opportunity (EEO) cases in the U.S. Postal Service (USPS). The number of EEO cases filed throughout the USPS dropped from 14,000 to 10,350 per year after the full implementation of the program. However, because of the difficulty of conducting comparative or control group studies, it is hard to know whether this is a result of the mediation process itself, the change in attitudes associated with the implementation of a new program, or other environmental changes—or to know how enduring such changes will be. It stands to reason that if agreements are voluntary, there is less of a chance that appeals will be filed since presumably people have agreed to the outcome. However, this suggests that the real comparison ought to be between mediated and other voluntarily arrived at outcomes, such as lawyer- or advocate-negotiated settlements. Since most court filings are settled without actual court hearings, this accounts for the bulk of court-connected cases, and we need additional studies comparing this type of settlement to mediation (McEwen and Wissler, 2002).

Consensus-based conflict resolution approaches may be cheaper and quicker—if consensus is reached. If consensus is not achieved, the costs and time may in fact increase. It is difficult to demonstrate clearly that conflict resolution saves time and money. This is a particularly hard case to make. How costs are measured, comparisons made, or opportunity costs evaluated pose major methodological challenges. Although participants often report cost savings (Wissler, 2002; McAdoo and Hinshaw, 2002), and some research on family mediation in particular appears to support cost savings (Kelly, 1990), it is difficult to identify the components necessary to make systematic cost comparisons. Some studies even suggest that under certain circumstances, mediation can be more costly and time-consuming than the alternatives (Pearson, 1982). Studies of court-based mediation services are mixed as to whether these produce results more quickly than more traditional approaches to litigation (see Wissler, 2002, but also Hann, Barr, and Associates, 2001). Obviously, unsuccessful mediations can cause a delay in reaching resolution, whereas cases that settle in mediation may indeed proceed faster to resolution. In discussing environmental or public policy disputes, comparisons are again almost impossible, but it is clear that these processes are resource intensive. One environmental activist described the process of consensus building as akin to "watching paint dry" (Golten, Smith, and Woodrow, 2002).

- *Characteristics of mediators and facilitators may not have much to do with the outcome or levels of satisfaction.* Neither training nor substantive expertise appears to have an impact on the outcomes of mediation. The single factor that seems clearly associated with greater levels of satisfaction and higher levels of agreement is experience: mediators who have completed a certain number of cases are more likely to be successful (Pearson, Thoennnes, and Vanderkooi, 1982). But other than experience, there is little evidence that background, training, or approach are correlated with satisfactory outcomes.

One study comparing process coordination, participant facilitation, and professional facilitation of water forums in California actually concluded that the presence of professional facilitators as opposed to volunteer participant facilitation was associated with lower levels of satisfaction and consensus (Leach and Sabatier, 2003). The authors speculate that professionally trained facilitators may be too occupied with process.

• *Long-term benefits from mediation processes have not been documented.* Even if there are high rates of agreement and satisfaction associated with collaborative processes, there is no clear evidence to date that these result in better relationships over time, improved long-term cooperation and adjustment (as in divorce), a changed organizational climate, or higher long-term levels of satisfaction. It may be a lot to ask that short-term interventions lead to long-term results, and even more to ask that these be documented. But to the extent that the goal of conflict resolution processes is to change the nature of how we relate, there is no evidence of success.

Perhaps unsurprisingly, an important conclusion from a review of research is that many of the benefits we aspire to and often advertise for conflict resolution services either cannot or thus far have not been clearly documented through research. Some of the worst fears about the impact of alternative dispute resolution have also not been borne out by research. But no news is not good news for conflict resolution practitioners. Unless we can document that the services we have to offer are worth the time, costs, effort, and emotional investment, it is difficult to make a strong case for investment in conflict resolution programs. This will especially be the case in the face of economic pressures, competing demands, and ideological opposition. Twenty-five years into the increasing presence of conflict resolution programs in courts, communities, schools, and the workplace, the failure to be able to document a clearer contribution should be a source of great concern to conflict resolution advocates.

## User Perspectives

In the absence of clear results from research, it is important to hear what users are saying and the stories they have to tell about their experiences with conflict resolution processes. Every established conflict resolution program can produce a whole slew of testimonials from people who have used these services, but we also have to hear the message, directly expressed or implied, from those less enchanted with conflict resolution processes. The nature of the stories told or concerns expressed varies depending on the substantive area of work. I believe it is important to look for the themes across these different areas of practice, but at the same time, we need to appreciate the specific concerns as well.

In this section, I reflect on what we can learn from users or potential users in terms of what they have said about conflict resolution processes and how they have used (or not used) them. I will look at these from the angle of several arenas of conflict resolution: environmental and public policy, family, organizational, and community.

## Environmental and Public Policy

Before we began the Furbearers Roundtable, the project director for the State Division of Wildlife stated that without a consensus recommendation, two things would happen. Trappers and hunters would go to the state legislature and have any restrictions on trapping and hunting overturned. Environmentalists and animal rights activists would then place an initiative on the ballot outlawing trapping. After an extensive consensus-building process that took place over a period of about six months, that is pretty much exactly what happened. Despite the good work of many people, representing many different viewpoints, and despite long hours, late night meetings, subgroups, bilateral negotiations, and considerable technical input, no consensus was reached.

Four policy proposals were developed, each representing the strongly held values of a group of participants. Each proposal was informed by the perspectives and interests of the other groups and was therefore more sophisticated and rounded than it might otherwise have been, but the essential policy recommendations fell along a predictable spectrum of values. One advocated a complete ban on trapping. A second called for banning trapping for recreational or economic gain, allowing it only to protect against serious, documentable damage and then only if "humane" traps were used and no other means were available. A third approach advocated the use of trapping for agricultural purposes with some loosely defined requirement that "humane traps be used." The final approach advocated no further regulation on trapping other than additional education of trappers, hunters, and the general public. The second and third approaches overlapped considerably, but since there was not going to be a single recommendation, the agricultural and more moderate environmental groups decided to submit separate recommendations.

The policy adopted by the division was an amalgam of the second and third alternatives. Soon after this, the legislature removed regulation of trapping from the purview of the Department of Fish and Game and placed it under the auspices of the Department of Agriculture, which took a much more liberal approach to trapping. In the next general election, the voters of the state passed an amendment putting considerable limits on trapping and requiring the use of so-called humane traps. For the time being, this issue seems to be dormant.

Participants in this process expressed a wide variety of views about this effort. Some government regulators felt it was a considerable waste of resources and that the same could have been accomplished through a more traditional policy-setting process. Others felt it was essential to give the different groups an opportunity to communicate and to see if consensus could be established. Those representing the more widely divergent interests (animal rights and trappers) probably agreed that there was no use trying to reason with the unreasonable but that some positive communication and education occurred and better personal relations were established. Those with less divergent views may have been both more frustrated because they sensed that consensus might have been possible among the vast majority, but not all, of the participants, and pleased to see the bulk of their recommendations reflected in the proposal that emerged from the division and in the policy that finally emerged from the political process.

Why consider this story of ambivalent, and to some extent frustrating, results? For one thing, we often learn more from our most difficult experiences than from the ones that result in more upbeat endings. But more to the point, this is how difficult policy-setting processes really work: with ambiguous results, a confusing overlap between politics and dialogue, and outcomes that are neither win-win nor win-lose. The outcome of this effort was in many ways very positive. A different kind of discussion among these groups took place, and this affected their interaction, how they framed the issues, and the policies they proposed. The public rhetoric was less caustic, less divisive, and in many ways more thoughtful. But because the stated purpose of this process was to achieve some consensus, it cannot be labeled a success. Perhaps the best evidence for that is that for several years after this, no further consensus-building initiatives occurred in this arena.

When genuine agreement among diverse stakeholders is reached and at a deep enough level that their most important concerns are addressed, participants tend to feel positive about these processes. The problem is that this is a tall order. Most consensus-building processes in the public policy or environmental arena will not stand up well unless they are viewed in comparison to and in the context of other elements of the policy-setting process. They can play a useful role in promoting dialogue, narrowing in on a decision, and arriving at agreements when other factors—legal, political, technical—fall into place. But they need to be viewed as part of more traditional policymaking procedures, not as independent from them. As an adjunct, a catalyst, an input mechanism, they are often valued by participants, but they are seldom the core component of how public policy disputes are resolved.

The problem is that they are time-consuming, expensive, and exhausting. The question that participants are almost always asking is whether this is a useful way for them to spend the limited resources they have to work on a project, and the answer is not always clear. Participants raise several specific concerns in the policy arena:

- *Local interests trump national concerns.* Community-based consensus processes tend to heighten the weight given to local concerns. National advocacy groups are often excluded from these processes or treated like interlopers. Focusing on local interests can be problematic. What was considered a very successful dialogue on forest policy in California and Oregon, for example, was criticized in this way:

> The past successes of most local conservation groups are due to the assistance of regional and national environmental organizations, which have supplied considerable scientific and legal help over the years. The strength of the local group is as the local member of a team that includes regional and national groups. To split off a local group and place it on its own in ambiguous administrative settings where its part time unpaid representative must deal with well paid professionals is a formula for failure [Britell, 1997, p. 3].

- *Structurally, consensus-based processes tend to support the status quo.* While some argue that an advantage of consensus-based processes is their flexibility, others point out that this usually leads to relaxing standards and enforcement rather than attaining agreement to more stringent parameters than dictated by policy. By using consensus norms, it becomes easier to prevent than to promote action. Therefore, the alternative to an agreement usually is the maintenance of the status quo or an escalation of involvement in political or legal processes, something that many stakeholders cannot endure.
- *Neutrals are not really neutral.* In the dialogue about trapping policies discussed above, the costs of the process, including our fees as facilitators, were borne by the state agency. Although the facilitators and the funding agencies were committed to neutrality and

transparency, in some sense we were accountable for our time and for the outcome to the agency in a way that was different from how we were accountable to the stakeholders. Furthermore, any time the facilitators had to make a decision about process (such as who would present a report first), there was a natural tendency for stakeholders to look for a motive based in this dynamic. The additional steps necessary to deal with this (working with a steering committee, negotiating agendas, and discussing process with the whole group) added to the time and intensity of the process. That is one reason that Leach and Sabatier (2003) believe that professional facilitators are less effective than volunteers from the group acting in that role.

Genuine consensus and commitment are hard to obtain, and the results are therefore often disappointingly general or superficial. While it is possible to obtain agreements on specific issues, it is difficult to get deep consensus on ongoing approaches to public policy problems that will result in a long-term commitment to the outcome. In a review of four water quality roundtables in the Great Lakes region, Landre and Knuth (1993) found that while most participants had high levels of satisfaction with the work of the groups, this did not necessarily result in high levels of support for the agreements reached or a willingness to advocate for them with their own communities or groups. In a review of stakeholder processes in the chemical and electronics industry (Mayer, Ghais, and McKay, 1999), we found a number of examples in which the hope of regulators and industry was that the community representatives would act as advocates for the work of the group within their communities. However, community participants were usually reluctant to play this role because they felt that this would place them in an untenable position with regard to the community and would in some respects make them public relations personnel for the industry.

• *Consensus-based processes seldom have real decision-making authority.* Decision making is usually reserved for an administrative, political, or legal body. As a result, collaborative processes are generally only as effective as the aggregate power of the participants and the degree of consensus reached. When decisions are reached, they can and often are overturned or at least significantly altered. I have been part of processes where a group was able to stick together in the face of an effort to overturn the results of their efforts and to see their proposals work their way through complicated political processes. But I have also witnessed the discouragement participants feel when they have reached an important level of agreement, only to see it overturned by an agency or political body:

> Larry is a well-respected and very experienced environmental activist who participated in a year-long dialogue concerning the clean-up of a major Superfund site that had been used for national defense purposes. Amazingly, through some incredibly hard work and creative leadership from a variety of stakeholders and the facilitation team, a consensus was reached about some very thorny issues among a highly diverse group of stakeholders. Larry and several of his associates devoted incredible amounts of time to this process, sometimes against their better judgment. A year later, when I ran into Larry and asked him about his thoughts about this project (which I was not part of), he told me that the process was great, but in the end it came to naught because the decision-making government agency had decided to ignore the results of their work. Had it been worth his while participating? I asked. He still was not sure, and to this day he questions the value of the good work done.

Larry's experience unfortunately is by no means unique. A more widely known example of the same problem occurred regarding the issues of logging in roadless areas and the use of recreational snowmobiles in Yellowstone National Park. In both situations, elaborate public input and consensus-building processes had taken place, resulting in some degree of agreement. These agreements were implemented during the last year of the Clinton administration, only to be overturned in the first year of the Bush administration.

We ought not be surprised that politicians or governmental leaders act in this manner because this is the nature of the political process. Furthermore, this does not mean that conflict resolution or consensus-building processes in these arenas are not valuable. But if the contribution of the conflict resolution field is limited to consensus-based processes guided by neutral facilitators or process designers, then we have carved out a very limited role. We have to see these processes as one part of a much larger policymaking system that is at times political, at times adversarial, and at times adjudicative. Our challenge is to work with the entire dimension of the policymaking process if we really want to have an impact on how conflict is conducted in this crucial arena.

## Family Conflicts

Whenever private matters intersect with state policy, systems of decision making clash. The emotional and developmental needs of children, the complexities of family systems, and the greatly varied values about parenting, family, and children in different cultural and social groups have made it hard to establish legal norms and social policies for dealing with family conflict. Perhaps this is why family mediation has been one of the mainstays of the conflict resolution field since the 1970s.

Mediation has offered the hope of allowing families to work out their legal and emotional issues in a nonadjudicative setting in the belief that to the greatest extent possible, families should be empowered to make the decisions that they will have to live with rather than turn these over to courts or other professionals. While we are most familiar with this in relationship to divorce and child custody, mediation has also been used in adoption, child protection, care of the elderly, family businesses, estates, special education, child welfare, and elsewhere (Kruk, 1997; Mayer, 1995). In addition to mediation, other conflict resolution approaches have also been used to resolve family disputes including: mediation/arbitration (med/arb), family group conferences, case management, settlement conferencing, and more recently collaborative law.

The contradictions families face when having to endure (and that is how it generally feels) legal processes to deal with life issues is great. The legal system asks, What does the law require? What is a legally defensible outcome? Families ask, How can I get through this crisis? How can I get my needs met? How can I be vindicated in some ways? These are very different ways of thinking. Representatives of the legal system often do not like the role they are forced to play by the structure of the system. Judges, lawyers, custody evaluators, child advocates, and other agents of the court have often expressed frustration and dismay at feeling that they are not really helping families and are in fact often making things worse.

These dynamics led to the mushrooming of the family mediation field, especially after the pioneering work of O. J. Coogler and John Haynes in the late 1970s and early 1980s (Coogler, 1978; Haynes, 1981). If ever there has been an arena that seemed like a natural fit for what conflict resolvers have to offer, this is it. Mediation of child custody disputes is mandated in many states or jurisdictions (for example, California and Florida). Professional organizations devoted to this arena have flourished. The family section is currently the largest section of the Association of Conflict Resolution. The Association of Family Conciliation Courts has been a leader in bringing together professionals who work with families in conflict: family court judges, family lawyers, child development experts, mediators, and related professionals. Family Mediation Canada has been a creative force for many years, as have similar groups in Australia, the United Kingdom, Ireland, and elsewhere.

With all this need, commitment, and action, this arena has also remained one of the most controversial and in many ways problematic as well. Feminist critiques of the impact of mediation have raised major concerns about how mediation may play into the power inequalities built into the structure of families and society (Grillo, 1991). The intersection between family mediation and domestic violence has been a major source of controversy. Many family violence workers have argued that mediation should never be used when there has been a history of domestic violence, with some suggesting that because of the hidden prevalence of this phenomenon, family mediation is always inappropriate. Issues around divorce are emotionally and substantively complex. Many critics have argued that substantive experts and advisers are necessary in order to carve out good agreements and that conflict resolution processes tend to exclude, minimize, or at least impede the participation of these experts (legal, financial, child development, and others).

Perhaps the most significant sign of the problems in using conflict resolution for family issues is the sparse voluntary use of mediation in this area. There is an oversupply of family mediators, many of whom are divorce professionals (therapists, lawyers, financial planners) who have wanted to move away from more adversarial roles. But where mediation is not mandatory or systemically referred by courts, it is underused. Where mediation is mandatory, it has been used extensively with relatively high levels of satisfaction (Hann, Barr and Associates, 2001; Macfarlane, 1995). But after twenty-five years of experience, it is still not a service people naturally turn to on their own. Why? Here are some typical reasons that divorce clients have given for resisting mediation:

> "I don't want to sit down with my ex. It makes me too angry [upset, sad, in pain] to be in the same room with him [her]."

> "She [he] is not trustworthy. How can I negotiate with someone who cannot be trusted?"

> "I don't want to be manipulated or taken advantage of."

> "I just want my lawyer to take care of it for me."

> "I don't understand how mediation works. What does the mediator do? Just sit there and smile?"

> "A mediator can't help in this situation. How can mediation help when someone is totally unreasonable and unwilling to compromise?"

"How am I going to know when I have been offered a good
  deal and when I am being played for a fool?"

"I can't afford a mediator, a lawyer, and an evaluator."

Each of these responses can be seen in some sense as a struggle
between an avoidance and engagement response. That is, mediation is seen as a mechanism that requires people to engage directly
in conflict, but without offering some of the tools people need to
feel safe and powerful as they do so. Mediation may also seem to be
an impediment to engaging in conflict because of a common view
people have that mediation is about compromising, "making nice,"
minimizing antagonism, and denying feelings at a time when they
are not feeling like finding a middle ground or being friendly. At the
same time as people want to avoid conflict, they also want to engage it on their own terms and they often view mediation as an
obstacle to this. (For a fuller discussion of this, see Chapter Three.)
Mediators can work with these dynamics, but the fact that people
so seldom choose it on a purely voluntary basis indicates how strong
these beliefs and assumptions are. This resistance requires more
than public relations or education to overcome, because it arises
from the structure of conflict resolution processes.

Another development in family mediation is also significant.
When the family mediation movement began, it was genuinely
multidisciplinary. Mental health practitioners, lawyers, accountants,
child development experts, and family court personnel all had a
strong presence in the family mediation movement. In more recent
years, two trends have changed the character of the field. One is the
increasing dominance of lawyers in the private mediation arena.
The bulk of successful private family mediators are now lawyers. This
may be due in part to the fact that lawyers are the major referral
source for private mediators, and in some circumstances judges have
been willing to refer cases only to lawyers. But this is also indicative
that many people feel they need the protection and assistance of
someone with legal training and experience—more so than someone with mental health skills.

There is no evidence that lawyer mediators achieve better outcomes or higher levels of satisfaction than nonlawyer mediators, but nonetheless, it is the legally trained who are making it professionally as mediators. There is an important message here: people do not simply want process assistance in the family arena (and maybe in other arenas as well). What they believe will help them engage effectively in conflict (give them voice, validation, vindication, impact, procedural justice, and safety) is something more than a communication, negotiation, or conflict guide.

A second trend is the bifurcation in training, background, experience, and approach of private and court-based mediators. Court-connected mediation programs and mediators in private practice seem to be offering very different services. Court-connected programs are not primarily staffed by legally trained mediators. They tend to focus more on parenting issues than financial concerns, they are very time limited, and they are more likely to have an evaluative or reporting component (Welsh, 2001b). This may be due to budgetary and resource considerations, but it also may reflect a different set of needs in an institutionalized setting. Perhaps when the power of the court is in the background and mediators have the amount of experience and support that is typical among court-connected mediators, there is less of a perceived need for legally trained mediators, and the role of the mediator may be different.

The issues around mediation and domestic violence provide some particularly interesting insights because of the passion with which this debate has been conducted. Family violence victims' advocates have been extremely skeptical about whether mediation could ever be appropriate where domestic violence has been an issue. They fear that mediation would fail to protect victims, would maintain a connection that should be broken, and would not provide a level playing field. In effect, they argue that mediation can revictimize people who have been abused. In response, mediators, as well as some victims, have argued that the alternative to mediation is not so effective in protecting people either. Many discussions have been held between advocates, shelter staff, the bench, and the mediation community. The debate continues, although some fairly commonly accepted principles have emerged:

- In domestic violence, mediation should always be voluntary.
- Effective screening mechanisms should be used to determine whether there has been a history of domestic violence.
- If mediation is used, victims (indeed all parties) need advocates, and the mediators should consider keeping the parties separate throughout mediation.
- Mediation should not be used if the victim is not immediately protected—that is, if the victim and perpetrator are still living together or if the victim will have to participate in an unprotected interaction before or after mediation.
- When the abuse has been serious and ongoing and substance abuse is also involved, mediation is not advisable even with protections.

Even with these principles, many still question whether mediation should ever be used when there has been a history of domestic violence. Yet others argue that mediation, when properly conducted, may be the safest way for victims to end a violent relationship (Zylstra, 2001). This debate highlights some of the important concerns people have about mediation more generally. Does mediation protect the less powerful? Can it create a safe environment when there has been a history of intense conflict and violence? Is the structure of mediation too presumptive of equality when society has an obligation to recognize the inequalities and inequities built into a situation? Can mediators really know what is going on in a conflict well enough to structure a process that allows for safe and yet powerful conflict engagement?

Family conflict in some respects highlights both the potential value and the significant limits of conflict resolution processes. The limits of adversarial or adjudicative processes are clear and the need for collaboration over time obvious. Yet mediation in particular has failed to make significant inroads into how family conflicts are handled unless it has been mandated. Whether mandating mediation is good policy or not, the fact that it must be required in order to be used in this arena shows the extent to which the public has not bought many of the premises of mediation advocates.

## Organizational Conflict

Some of the most successful conflict resolution programs have been those instituted in the organizational arena, if a measure of success is how far conflict resolution has been institutionalized and systematized as part of overall organizational decision-making processes. Mediation, advisory mediation, conciliation, and ombuds functions are integral to many organizational processes for dealing with equal employment opportunity issues, grievances, and other workplace disputes.

Many government organizations provide for internal and external mediation. The U.S. federal government has established an extensive shared-neutral program. Each department of the U.S. government is required to designate a dispute resolution coordinator with responsibility for promoting effective approaches to dealing with conflicts within the department. Several agencies, notably the USPS, the Environmental Protection Agency, the Department of Agriculture, and the Department of the Interior, have established extensive programs to resolve conflicts in a productive and appropriate way and have devoted considerable efforts to train dispute resolution specialists. Many state agencies have established similar programs.

With all this activity, an important question to consider is whether the culture of conflict and conflict resolution has changed significantly in these organizations. Perhaps an even more important issue is whether there has been a significant change in the overall tenor of employee-employer relationships and in the relationship of workers to the management of the organization. Are we seeing the paradigm shift that has been written about in so many popular books about organizational culture (for example, Senge,

1990, and Robson, 1982)? Have we seen a shift to more participatory forms of management, flatter organizational structures, and more consensus-based decision making, and has this made a genuine difference to the experience of workers and to organizational performance?

These are still largely unanswered questions. Many studies point to the high levels of grievances and EEO complaints that are being resolved without going to adjudicative or rights-based processes and to the generally high levels of satisfaction with these processes (Bingham, Chesmore, Moon, and Napoli, 2000). Others point to the increasing use of an integrated conflict management system in corporations (Lipsky, Seeber, and Fincher, 2003). But it is not clear that these programs have had an impact on the overall culture of the organization. What is clear is that for the most part, neither workers nor organized labor nor management are demanding programs like this, and although they may be viewed as a benefit, they are not yet embraced as key to the overall health of an organization. In fact, there has been significant suspicion that participatory management, quality circles, Total Quality Management, and employee involvement programs, among other new approaches, are by and large more cosmetic than substantive or, even worse, more about employer control than employee empowerment.

Large organizations, such as government agencies and corporations, are complex systems that can easily swallow up major new initiatives without fundamentally changing their way of doing business. There seem to be major new management trends promulgated all the time, and there is an understandable suspicion or even cynicism about these "flavors of the month." Many approaches such as Total Quality Management, organizational reengineering, and creating learning organizations have been initiated and have failed to change organizations fundamentally. This is not because the concepts or approaches were problematic so much as that organizations cannot be changed easily or intentionally. Unfortunately, many managers and workers have seen conflict resolution programs and conflict management systems in this light.

This is an area in which we may yet see considerably more integration of conflict resolution processes into the overall way in which conflict is being conducted, but at this point, despite a great amount of activity and efforts in the area, these programs still by and large exist at the margin of organizational life. Many large corporations are turning to some form of conflict resolution to assist with internal disputes, but these programs are used to address a rather limited set of issues—EEO, grievances, some issues of sexual harassment—but generally not systemic or fundamental concerns such as reductions in force, relocation, mergers, automation, bankruptcy, acquisitions, or major new organizational initiatives. When extremely serious conflicts do arise in an organization, short of a formal work stoppage, conflict resolution programs are not widely viewed as central to returning an organization to health. (The CPR Institute for Dispute Resolution offers members a corporate pledge that undertakes to "seriously explore negotiation, mediation or other ADR processes in conflicts arising with other signatories before pursuing full-scale litigation." CPR claims four thousand corporate signatories and fifteen hundred law firm signatories. See www.cpradr.org.)

Moreover, when organizations have had major conflicts throughout their management structure or with other organizations that they do business with, short of mediation or arbitration to settle lawsuits, they have not often turned to conflict resolution practitioners for assistance. We may occasionally be asked to facilitate management retreats or labor management dialogues, but we are not seen as major resources for working through the serious and often ongoing systemic conflicts that organizations deal with daily.

In the 1980s, several government organizations (notably the U.S. Army Corps of Engineers) instituted partnering programs to try to anticipate potential conflict with large contractors and to create effective working relationships. These were largely very successful, but this approach has not been used on a wide scale even within those agencies that have had positive experience with them. In this arena, we see that when conflict resolution and related processes are used, people are generally positive about the results, but nonetheless there is a great deal of resistance to using these procedures in a systematic way outside of very limited and defined areas.

## Community Conflict

Some of the most innovative and creative approaches to conflict resolution have emerged in the area of community conflicts. Perhaps the most quickly growing new approaches involve a series of initiatives under the general rubric of restorative justice. These have taken root in communities and schools as an alternative way of dealing with conflicts in which the goal is restoration and healing rather than retributive consequences.

In addition, many communities have established a variety of mediation programs—landlord-tenant, small claims, neighborhood, and zoning, for example—all intended to promote a different kind of community ethos and to divert issues from more formal complaint processes. Another aspect of this work are the many programs that schools have initiated to bring conflict resolution skills and practices to students, parents, teachers, and staff.

Most of these programs are staffed by volunteers, many of whom are dedicated, skilled, and very hard working. Most are also underfunded, underused, and probably underappreciated. Sometimes the very diversity of programs is confusing to potential users and referral sources, and the differences in approaches—restorative, victim-offender, transformative, neighborhood, community panels, and so on—are often of far greater significance to practitioners than to potential users or referral sources.

In one community where I participated in reviewing the range of conflict resolution services offered, I was struck by the number of dedicated, creative, overlapping, competing, and underused programs. There were several city- and county-based mediation programs, restorative justice programs, victim-offender mediation programs, school-based conflict resolution services, services provided through a nearby college, a special program operated through law enforcement, and quite a few private mediators as well.

In talking to several of the agencies and individuals who were frequent sources of referral to mediation (municipal courts, city attorney, police, schools, and others), we found two common responses to this multiplicity of services. People either selected one particular service and approach, usually because they had had positive previous experiences or personal connections with key program staff, or they threw up their hands and did not use the services at all.

Another problem that community conflict resolution programs face is common to many other arenas of practice as well. Either people do not want to engage, and therefore avoid any acknowledgment of conflict and the use of any conflict resolution service, or they are so far into the conflict process that they avoid anything that smacks of collaboration, cooperation, or compromise (see Engle Merry and Silbey, 1984). One court officer said, "There are wonderful mediation services and wonderful mediators, and they do a good job. The problem is that by the time people get to us, it is too late. They feel they have been violated, and they want their day in court."

That these programs can provide a useful service is clear. That they are especially meaningful and valuable to the volunteers and staff who work with them is also clear. Unfortunately, as in so many other arenas, it seems that the public sees them as tangential to how they want to deal with community conflicts.

One of the most successful efforts of conflict resolution professionals to engage in a major community conflict occurred in Cincinnati partly in response to the rioting that occurred several years ago. After a police shooting, the Cincinnati community erupted, and considerable anger was expressed around issues related to racial profiling. An extensive community dialogue was organized under the auspices of the court and coordinated by Jay Rothman, president of the Aria Institute in Yellow Springs, Ohio. After many meetings, surveys, discussions, and public input, a stakeholder group, including community leaders, police officials, police union members, city officials, and the churches and synagogues of Cincinnati, developed a protocol around racial profiling and police-community relations. This was an example of how effective creative approaches to conflict resolution can be, but it was also an exception.

Racial profiling is cause for significant public concern in many communities. So are issues about public housing, school closure, location of shopping malls or transportation facilities, allocation of diminishing public funds among competing service needs, and a range of racial conflicts. Examples of effective conflict resolution efforts can be found in each of these arenas, but they continue to be the exception, despite the fact that, as in Cincinnati, their potential to make a major contribution has been demonstrated.

A common dilemma for people who operate community mediation programs is the disparity between the enthusiasm of newly trained and excited volunteers who are eager to get going and the relative lack of cases. In some programs, volunteer mediators may participate in one or two cases a year at best. This is not enough involvement to maintain either individual commitment to the program or intervention skills. In this arena as in others, the paradox of satisfied users and an uninterested public remains. We have not been short of creative approaches to conflict and new ways of bringing people together, but we have not been effective at facing the root causes of the public's resistance to engage in a fuller and more systemic way.

We can look at the enthusiasm for community-based conflict resolution programs as a sign of the interest and potential value of this approach to building and preserving community. The excitement that these programs generate from potential volunteers is also a sign that conflict resolution touches on a fundamental value and need that people have. But there is a less promising and equally clear message in the underuse of community programs, the poor and perhaps diminishing public funding of them, the lack of balance between those interested in mediating and those wanting mediation, and the peripheral role these programs play in the most fundamental conflicts that communities face.

## Facing Resistance and Learning from It

Has conflict resolution been rejected? It has by some for sure, but perhaps the fairer conclusion is that conflict resolution has not been very widely or warmly embraced by most of the public or organizations we might potentially serve. There are conflict resolution programs everywhere, as well as skilled and committed practitioners. But there is a consistent pattern of underuse, marginalization, and skepticism. Call it rejection, call it resistance, or call it a natural developmental trajectory of a new field of practice. Regardless, this is a pattern that cannot be ignored or wished away. It must be confronted and dealt with if our field is going to flourish and reach the potential that I believe it has to have a positive impact on the way we conduct ourselves in conflict and thereby influence our communal experience.

In order to deal with this crisis, we need to learn from this tepid public and institutional response and from the broad criticisms that have been leveled against our field. Several key themes emerge from the critiques, the research, and the experience of users across different arenas:

- *The more intense or vital the conflict is, the less likely it is that people will use conflict resolution services.* There is a middle ground of conflicts—sometimes a very narrow middle ground—for which conflict resolution services are used. When the conflict is seen as too intense, too crucial, or too frightening, then more traditional approaches are more comforting or acceptable. Also, even when people are willing to use conflict resolution services, they tend not to believe that the really important decisions are made in this context.

- *Conflict resolution processes are not viewed as genuinely impartial, neutral, or even-handed.* In many arenas where power is an issue in conflict (as it almost always is), people do not feel that conflict resolution processes can help to level the playing field fundamentally. Where there is a need for affirmative steps to be taken to counter a structural inequality, conflict resolution is seen at best as ineffective and at worst as a forum that exacerbates these inequalities. While the conflict resolution professional may be seen as neutral, the nature of the process itself is viewed by many as reinforcing existing inequalities. Perhaps even more important, the concept of neutrality itself is suspicious to people embroiled in conflict. Neutrality too easily translates into not caring, not engaging, not being genuinely supportive, or not really hearing and understanding what people have to say. Disputants are often more willing to listen to advocates counsel cooperation, collaboration, or compromise than to people who present themselves as neutral.

• *Conflict resolution programs are not effective at helping people deal with the avoidance-engagement dilemma.* In essence, most conflict resolution approaches ask people to engage in conflict, to overcome the many ways in which they normally chose to avoid conflict, but to do so without many of the structural safeguards offered by adjudication, political processes, or advocate-centered efforts. We all struggle with wanting both to engage in and avoid conflict. This is true of institutions, groups, and communities, as well as individuals. Effective approaches to conflict have to help people negotiate these competing tendencies. There are good reasons for people to engage in conflict directly, take ownership of it, and employ alternatives to rights- and power-based approaches. However, the mechanisms that we have developed for helping people to do so have not provided adequate enough structures to help them feel safe, effective, and heard once they do engage. So far, conflict resolution programs have not measured up to more traditional approaches to conflict in helping people handle the competing tendencies to avoid and engage in a way that feels safe.

• *Consensus-building efforts are often viewed as shallow, inefficient, and facile.* When serious conflicts need to be seriously engaged, collaborative dialogue, facilitated problem solving, and third-party neutrals are not seen as effective or efficient. Often they seem to result in shallow solutions that do not address the deepest concerns people have. It often seems to participants in conflict that they will have to give up the depths of their feelings or compromise on issues important to them if they are going to work on a conflict through a collaborative process.

• *Conflict resolution processes do not deal with power effectively.* Much of this comes back to the question of power. When people feel that they are powerless or powerful, they question the wisdom of conflict resolution processes. Those who are less powerful (or who represent the less powerful) often worry that they will have to sacrifice the one important source of power they have—their rights under the law or another existing formal structure—in order to participate in a consensus-based process. Those who believe they have the power or authority to get their interests met often feel they will have to compromise this in order to participate in conflict resolution efforts. Ironically, in a way, the powerful and powerless share this challenge. Systems based on neutrality and on consensus problem solving ask people to set aside the normal power they might have and try to get their needs met on a very different basis. This requires faith that productive results can come from a process that specifically addresses power differences, and many people, particularly in the midst of serious conflict, do not have this faith. We have to ask ourselves whether we can genuinely offer people approaches to conflict that address power issues, especially from a third-party stance.

---

The critiques or conflict resolution outlined in this chapter reflect fundamental concerns and perceptions that will not go away with education or the continued application of the best mediation or collaborative problem-solving processes. They are built into some basic realities about how people function in conflict. To address these too simply or in too facile a manner reinforces the basic nature of the problem. We have not taken conflict seriously enough, or perhaps more accurately, we have tried to address very serious conflict with overly simplistic tools. We have been too confident that a third-party neutral, using a well-designed collaborative or consensus-building process, can help people in serious conflict address their most important issues. In some specific conflicts and settings, we have been able to do exactly this. But across the whole set of conflict arenas that we work in, people are skeptical as to whether our current tools and models are adequate to tackle their issues in an effective, deep, powerful, and efficient way. We have to come up with better and deeper answers than we have so far if we are going to be able to break out of our limited presence in serious conflict.

In order to consider this further, let's look at the single approach to cooperative conflict resolution most associated with our field: mediation.

# 3

## The Use (and Misuse) of Mediation

Conflict resolution as a field has largely been identified with the third-party neutral role and especially the role of the mediator. Therein lies a great strength, but also a significant limitation.

By maintaining this rather narrow identification, the field of conflict resolution has presented a more tangible representation of what we do and who we are. Rather than discussing our work by focusing on communication, integrative negotiation, process design, or conflict analysis, which are often hard to explain simply, we have instead been able to explain our field in terms of the neutral and procedural role of mediators. Furthermore, we have been able to create training, certification, ethical guidelines, and organizational membership categories based on this role.

If I say that I work in the field of conflict resolution, relatively few people will have any idea of what I do, but if I say that I am a mediator, most people will have some sense about the nature of my work. If anyone wants to experience this difference, try answering an immigration official's question about your work by saying you are a conflict resolution professional. Or try answering questions on loan applications or insurance forms in this way. Very likely you will confuse people, raise questions, or arouse suspicions.

Having a concrete and clear role has also allowed us to market ourselves more effectively. Identifying ourselves as a mediator or facilitator helps declare to ourselves and to the public exactly what can be expected of us and to what standards we can be held accountable. This clarity of accountability is an important part of what distinguishes a profession.

So there are many reasons that we have gravitated toward an identification of conflict resolution with the third-party neutral role and in particular with mediation. But we also pay a big price for doing this.

Many (although not all) of the concerns outlined in the previous chapter are particularly directed at the third-party neutral role. For the most part, when people do not feel the need for third-party neutral assistance, or when conflict resolution practitioners have not seen a way of gaining entrée into a conflict as a neutral, conflict resolution has been seen as irrelevant.

## The Problem of Neutrality

One reason that third-party neutrals sometimes seem irrelevant is the difficulty in defining neutrality. Neutrality is a hard concept to nail down. It has different meanings in different cultural contexts. In some contexts, the term *neutral* is associated with being inactive, ineffective, or even cowardly. In others, it is viewed as a sine qua non for third parties to establish respect. But even in a middle-class North American context, the acceptability of a neutral stance varies greatly from conflict to conflict. In the middle of intense conflict, many do not believe anyone can or should be neutral. Someone who professes neutrality is therefore likely to be viewed with suspicion or even disdain. Our ability to assist people in conflict can therefore be seriously constrained by the neutral role.

### The Third Party

Being a third party is not the same as being a neutral. Third parties are present in one form or another to assist people in conflict in almost every society and perhaps in every social system, but these are not usually people who approach problems from a neutral stance or from a primarily procedural point of view. Parents trying to help children resolve a dispute do not generally view themselves as neutral. When an elder in a clan or tribe is looked to for assistance in resolving a conflict, that person is not generally viewed as neutral either.

Generally, the commitment of third parties is to help people work through a conflict in a wise way and in keeping with a certain set of values or standards, but not necessarily without taking sides or having one's own interests at stake as well. In one of the most famous examples of successful international mediation, the Camp David negotiations between Anwar Sadat and Menachem Begin, which was one of the accomplishments cited when he was awarded the Nobel Peace Prize, President Jimmy Carter was certainly not a neutral. He had to represent the interests of the United States, and he also had a great deal of resources to draw on to reward the parties for reaching an agreement (or sanction them for not).

In our field, however, most of us equate the third-party role with being neutral, process focused, and interest based. Usually this means mediation or facilitation. Despite the argument that many have made—that we should think of the field more broadly—mediation still seems to be the defining role, the fulcrum of the modern conflict resolution movement.

In the previous chapters, I have focused on a broader discussion of conflict resolution, but since mediation is perhaps the key identity of so many in the field, attention needs to be given specifically to this function. If we are going to face the limits of conflict resolution, we also have to face the specific limits of mediation. If we are going to grow beyond these limits, we also have to be clear about what is effective and powerful that mediators offer, and this means understanding the heart of what mediation provides to people in conflict.

The focus of this chapter is on mediation's challenges, shortcomings, and strengths, taking a broad view of what we mean by mediation. I view mediation as inclusive of many types of third-party, nonbinding interventions ranging from evaluative to transformative, directive to facilitative, active to passive, and substance focused to process focused.

## Defining Mediation

It's important to take this broad approach since we won't move our field forward if we create a mediation orthodoxy. Many different approaches to mediation can work, depending on the conflict, the parties, and the skills of the mediator. But taking a broad view of mediation raises its own questions about where the boundary between mediation and fundamentally different approaches to conflict and decision making lies, so I first suggest some definitions of mediation.

The essence of mediation, as I see it, lies in four characteristics:

- *Impartiality.* Mediators do not see their job as trying to promote one person or group's interests at the expense of another.
- *Process orientation.* Mediators conduct a process to assist people in communicating about the issues that are of concern to them. They do not focus on the substance of the issues alone (although the role mediators play with regard to substance may vary considerably).
- *Problem solving.* Mediators do not simply try to decide what the law dictates; they endeavor to help solve the problems that underlie the conflict. Often, but not always, this means taking an integrative or interest-based approach.
- *Client focused.* The mediator's goal is to attain a solution that the disputants will accept rather than to impose one on them. Usually this means focusing on clients' interaction, communication, emotions, needs, and decision-making process.

The key question is, When does an approach exhibiting these characteristics provide something people in dispute want, and when does it not? Two other important questions are implied by this: When do people really want mediation, and when do they resist it? What type of mediation do people want, and why? My belief is that as a field, we have tended to view mediation as the preferable approach to most conflicts. When mediation has not been possible or desirable, we have not been very effective about figuring out other ways in which we might have an important or constructive role to play. And when mediation has been possible, then we have gravitated to that role as the only and most important one for us to fulfill. Instead, we should view mediation as just one tool at our disposal for dealing with conflict. We should be clear about when and how it can be used effectively, but not let ourselves be boxed in by our identification with mediation, or we will not get past the current limits on our work.

## Why Has Mediation Been Rejected?

Let's start with the bad news. Why and when have people rejected, resisted, or simply avoided mediation? For the most part, the widespread use of mediation has been limited to a fairly narrow range of conflict situations: those that are not too difficult or not worth the trouble. Mediation is not generally sought after and may be actively resisted if

- The conflict is too intense or not intense enough.
- The stakes are too high or too low.
- People are too angry or not angry enough.
- People feel too powerless or too powerful.
- People have an excellent alternative to negotiation or no alternative but to capitulate.
- Issues are too complex, or there is only a single issue involved.
- There are no relationship issues involved (it's all about substance), or the main concern is an acrimonious relationship.
- There has been no history of conflict, or the history of conflict is extremely long.

These are factors, not absolute criteria for when mediation is sought or avoided. Mediation is sometimes used in conflicts that have a very long history, with a great deal of violence, the stakes are high, and there are major power differences. And it is sometimes used in conflicts that have been chronic and long enduring among people who know each other well. But mediation, in the sense of involving third-party neutrals with a process orientation, is not usually sought after in these situations. Why?

Each of these factors describes a continuum along which a conflict may exist. If a conflict falls at one end or the other end of the continuum, then mediation is less likely to be used. For example, if a dispute is too intense, people may well feel unsafe in mediation, but if it is not intense enough, then the effort and engagement that mediation requires may not seem worth the trouble. When a conflict does not fall in the middle range of these continua, mediation is resisted, rejected, or avoided.

Often mediation is rejected even though it might have something of value to offer, but despite this, parties still find it either too demanding or not sufficiently powerful or safe. There is a very small, sometimes nonexistent distance between when a conflict seems worthy of the effort and commitment required in mediation and when it seems too important or complicated to be sorted out without the involvement of advocates or those with decision-making or enforcement authority.

Mediation demands a commitment of time, emotional energy, intellectual effort, and financial resources. It also requires a willingness to take risks and accept responsibility for searching for acceptable solutions. Most important of all, it requires that people own up to the fact that a conflict exists and they must face it. Often a conflict does not seem worth all the effort involved in mediation.

In the workplace disputes I have mediated, people have almost always tried three approaches before they have asked for mediation:

- Ignoring the issues
- Asking for a change
- Using informal resources (friends, colleagues, or a supervisor's intervention)

Taking the next step of filing a complaint or asking for mediation generally involves an important shift in outlook or energy: accepting that there is a problem that cannot be solved (or is much less likely to be solved) without outside help. Sometimes the most important and constructive aspect of a mediation occurs simply because someone has opened up an issue by asking for help. But once an issue is opened up, people have admitted to themselves that it exists, then it can suddenly seem enormous—far too serious to be solved in a voluntaristic way, using primarily process-oriented assistance.

The jump from avoiding conflict to seeking a powerful intervention tends to leap right over mediation. As a result, and at some cost to the spirit of mediation, we rely on the mandatory programs as an ongoing necessity.

In many different areas, we can observe a similar leap from a desire to avoid to a wish for more power- or rights-based approaches. In the child protection arena, child welfare agencies tend to either avoid intervention entirely or prefer more authoritative court-based intervention processes. In divorce mediation, the vast bulk of cases are settled through direct negotiation or lawyer-assisted negotiation between the divorcing couple. Of those that are not settled through direct negotiation, especially in which the conflicts are too great or the stakes too high, mediation is relatively rare when not mandated (Kakalik and others, 1997). In community conflicts, the easy conflicts often do not require mediation, and the really intense ones usually rely on other processes. This pattern can be seen even in international conflicts, where mediation is reserved for a very small and specific category of conflicts, and mediating organizations, such as the United Nations, are often viewed with skepticism.

## Working on Major Conflicts

Those conflict resolvers who have engaged in conflicts of a more serious nature on a regular basis have generally done so in some role other than mediators in the sense we have been using that term.

They have been advisers, coaches, power figures, resource providers, or advocates. When mediators have engaged in more serious conflicts, it has often been after court decisions have been made, political contests decided, or some other occurrence has played out that has defined the alternatives much more narrowly and thus lowered the stakes considerably.

Many critics of mediation might argue that this is a good thing, because mediation is not ideally suited for establishing fundamental policy. Some mediators would agree that the courts or political processes are more effective when fundamental policy needs to be hashed out, power differentials are such that the rights of weaker parties cannot be protected through mediation, or value differences are extreme. Others might argue that mediation can be as effective as, or maybe more effective than, any of the alternatives available to parties to solve these types of disputes in a fair and constructive way.

But what we argue does not really matter. The fact is that mediation is not usually selected and may be very actively resisted when the conflict is too severe or the stakes are too high, or when the conflict has not become serious enough to encourage attention at all. We can argue all we want that its use should be more extensive, but that will not alter the fundamental attitudes that people bring to a procedure defined by neutrality, a focus on interests, and a process orientation.

## Indirect Resistance

Mediation is sometimes rejected passively, sometimes actively, and the rejection is sometimes institutional, sometimes personal. Probably the most common rejection occurs through simple lack of use: people do not make use of available services. But even when there is an expectation that mediation will be used, people often find ways of bypassing it, delaying its use, or finding ways to get around it. I am impressed by the creativity people sometimes use to avoid engaging in a mediation, even when they have ostensibly agreed to participate:

Marie and James filed a grievance claiming discrimination against their supervisor at a public agency. They also agreed to mediate. In my preliminary discussion with them, they described a history of actions that they considered examples of disrespect and favoritism on the part of Don, their supervisor. Don felt that they were unwilling to accept any standard setting on his part, but said that he really wanted to work with them. All appeared to want to work this out, and the issues on the surface did not seem insurmountable.

But when it came time to set up the actual mediation, a series of problems occurred that led to a six-month delay. Weather problems, car breakdowns, medical appointments, training programs, family emergencies, and an unrelated court hearing all played into the picture. On at least two occasions, I appeared for a meeting, only to find it had been cancelled. Finally, by the time we did meet, Marie and James started out by saying how much they actually liked Don (who reciprocated) but how strongly they still felt about the substantive issues. They also said that they had decided to transfer out of this department, so the mediation was moot.

This was a case where, from their point of view, both too little and too much was at stake to mediate: too little in that the substantive issues were actually quite small and the outcome might not have warranted the emotional effort; too large in that very basic relationship issues were involved that they did not want to face or did not feel that they could effectively address with each other in mediation or perhaps in any forum involving direct interaction.

## Direct Resistance

People and institutions openly and actively resist mediation as well. They do this by outright refusal to participate and by using all the open means at their disposal to avoid mediating, including court action, no-shows, failing to agree on mediators, being completely uncooperative in mediation, or setting up unrealistic time or logistical parameters for mediation. Often this open and active stance is easier to deal with than the passive or indirect refusal. For one thing, we can more easily work with people under these circumstances to assess whether mediation makes sense. Second, the issues or concerns are likely to be more obvious and thus can be more readily addressed.

Organizations and groups often take more systemic approaches to resisting participation in mediation, both passive and overt. Resistance is sometimes linked to elaborate efforts to set up mediation programs, but these are then underfunded, underpublicized, underused, and undercut. In several public agencies I have worked with, there has been an ostensible commitment to incorporate mediation into all personnel disputes, and potential mediators have been selected and trained. These mediators have become excited, committed, and eager to get going. What they have then faced, however, has been agency resistance to giving them time to mediate; inadequate funding for support, consultation, program administration, and travel; and a widespread resistance of key people, both managers and workers, to use these services or bring the real issues to the table in an open way.

There are many reasons for rejecting, resisting, or simply not using mediation. But in the end, they all come down to the very small and somewhat rigid boundaries within which most people are willing to accept the use of an approach that is based on neutrality, process, and interests to address the conflicts that they face.

## When Mediation Has Been Marginalized

In many circumstances, mediation has been accepted, but only in a very specific or marginal manner. Where many of us who are mediators have seen the potential for helping in a much larger context and are eager to do so, we are often constrained to play a marginal role at the edge of the major issues. These three examples, from different arenas, will be familiar to mediators:

• *Family: "Mediation is fine, as long as there are not big bucks involved."* I have heard many versions of this statement. In many jurisdictions, mediation is mandated or court mediation services are provided for parenting issues, but mediation is not promoted for financial issues. Another variation is when family mediators are deemed useful for minor or simple financial matters, but for complex issues involving large amounts, people tend to want to go to retired judges or rely on a more traditional approach to problem solving. This assumes that parenting and financial issues can be separated, which may be possible legally but is often not practical.

• *International: "Mediators have really helped with 'track two diplomacy,' but for real negotiation we need the power players."* Track *two diplomacy* refers to citizen-to-citizen dialogue, as opposed to government-to-government negotiations. While mediators have been used in places like Bosnia and Northern Ireland, the third parties, more often than not, are not mediators in the sense we have been using the term. Senator George Mitchell played a critical role in Northern Ireland, as did Richard Holbrook in Bosnia, Jimmy Carter and Colin Powell in Haiti, and Presidents Bush, Clinton, and Bush in the Middle East. But all of these were mediators who represented powerful interests and could bring important resources to bear as incentives or consequences. When mediators have been used in track one situations, it has been on peripheral issues. I facilitated discussions between the Russian, U.S., and Norwegian defense departments about issues related to Arctic military waste. But although everyone found the facilitation useful, they also thought it very unusual and even strange to be using an employee of a nongovernmental organization for these purposes.

• *Employment: "Mediators are great for grievances, as long as they don't touch anything that has to do with workers' rights [or management prerogatives]."* This is an area in which very effective mediation has been provided by federal mediation services (the Federal Mediation and Conciliation Service in the United States, the Employment Tribunal in New Zealand, the Canadian Industrial Relations Board, and similar agencies elsewhere). In this arena, neutral, process-oriented, interest-based mediators have played a role in some of the most significant conflicts. But their work primarily occurs in two ways: during the collective bargaining process itself or in relationship to specific grievances. Major issues that arise outside regulated collective bargaining processes are less likely to involve mediation. In these situations, if direct negotiations do not work, power- or rights-based approaches are more likely to be employed.

In each of these situations, the use of mediation is to some extent accepted and sometimes even sought after, but in very circumscribed ways. Why has the use of mediation been limited or marginalized in so many different arenas? Many of the reasons are similar to those leading people to reject mediation altogether, but there are some additional factors to consider as well.

Two elements seem critical: a conditional realization of the need for conflict resolution assistance and a fear about the impact that mediation will have on the precarious equilibrium of the power system.

## Conditional Realization

In many circumstances, people are uncomfortable with the array of approaches to conflict normally available to them, and they want help to change how they or the groups they represent deal with conflict. This accounts for the considerable growth of mediation over the past twenty years. Fundamentally, people know that there has to be a better way—that too many resources are being spent on unproductive conflict interactions. Whether we are talking about labor-management problems, community disputes, or family conflict, this awareness is widespread.

Mediation and closely related approaches have been presented as a significant alternative, and when people have tried to use these, they have been generally satisfied, but they have also sensed that these do not address the more fundamental conflicts that are the foundation for the more specific issues that are taken to mediation.

So while people want alternative ways for dealing with the important conflicts they face, and therefore are attracted to mediation, they also sense that it may not be a powerful enough approach to the basic struggles they experience. But people are also fearful of rocking the boat, of taking on these struggles. Mediation can appear to be an unpredictable process that may take people to a level of conflict they are not prepared for. This has resulted in an approach-avoidance dynamic that causes people to accept mediation but to marginalize it.

## Fear of Impact

This is related to the second dynamic: concerns about disrupting the equilibrium of the system of power. In many conflicts, people want change but are afraid of it, and one of the things they fear is upsetting a precarious but important set of power relationships. Between workers and management, serious conflict may exist, methods of interacting may be unproductive, and everyone may feel frustrated, but at the same time, the allocation of power and the interactions about power among different parts of the system are often the result of hard-fought and costly previous struggles.

Often whole systems of relationships have been built up around the outcome of these struggles, and any alteration of the fundamental way in which power is wielded threatens this system of relationships. Executives, human resource personnel, labor relation specialists, outside counsel, supervisors, stockholders, the board of directors, and others have evolved a network of relationships, in part defined by the relationship between workers and managers. Similarly, union officials, union staff, union counsel, shop stewards, negotiating committee members, and members in general have developed their own internal network.

Accepting mediation into the core of this relationship, with its different values, assumptions, procedures, and structures, can threaten to disrupt this web of relationships, or at least force it to reorganize in a different way. To many, this feels like more of a roll of the dice than they are ready for. A better alternative is to allow mediators in to help change how conflict is handled, but in a very encapsulated way, away from the areas of major conflict and major concern.

When I have been allowed into the arena of major conflict in organizations, it has been because the system of power relationships had significantly broken down and people felt they had little to lose by trying something very different or because the alternative for them was to exit the system.

In this pattern of marginalization, there is both a warning and a hope. The warning is to be wary of trying to push mediation into areas where people feel their fundamental position or source of influence is at stake. The hope lies in the recognition that many disputants have that something different needs to happen. People often do not like the way conflict is handled and the alternatives open to them seem inadequate, but they do not see the answer for their most fundamental concerns to lie with mediation as we normally construe it. If we can recognize the essence of the need at the same time as we are realistic about the limits of what we have to offer as mediators, then we have a major opportunity to help people with the most essential conflicts they face.

## The Misuse of Mediation

Consider these illustrative stories:

Some years back, I was approached at a social gathering by an attorney who had represented several people involved in mediations that I had conducted. Maybe because of the social atmosphere, maybe because of his liquid consumption, he seemed to feel the need to share his "mediation secret" with me. I wished he hadn't because it caused me an ethical dilemma whenever future clients of his came to mediation. He said, "I really like sending my clients to mediation, and I do it all the time. I don't ever want them to settle, but I obtain lots of useful information that way, and it prepares them to go to court."

At about that same time, a partner and I were asked to serve as comediators in an organizational dispute. We found out, after a day of meetings, that a decision had been made to fire several key staff. The leadership of the organization had ratified this decision, and an elaborate letter of dismissal had been prepared. However, since the staff had been promised mediation, they were going to go forward with it, but they were also committed to its failure.

Over the years, my colleagues and I have been approached by a number of organizations that have requested assistance in setting up mediation programs with the express purpose of avoiding unionization. When we have asked whether they were primarily interested in forestalling unions or in setting up more effective ways of dealing with organizational disputes, we have usually been given the "correct" answer—solving disputes fairly and collaboratively—but not always. Sometimes, however, people have come right out and said that avoiding unionization was their number one motive.

The director of public works of a midsize city asked me to facilitate a negotiation between a neighborhood and the city about a plan to redesign a major thoroughfare through the neighborhood. As is my normal practice, I spent some time asking whether this was a "whether" or a "how" question (whether to do the redesign or how to do it) so that the parameters within which the city was willing to negotiate were clear to the community as they decided whether they wanted to participate. The city insisted that it was both, but on pressing them a bit, I found out that they were willing to discuss the "whether" because they were completely sure they could convince the neighbors to proceed with the plan. "What if you can't?" I asked. "We will be able to," was the reply. "But what if you can't and they really do not want to go forward? Are you willing to consider alternatives?" And so it went. The city representatives persisted in maintaining their willingness to discuss the "whether" because the wise course of action seemed so obvious to them and they were sure they could sell it to the neighbors. They never entertained the possibility that the project would not go forward. But the neighborhood had a different idea about what constituted a wise course of action, and the redesign never occurred.

What is most interesting to me about these stories is not the questionable motives or manipulative approaches to mediation, but how open people were about them. They make me wonder about the many times that such motivations are present but we are unaware of them. I always assume that some less-than-straightforward motives are present, usually mixed in with a genuine desire to make progress, and I have no problem with this. But when the fundamental intention is to use mediation for something other than its ostensible purpose, a serious ethical and practical problem is present.

The ethical problem is obvious: mediation is being used not to help deal with conflict in a constructive manner but to take advantage of others and to manipulate and mislead them. In each of these situations, a useful and valuable interchange might have been possible, but instead people were choosing a more manipulative and less transparent path. The more practical problem is that these motives eventually become clear, perhaps not in every case but as a pattern of behavior. As a result, the whole mediation field, and conflict resolution more generally, loses credibility and is viewed with increasing suspicion, and people become more reluctant to be disclosing and risk taking when in mediation.

How prevalent is this tendency to use mediation for manipulative purposes? In her groundbreaking study on mediation and culture change, Macfarlane (2002) studied the impact of mandatory mediation of commercial disputes in Toronto and Ottawa and identified five "ideal types" of litigator response to this mandatory program: the pragmatist, true believer, instrumentalist, dismisser, and oppositionist. Consider her description of the instrumentalist: "This lawyer has assimilated mediation as a procedural tool to be efficiently utilized or alternatively avoided or neutralized by showing up but not engaging. Favorite instrumental strategies include using mediation to reduce the expectations of the other side, or as a fishing expedition to obtain early discovery" (p. 257). Macfarlane cites two statements from lawyers she interviewed to illustrate this archetype: "Mediation is the perfect opportunity for the fishing expedition, which prior to this was not available to counsel" and "You can tie everyone up and keep them further away from getting their dispute resolved through . . . a mediation process than anything else" (p. 257). In her research, Macfarlane found that these attitudes were fairly prevalent, particularly in the larger and more intense commercial climate of Toronto.

Although it is tempting to ascribe the misuse of mediation to unethical behavior on the part of advocates or disputants, and that certainly is part of the picture, we would be missing the real message of this by doing so. Mediation is in fact an opportunity for "fishing expeditions," delays, offering false hopes, pretending to collaborate, and so forth. Disputants and their advocates know this, and they sometimes use it for opportunistic purposes. Depending on how blatantly manipulative or dishonest people are and how much this instrumental approach is tempered by a reasonable effort to make progress, this behavior is more or less unethical. But whether it is ethical or not, mediation is subject to this type of use, and this explains some of the reservations and misgivings people have about it.

While mediation can be misused in many different ways, several seem particularly prevalent:

- People are not trying to make genuine progress on a conflict but to gain an advantage so that they can pursue distributive ends in another arena.

- Mediation is used to avoid dealing with a conflict through delay, muddling the issues, or misdirecting people's attention.

- Mediation is used to prevent people from gaining access to legitimate sources of power that they would otherwise have access to that could help address a major source of inequality.

- Mediation is used to sell an outcome that has already been decided on.

- Mediation is used to give the pretense of cooperation, collaboration, or participation in decision making when the actual decision is being made elsewhere.

- Mediation is used to intimidate, threaten, or further disempower someone in a vulnerable position.

- Mediation is used to translate social problems into individual problems and structural concerns into psychological issues.

- Mediation is used to impose a dominant cultural set of values and approaches to decision making and communication on other cultures.

The problem we should face is that these are not rare or hypothetical concerns, but frequent phenomena that the very structure of mediation invites and allows. This does not mean mediation is in itself a problem or a socially undesirable approach to conflict. It does mean, however, that the concerns that many have about entering into mediation are not unfounded and that conflict resolvers cannot be naive or simplistic in their approach to these if they expect to be taken seriously when serious conflict is involved.

## Why Mediation Has Been Embraced

With all the resistance, limitations, and misuse, mediation and related activities nonetheless continue to play a vital role in conflict. With all the problems I see our field facing, I do not for one minute doubt the continued importance and value of mediation as a tool for dealing with interpersonal and intergroup conflict. The number of mediations that are occurring, the number of organizations and communities that have instituted mediation services, the schools offering mediation programs, and the people interested in studying and practicing as mediators continue to grow. Clearly, mediation as a field offers something very important to people in conflict. In understanding the challenges to our field and the opportunities that await us, we must not lose sight of this or weaken our ability to deliver this service.

Much has been written about how mediation can help people in conflict and the different ways in which people can use mediation. My concern in writing this book is that as a field, we have not adequately confronted and learned from the problems that we have faced, but we must keep those problems in perspective. We must not lose sight of the continuing value of mediation and the circumstances in which mediation is genuinely embraced. This suggests two questions for us to consider. When is mediation embraced? and What is the essence of the attraction of mediation?

## Key Factors in Acceptance

I believe mediation is embraced under three circumstances:

- A conflict falls in the middle range of seriousness and intensity.
- The use of preferred alternatives to mediation is unavailable or impractical.
- People have sufficiently engaged in conflict that they are ready to move to a resolution phase.

When these factors are present, disputants are more likely to embrace mediation, and to the extent they are absent, resistance is more likely.

I have suggested eight variables that could help explain the rejection of mediation. These variables, of course, can also suggest when mediation might be embraced. For example, when people are angry enough to feel they have to do something about a conflict, but not so angry that they cannot imagine directly interacting with an adversary, then mediation may well be appropriate. Or when a dispute is serious enough that people are encouraged to overcome their avoidance tendencies, but not so serious that the "big guns need to be brought out," mediation is more likely. Of course, mediation is sometimes sought even when anger levels are extreme or a conflict is very serious, but under those circumstances, mediation is more likely to be resisted. What can overcome this resistance is the absence of acceptable alternative avenues for resolving a dispute:

> One of the earliest child welfare cases I mediated was also one of the most distressing. A young child about three years old had been in foster care since about the age of one because of a history of abuse and neglect. One of the suspected abusers was her older brother, but the single parent was also involved. Even with the child in placement, it had been hard to control the abuse, and a serious incident of abuse occurred during a supervised visit at a department of human services facility.
>
> Despite this, the case for termination of parental rights dragged on, and although termination was the likely outcome, it was by no means certain. I was asked to consult about this case in my capacity as a child and family therapist at that time, but instead—without clearly knowing how this might look—I suggested mediation. With some skepticism, everyone agreed, and the outcome was a voluntary relinquishment of parental rights and adoption by the foster family.
>
> The thinking processes that led each of the parties involved to agree to mediation was very instructive. The attorney for the birth parent felt he had a case, due to procedural irregularities, to delay and obstruct termination, at least for a while and maybe for quite a while. However, he was wise enough to recognize that the child probably would not be returned home for a long time and that dragging the case on was not in the client's interest. The birth parent had her hands full as it was and did not want to face the reality of abuse, but she was having a hard time accepting the necessity to give up her parental role entirely. The child protection agency representatives thought they had little to lose by trying mediation, that the court process would be very difficult and somewhat uncertain, but that they could not

let the child return to the birth parent under any circumstances. Key to this were the foster/adopt parents, who were almost desperate. They felt let down by the courts, the child welfare system, and all the lawyers involved, and they felt that to return the child to the parents would be completely unconscionable. For them, the conflict could not be more serious from an emotional and substantive point of view.

## Mediating the Elian Gonzales Case?

Years later, when the Elian Gonzales case was in the news, I wondered why there was no serious attempt to mediate that situation. The head of a local Catholic college, Sister Jean O'Laughlin, did act in a mediating capacity, but she ended up playing a fairly public and in the end nonneutral role, and from the outside at least, it appeared that this attempt at mediation was more for show than to work out a solution that could allow Elian some ongoing relationship with all elements of his family.

Why was it that mediation was embraced and used well in the one situation but manipulated and resisted in the other? Both were extremely serious from the point of view of the participants. In both cases, emotions were running high, and in both cases a variety of integrative solutions were at least possible.

One obvious answer is that the Gonzales case was highly politicized and very public, and represented far wider community interests—in other words, the stakes were much higher. In addition, perhaps partly as a result, key players seemed to think there were preferable available alternatives to mediation. The Miami-based family of Elian Gonzalez felt they could rally the considerable support of the local Cuban American community, local politicians, and local media. They also knew they would lose that support if they agreed to any solution that would result in Elian's return to Cuba. The U.S. government did not want to remove Elian forcibly but knew that it could and that large numbers of Americans probably would support this. Elian's father believed that he could rely on the U.S. government to back him up and that any compromise with the American family would reduce his support in Cuba. So from his point of view, there was a preferable alternative to mediation.

Elian's family was not ready for resolution, at least not of an integrative nature; they were still in an engagement mode, possibly because the conflict was not just about Elian but about the Cuban government and Cuban-American relations. In the termination-adoption case that we mediated, although the stakes were extremely high, there was no acceptable alternative to mediation for several players, and most parties were far more interested in resolution than in engagement.

In general, when a dispute falls in the middle level of seriousness and when all the parties have some degree of power but no one has an overwhelming superiority of power, when acceptable alternatives to mediation are not readily available, and when the primary goal of disputants is no longer engagement but resolution, then mediation is very likely to be sought after and embraced. Why?

## When Mediation Works

Mediation works, and people who use it generally like it. But why is it that mediation works when alternative approaches that are more desirable in some respects are less satisfactory? Mediation brings some important assets to people in conflict:

- *Enhanced communication*. The structure of mediation and the presence of the mediator add new opportunities for confidential, nonprejudicial, nonbinding, and open-ended communication. This can occur at the table, with the assistance of the mediator, or using the mediator as an intermediary.
- *Confidentiality*. Often mediation provides the most confidential forum available. What occurs in mediation is generally not admissible in court, and often parties enter into nondisclosure agreements.
- *Ownership*. Mediation encourages people to take responsibility not only for raising their concerns and their requests in an

effective way, but for finding a wise solution. Agreements that are reached belong to the participants in a way that adjudicated or advocate-negotiated agreements may not.

• *Value congruence*. In many circumstances, mediation allows people to participate in a negotiation or dispute resolution process in a way that is in keeping with their values about cooperation and that allows them to feel good about the role they are playing.

• *Creativity*. Many other forums for dealing with conflict impede creativity because of the difficulty in brainstorming, floating trial balloons, or disclosing sensitive information or ideas. Mediation has the potential for counteracting some of these hindrances to creativity and employing tools that create a safe atmosphere for allowing creativity to flourish.

• *Negotiation*. Mediation can assist people in being competent negotiators and in handling the tension between distributive and integrative negotiation tactics effectively.

• *Reality testing*. Mediation can help people face their real choices and make appropriate decisions with dignity and without undue pressure.

• *Bridge building*. Mediation provides an additional bridge among people who are at odds with each other, and it can help them reach out to each other in new ways. Structural or psychological barriers may exist that make any communication or contact difficult, charged, or impossible, and mediation can sometimes be the mechanism that allows for the initiation of more constructive contact.

• *Relationship building*. Mediators can sometimes help build a stronger relationship or address the negative elements in a relationship that have exacerbated a conflict and interfered with its progress toward resolution. Sometimes, in the absence of building a direct relationship between antagonistic parties, the mediator can establish a strong relationship with each of them, and this can be used to help make progress in conflict.

• *Process design*. The mediator can help design a process of interaction and problem solving that can help in conflict. Often it is not what the mediator does to facilitate direct interactions that is most important, but all the different elements of process design, such as arranging for subgroup meetings, data gathering, proposal development, and agenda formation, that are key to the resolution of conflict.

Mediators do many other things to assist with conflict (see Mayer, 2000), but I believe these are the key assets of mediation that explain why people embrace it when the circumstances are right. Because these are powerful contributions, mediators will continue to have an important role in conflict. Furthermore, in considering how to redefine our field, it is important that we remember that people need and, under the right circumstances, want this kind of assistance. A challenge for us is to find ways of bringing these assets to people in conflict when they are not open to mediation and when mediation in fact may not be appropriate.

## Our Hidden Ideological Agenda

Mediation to a large extent is an ideologically driven field. Most mediators do this work not simply out of an interest in the field or a sense that this is a reasonable way to make a living, but because they believe mediation is contributing in an important way to improving our world.

As a result, mediators tend to be committed to an approach that does not just help people resolve their disputes, but has a further, if not always articulated, agenda of changing the way people handle conflict and interact with each other. Not all mediators come from this perspective. Some would say that they are here simply to guide people to a solution to the dispute. But many mediators speak of using mediation to transform people, empower participants, open up new ways of communicating, and help promote a more peaceful world. These goals stem from a view of how people ought to interact, how decisions ought to be made, and how society should approach conflict, and as a result we are fairly ideologically driven in how we approach our actual practice.

Among the values and beliefs embedded in our practice are these:

- Resolution is better than conflict.
- Cooperation is better than competition.
- Integrative solutions are better than distributive solutions.
- The coercive use of power is bad.
- Interests are important; positions are a problem.
- Communication among antagonists is desirable.
- Pressuring people to accept a solution is not helpful.
- Empowering disputants to solve their own problems is important.

There is nothing wrong with these values. Indeed, I share most of them. The problem is that they are not necessarily the values of our clients. When they are and we share these values with our clients, particularly when all parties to a dispute share these values, we are able to provide especially rich services.

But there are two other possible dynamics that we have to consider. Our clients may not share our values, but our values may not be in significant conflict with theirs, or we may have conflicting values. For example, clients may not care about being able to communicate or finding an integrative solution—but they might not object to it either. Or clients may actively want to win, continue to be antagonistic, or maintain negative communication with each other.

We will explore these beliefs and how they can get in our way in the next chapter, but for now, what is important to consider is how this can lead to a disconnect between the type of mediation clients want and the type many mediators offer. This is not necessarily a problem if the mediator and the client, in a process akin to an interest-based negotiation, can work through these differences or if the mediator can "start where the client is at" and work toward a broader social goal. But this disconnect can often lead to a situation where clients want something different from what we offer and are reluctant to use our services because they do not see these services as meeting their needs. Clients may want some of the following things, but many mediators do not feel they can accommodate them:

- Clients want to be told who is right and who is wrong.
- They seek vindication.
- They want to be told whether a solution being suggested is fair and reasonable, or whether they are being played for a fool.
- They want help in convincing other parties of the merits of their case or the reasonableness of their proposals.
- They want substantive information and advice.
- They want to know how other people have solved the same problem.
- They want the mediator to guide the process with a firm hand, making sure that they do not waste time and that they are not subject to attacks, dirty tricks, or a level of emotional engagement that they are not prepared for.
- They want to get out of the room.

Of course, not all clients wish these things, and many mediators will accommodate some of these needs, particularly if they approach their work from an evaluative perspective. Evaluative mediators will provide substantive input, give clients a sense of how others may have solved the same problem, provide input as to the reasonableness of a proposal, and pressure parties to accept each other's offer. However, in the process, they give up some of the potential benefits of mediation. Sometimes clients may well be advised to "watch out for what they ask for because they may well get it." That is, clients may want something that will not serve their interests particularly well in the long run.

In many circumstances, clients or advocates seek a very particular type of mediation that is not in keeping with the underlying ideology or values of the conflict resolution field. That may in part account for the popularity and growth of judicial mediation, med/arb, evaluative mediation, and in general the growing dominance of lawyers in many different segments of mediation.

As a field, we have every right to maintain our values and to push the public and our client population to reorient their thinking. Other professions have done this fairly successfully (mental health, public medicine, child development, urban planning, education), but we are also in danger of creating too big a divide and having a difficult time broadening the reach of our services. In response to this concern, evaluative mediators might argue that their approach is the only one that will work from a business point of view over time, and many referring attorneys would agree. The downside of this approach is that it does not really change the way conflict is addressed in keeping with the broader needs of society and the values of most of us in this business.

## Our Failure to Embrace Mediators with Power

Up to this point, I have primarily been considering the dilemmas faced by mediators who are not only neutral but have no substantive power or authority. When most of us mediate, we have a certain amount of normative or persuasive power to bring to bear, we may have built an emotional or psychological dependence on us that gives us power, and we have a certain amount of power over the process. But we do not have the power to bring resources to bear, command public attention, threaten consequences, or speak for a governmental entity.

Most of us are not George Mitchell, Kofi Annan, Jimmy Carter, Colin Powell, or Nelson Mandela, all of whom have played mediating roles from a position of relative power or authority. Many mediators are former judges, and some are sitting judges who also function as settlement judges. An increasing number of former judges have found it very profitable to work as "judicial mediators" after stepping down from the bench. In many community disputes, city officials, legislators, and city staff may act as mediators. Courts sometimes appoint special masters or settlement judges to oversee the progress of a dispute, and these often function as mediators or facilitators. An interesting and very public example of this occurred when Ken Feinberg was appointed as a mediator to oversee the distribution of relief funds for victims of the 9/11 attack on the World Trade Center. He was charged with mediating, organizing, and distributing available funds as a representative of the U.S. Congress.

Mediators with power have made a significant contribution to people in conflict and have changed the way a whole range of issues is settled. They have developed some very interesting hybrid processes that incorporate mediation with judicial decision making, for example, and they certainly have challenged our normal notions about the boundary between mediation and traditional diplomacy and problem solving.

One approach that has been developed by some former judges is to combine the mediation function with the judicial function. A former judge may be appointed as a settlement judge for a case in dispute. This judge can then move in and out of a number of roles, such as acting as a facilitator, taking formal motions, and making judicial determinations on procedural issues such as disclosure.

## Professional Identity

In many ways, these new, interesting, and varied approaches are a healthy sign and are all contributing something of importance, but there are several noteworthy concerns as well. One is that these "mediators with power" do not necessarily identify with the conflict resolution field, and we as a field have not seen them falling within the boundaries of our own profession.

This has meant that we do not gain from their experience, standing, understanding, and involvement, and they do not gain from our experience and perspective on conflict and its resolution. I do not know how many of these mediators with power see themselves as part of the conflict resolution field, but I do know that our journals, conferences, literature, and practice standards do not tend to address their work very fully. For the most part, they have remained at best a low-profile presence in our professional organizations.

This dynamic is not just about high-profile stars but also about much more localized interventions, such as when a city councilor or school board member enters into a dispute. Disputants do not necessarily distinguish between these approaches and those of other mediators—or they may not see this as mediation at all—but in fact, for many people, these are exactly the mediators who will have the greatest impact on the disputes most important to them.

## The Value of Clout

What accounts for the popularity of mediators with power? They are not necessarily more skilled at understanding the underlying interests or choices people have, encouraging creative solutions, promoting communication, or dealing with the various procedural challenges that mediators face. But they do offer several things that we have seen over and over again as important to disputants.

They offer a different potential for voice, impact, validation, and procedural justice. They may carry the appearance of increased safety because of the forces arrayed behind them. Sometimes it is easier for people to sit down with a mediator who has personal standing in a community because it does not appear to be as much a sign of weakness or vulnerability as when they work with a neutral who has no ostensible power. When George Mitchell comes to town or Dennis Ross (President Clinton's envoy to the Middle East), then it can be viewed as simply foolish not to talk to them, whereas why should people embroiled in deep and potentially deadly conflict sit down with someone who has no public standing?

There is also an important cultural reason for the popularity of mediators with clout. In many cultural settings, the concept of neutrality is suspect at best and perhaps even unbelievable. Disputants may actually look for someone to declare their nonneutrality—where they stand on the issues or the people involved—before they will consent to allow them into the conflict process.

Navajo peacemakers, for example, often start out a peacemaking process by declaring their clan affiliations, and they continue this until everyone involved experiences some affiliations with the peacemaker and with each other. In many cultural contexts, the only accepted mediators are people with standing in the community: elders, religious leaders, governmental officials, or others who are respected for who they are as opposed to being respected for their neutrality or mediation experience.

We have often invited these types of mediators to speak at our conferences and have had some interesting dialogues with them, but I do not think we have embraced them as members of our field, nor have they really looked to the field of conflict resolution as a source of personal and professional support and belonging. We have a lot to offer each other, and connecting with mediators with standing is one avenue for us to take to expand our self-conception and ability to have a broader impact on conflict.

## Mediation's Hostile Dependence on Mandatory Programs

Much of the expansion of mediation during the past twenty years has been connected to mandating the use of mediation. This has been the source of a considerable amount of cognitive dissonance for a field that values voluntarism, client empowerment, and self-determination. To be sure, there is an irony in having to force people to engage in a voluntary process. Mediators have discussed this apparent contradiction or paradox extensively, and there has been a great deal of hand wringing about it. In the end, two things seem clear: without mandatory programs, the use of mediation would be much diminished, and mandating mediation does not mean that clients are necessarily unhappy about or resistant to mediation.

There is a legitimate cause for concern about this trend, but there is a lot of unnecessary angst as well. The fact that mediation's growth has been so dependent on mandatory programs is an indication that given a choice, mediation is not often the route people naturally take. Mediation may be avoided in part for structural and systemic reasons. That is, the system of dispute resolution is organized and staffed in such a way that mediation as an alternative does not naturally present itself or will not readily be used.

The culture of courts, of adjudicative decision making, of advocate-based negotiation, of political give and take is very different from that of mediation or conflict resolution. When people decide to take a conflict through the dispute resolution system, their most likely first stop is to someone who has a rights-based or power-based approach. Furthermore, those who staff these systems may see mediators as competitors in some sense. So there are systemic forces to overcome, which is one reason that mandatory programs have been initiated.

Also, as McEwen and Milburn (1993) point out, mandatory programs may actually help people enter into a settlement process that they would like to participate in without appearing weak and unsure of their case. That is, mandating mediation may make it possible to participate in a process that people find desirable but would have a hard time entering into without a structural setup that normalizes such participation.

But in focusing on the systemic or structural factors that have caused resistance to mediation, we can easily overlook the importance of the many other reasons that people have not independently chosen mediation, reasons that I have been discussing in this chapter.

The good news for mediation is that mandatory programs have been accepted and there does not seem to be a rising resistance to them, although that could still happen. The unfortunate news is that they are still necessary, that the culture of advocacy and conflict has not fundamentally changed because of mandatory programs, and that the field of mediation is vulnerable to a change in policy about mandating mediation.

There may be an even more problematic side effect of mandating mediation: the impact on the practice of mediation itself. Arguably, rather than changing the culture of disputing, mandating mediation may have more significantly changed the culture of mediation and conflict resolution, promoting more evaluative, adjudicative, and pressure-laden models (Alfini, 1991; Macfarlane, 2002; Welsh, 2001a). Mediators may be induced, seduced, or pressured to adopt norms and approaches more in keeping with the systems they are entering into in order to gain acceptance, avoid provoking a backlash, and meet the expectations put on them. This would hardly be surprising, but it is concerning.

There is no reason to label evaluative mediation as a negative development. Along with other approaches, evaluative mediation ought to be a service available to people in dispute. But if it is crowding out more facilitative approaches, then the prospect of transforming how disputes are handled will diminish. Furthermore, I do not think a field primarily consisting of evaluative mediators will survive as an independent field of practice. If all the training and promotion of mediation is based on the values of communication, integrative negotiation, client empowerment, and noncoercive settlement procedures, but all the real work is being done by mediators using evaluative and settlement conference approaches, then our field is based on a misconception or, worse, a deception. This is not yet the case, but it may be the direction in which we are heading.

## Beyond Mediation

Mediation has come to be the core service around which the field of conflict resolution has been defined. Some have argued that mediation is the professional identity around which we should organize.

Yet the reluctance to embrace mediation and the tendencies to marginalize or misuse it are symptomatic of the reactions that people have to the entire field of conflict resolution. By considering the attitudes that people show toward mediation, we can understand better the challenges that face the whole conflict resolution field. Under the right circumstances, mediation is embraced, even eagerly, but those circumstances are narrow. And even when mediation is embraced, what the public wants and what mediators offer are often at odds.

Furthermore, we have had to rely on mandatory programs. This reliance is symptomatic of the more general problems people have with mediation, and it endangers the field in several ways. Our reliance on mandatory mediation makes us very vulnerable to the vagaries of social policy, and the nature of our services is dramatically altered by participating in mandatory programs.

Mediation always has played an important role in helping people through conflict, and it will continue to do so. Whether we are talking about formally identified mediators or the informal mediating roles that all of us play from time to time, mediation is a key component in a conflict resolution system. But it is not the role around which the future growth of the field can rely to the extent that it has in the past. Although we will continue to see the growing use of mediation within the boundaries of acceptability I have discussed, we are unlikely to see a continuation of the dramatic growth of the past two decades.

More important, mediation is unlikely to be the route by which we can enter more fully into the deepest and most profound conflicts that we are facing. We need to offer mediation in an ever more diverse and creative manner, but the field of conflict resolution needs to grow well beyond the boundaries of a process-oriented third-party neutral role.

If we are to succeed in this, we will need to consider more fully the values and beliefs that have constrained our thinking about who we are and what we do. We begin to do this in the next chapter.

# 4

## Ten Beliefs That Get in Our Way

Probably the biggest obstacle we face in confronting the challenges to our field lies in our own belief systems. We can contend with the challenges of use, resistance, rejection, and suspicion only if we overcome the limits we impose on ourselves by the constraints of our own thinking.

Surrounding some of the guiding insights and principles of conflict resolution are many operational norms, constructs, and assumptions that we need to examine, broaden, and in some cases let go of. While the fundamental concepts and insights that guide our field—for example, our focus on process, communication, decision-making structures, power, culture, and relationships—are the tools we will continue to use as we struggle to grow beyond our current limits, they are surrounded by a set of operational attitudes and beliefs that limit our flexibility, creativity, and the range of responses we bring to conflict. These are beliefs that we need to examine and challenge if we are to grow beyond the existing limits on our work.

Ten key assumptions or attitudes seem particularly problematic. There is truth and value in each of them, but they are nonetheless constraining and overly simplistic. We can and should move beyond them.

## Belief One: We Are Neutral
## Third-Party Conflict Resolvers

We have defined a limited role for ourselves in conflict, and implied in this is a limited view of conflict. That role is as third-party neutrals, and for the most part we mean neutrals with a procedural, as opposed to a substantive, focus. We understand our value to people in conflict in terms of our ability to remain neutral and to guide them through a decision-making process.

But most conflict is not carried out with the assistance of neutrals, and most resolution is not achieved in that way either. In the abstract, most conflict resolvers might agree that there are other valuable roles we might play, but when a conflict is referred to us, we almost always view our role through the third-party neutral lens.

In Chapter Seven, I will consider other roles that we can and occasionally do play, including coach, trainer, adviser, decision maker, designer, organizer, case manager, evaluator, and advocate. Many conflict resolvers already fulfill these roles from time to time, but they still remain peripheral to how most of us think of ourselves, and certainly to how the field defines itself.

### The Third Side and Beyond

In *The Third Side* (originally published as *Getting to Peace*), William Ury suggests that the critical way to deal with conflict is to provide richer and more varied "third-side" resources. As Ury sees it, the key requirement for altering the destructive nature of many conflicts is to add a third side to the polarized dynamics of two-sided conflicts. By thinking of conflict as a three-sided process rather than a two-sided struggle, we can help conflictants engage in and resolve conflict in a much more productive manner. Ury (2000) identifies ten third-side roles geared to the three fundamental purposes of preventing, resolving, and containing conflict: provider, teacher, bridge builder, mediator, arbiter, equalizer, healer, witness, referee, and peacekeeper. While some of these are roles for conflict resolvers, he is mainly interested in creating more social capacity to play third-side roles in everyday life as well as in protracted large-scale conflicts. The third side consists of all those individuals and institutions, such as schools, relief organizations, churches, mediation programs, individuals with connections to both parties to a conflict, or even what Ury calls the "emergent will of the community" (p. 14), that change the way in which the primary disputants engage with each other so that the conflict is less destructive.

Ury has opened the door for a far broader and more creative concept of the roles we can play in conflict. I suggest we open that door even wider. We need to think of our roles in terms of Ury's broadly conceived third-side functions, but we also need to understand how we can assist conflicting parties from a nonneutral, non-third-party stance. That is, we need to think about how we can directly assist disputants to engage in conflict—in essence, to participate as part of one of the sides to the conflict—even when no third side is sought after or involved. This means helping people to engage in conflict by serving as advocates, coaches, advisers, and representatives.

Ury alludes to this direct assistance most clearly through his discussion of the equalizer role, which occurs when a third party intervenes to help counteract a severe power imbalance, such as when a high-status group member insists that an authoritarian leader listen to a low-status member's complaints. But there are many other ways in which we can assist people in conflict without acting as neutral third parties. For example, we can act as an advocate, representing people in conflict, or as a strategist who assists parties in figuring out how to conduct themselves in a conflict in a way that will help them attain their goals (which may or may not include resolving the conflict). I discuss these further in Chapter Seven.

If we can view ourselves as conflict specialists (or conflict engagement specialists) who have something of value to offer by directly participating or assisting others to participate in conflict, then a whole new range of opportunity opens up for how we can deal with conflict constructively and dramatically. We can then be in a better position to help people engage instead of avoid, listen instead of attack, organize instead of retreat, connect instead of isolate, and much more. In this way, we can help transform the way conflict is conducted.

## Neutrality and Advocacy

I am suggesting that conflict resolution professionals have the potential to make a major difference if they can incorporate genuine advocacy into their work. I am not talking about simply advocating for a process or advocating for all parties equally. I mean acting as advocates for particular disputants. This is a major change for how conflict resolution professionals have viewed themselves and how they have presented themselves to the world, but it is an essential change if we are going to make a real difference. How we make this change and bring those who are already functioning as advocates into our field is explored in Chapter Eight.

Conflict resolvers face perplexing dilemmas in expanding beyond the normal third-party roles they have played. How can conflict resolvers be advocates in some cases when they are neutrals in others? Maybe the same person cannot serve as a mediator for an environmental issue one day and an advocate in a similar dispute the next, but already we often have to clarify which among the many different roles we play in conflict we are going to occupy in any given situation: mediator, facilitator, arbitrator, counselor, adviser, or trainer.

Many of us have found ourselves in situations where we've had to create hybrid roles, which are mixtures of more defined and established roles, such as med/arb, therapeutic mediators, trainer/facilitators, or system designer/mediators. We can make mistakes by failing to clarify our roles or by switching too readily from one to the other, but mostly we have handled these potential role contradictions fairly effectively. Furthermore, many of us have come from professions of origin where we have acted as advocates (lawyer, union organizer, management representative, child advocate, or political activist for example), substantive experts (scientists, financial planners, psychologists), or advisers (counselors, therapists, teachers). Many split their practices among these professional roles. And even when individuals cannot straddle these roles, the field can certainly embrace people who play profoundly different roles in conflict.

When we serve as advocates, we can still think of ourselves as conflict specialists, bringing to our work the same insights, values, and skills that we may use as neutrals, and we can also urge our field to think of us in that way.

## From Resolution to Engagement

As hard as it will be to expand our self-concept beyond that of the third-party neutral, there is another way in which we have to challenge our thinking about our role and purpose that may be even more difficult.

Our field has been defined as the conflict resolution field. The implication is that we are about resolution. In most of my work, I have had the implied or stated a goal of helping people reach resolution. Under the right circumstances, that is an appropriate and powerful mission. But conflict is a process and a system, and resolution is not always a timely or useful goal. To build our field around the resolution phase of the conflict process is to limit our role significantly and misread the essential nature and challenge of conflict. Moreover, we deliver a message that says people in conflict should always want resolution.

Most of us have experienced the value of helping to raise the level of conflict, risky though this may be, in order to get the real issues on the table and available for discussion. But we don't take this far enough. We generally see this as something that needs to occur in the service of the goal of reaching resolution. We often need to help raise conflict, knowing that this may genuinely exacerbate relationships or the smooth functioning of a group.

Why? Because otherwise we will not be genuinely addressing people's needs; we will instead be contributing to the suppression of issues that will come back in a more serious way later or contributing to the ongoing repression of vulnerable individuals or groups. Furthermore, I think people often want help raising conflict, not necessarily in resolving it. When the time for resolution comes, we can be there to help too, but we should not go there prematurely.

In the end, the value of helping people to raise, escalate, and continue a conflict is in part about resolution at a deeper level, but if we focus on that instead of on helping people engage in conflict, then we are contributing to the avoidance problem. If we can genuinely liberate ourselves in all that we do from this resolution bias—that is, from the automatic assumption that our role is to bring about resolution—and instead see our role as helping people engage constructively at all phases of the conflict process, then our ability to have a constructive impact on conflict will dramatically increase.

Our sense of our role in conflict is the core attitude that we must examine and challenge. In some ways, all the other restraining beliefs flow from this. But other assumptions reinforce this one.

## Belief Two: Competition Is Bad; Cooperation Is Good

We often discuss our work in terms of cooperative problem solving, a cooperative approach to working through conflict, and an alternative to competitive processes. The clear implication is that competition is bad, and cooperation is good.

I would not want to argue that cooperation is a bad thing, unless we are cooperating with evil. (One of Gandhi's central principles of nonviolence was refusing to cooperate with evil.) On the whole, when people are ready to cooperate in moving through a conflict, that is good. If divorcing parents can cooperate in making decisions about what is best for their children, that is better than if they are competing for their children's affections or approval or time. If labor and management can cooperate in dealing with an economic crisis in a company, that company may have a better chance of surviving and thriving.

When people are ready to cooperate, that can encourage mutually beneficial solutions to problems, creativity, more complete disclosure of information, and better interpersonal relations. But people in conflict are not always ready to cooperate nor should they be. Just as cooperation is productive under the right circumstances, so is competition.

If we are only about helping people cooperate, then how can we be of use when people want to compete or should compete? People will either avoid us (and do) because they do not want to cooperate and they realize that when they come to us, that is exactly what we will ask them to do, or we will find ourselves in the position of having to persuade people to try to be cooperative when their instincts tell them not to be. Sometimes those instincts are right on the money. Competition can be a wise and realistic course for people to take as they engage in conflict, and one that we should sometimes encourage.

What do we mean by *cooperation* and *competition* anyway? These are nebulous terms that limit our thinking. I think we mean a variety of things when we talk about competition and cooperation. Sometimes we mean working with each other when we cooperate and working against each other when we compete. Sometimes we mean trying to achieve mutual gains (integrative solutions) when we cooperate, and a larger piece of the pie for ourselves (distributive solutions) when we compete. Sometimes we mean playing to win versus helping each other. Sometimes we mean being friendly, warm, and helpful as opposed to angry, cold, and oppositional.

But these all have different implications. I do not like to play basketball or volleyball without keeping score. Generally, it's fun to win, but I don't especially mind losing. I just like to keep score. Maybe it's a gender thing, but I don't think so—and I do not feel as if I am being unfriendly, grasping, greedy, or noncooperative. It is about motivation, knowing how well I am doing, comparing myself to others (often unfavorably), and letting down my professional guard.

This is a very different type of competition from trying to compete for a job or the affections of a potential partner or a desired office. It is also different from trying to win election to office or win a war. Intuitively, I think we all know that some kinds of competition are healthy, necessary, and productive, and other kinds are not.

We tend to view competition and cooperation as being opposites or mutually exclusive. In fact, we think that there is a sort of a competition between a cooperative and competitive framework. Sometimes there is, but not always. We can cooperate in competing with each other, as when we play competitive sports. Even in extremely serious conflicts, people cooperate in competing. Political parties cooperate in many ways during furiously fought elections. They cooperate over the rules of the game, over how they are going to stage debates, over the parameters of the political discourse, and over excluding third parties from equal participation. In fact, without some form of cooperation, competition is probably impossible. Both, after all, involve engagement.

Can we imagine a healthy or constructive approach to competitive problem solving? I think so, and often this is the most productive thing we can offer people in conflict. Competition is often necessary and inevitable. There are often fundamentally different interests and needs in play, and the outcome is not simply a matter of rational discourse or objective problem solving but a serious struggle among opposing and incompatible goals, values, resources, or world views. Sometimes this occurs against a background of a seriously inequitable distribution of power. Under these circumstances, our challenge is not necessarily to focus on cooperation but on constructive competition. Can we help people compete in a constructive way? I believe we can and we do.

Competition can be constructive when participants are wise, informed, skillful, and ethical:

- *Wise* in the sense of understanding their choices, making good judgments about when to hold firm, when to make concessions, when to reach out, when to wait, whom to communicate with and in what way
- *Informed* about the key data; understanding other players' interests, issues, and alternatives; having a good handle on the overall context within which the conflict is occurring; and being clear about one's own interests and alternatives as well

- *Skillful* in the art of negotiation, communication, framing proposals, organizing one's support systems, and knowing how to use one's power effectively

- *Ethical* in playing by some explicit or implicit set of rules or norms of conduct—usually about honesty, coercion, follow-through, and principles of interaction

One of the greatest gifts conflict resolvers can give to people in conflict is to assist them in competing constructively when competition is appropriate. This means helping people try to get their needs met at the expense of others if that is what is necessary, but doing so in a wise, informed, skillful, and ethical way. Of course, we also know that people in conflict often do not see the cooperative or integrative potential that does exist, so our role is also to help them recognize these as well. But if we think that competition is always inappropriate or not quite worthy, we are being very naive about conflict and will be treated accordingly.

## Belief Three: Our Goal Is a Win-Win Solution (the Integrative Trap)

Related, but not quite the same as our beliefs about cooperation and competition, is the win-win trap. We are generally focused on achieving win-win outcomes, and this makes us less effective or credible when a purely win-win outcome is not possible within the value system and cognitive framework of disputants.

As far as many disputants in many conflicts are concerned, no matter how much we try to influence their thinking, the choice is either winning or losing, and they view their tactical choices as either being hard-headed and realistic in protecting their interests and pursuing their objectives or being naive, unrealistic, and therefore vulnerable to exploitation. If we always preach a win-win gospel, we too will appear to be naive and unrealistic.

As conflict resolvers, we are aware that all conflicts have an integrative and distributive component. That is, all conflicts pose a challenge for how to expand through creativity and cooperation the amount of value to be divided up and how to divide up limited resources, which usually entails a more competitive process. Effective approaches to conflict have to take into account both dimensions without denying the reality of one in service to the potential of the other. As a general rule, it is easier to deal with the distributive elements of conflict if we have explored the integrative potential.

For example, when divorcing parents can figure out creative ways of assisting each other with child care responsibilities, thereby allowing them to pursue professional and personal goals while fulfilling their parenting roles, then it often becomes easier to divide up the time the children will spend with each of them.

But two things temper this. One is that people often arrive at the point of engaging in a conflict only after they feel they have to some extent explored mutually beneficial approaches and gotten stuck. The closer to arriving at Pareto optimality (the point at which further benefit cannot be obtained by one party except by diminishing benefits to the other), the harder it becomes to achieve more mutual gains. Effective resolution processes can sometimes break through a deadlock by identifying previously unrealized mutual gains, but just as often people are stuck because after having explored these possibilities, they find it hard to face difficult but necessary distributive decisions.

The second thing standing in the way of a focus on integrative opportunities involves people's emotional take on being in conflict. The anxiety, fears, hopes, anger, and doubt of disputants are almost always focused on the distributive elements in a conflict—the win-lose dimension. To go too quickly and blithely to the win-win options can often fly in the face of people's emotional reality.

Conflict resolvers tend to focus on the integrative elements because these are easier and nicer. They are easier in the sense that they do not require the difficult, painful, and sometimes ugly interchanges that distributive choices involve. This is not to say that good integrative decision making is simple; it in fact requires a great deal of creativity and an ability to think deeply about the range of interests or needs involved. But when this creativity can be achieved, it is not as painful as the distributive aspects.

Integrative negotiations are also "nicer" because they are less likely to involve negative labeling. When we can genuinely separate the people from the problem, we can create a friendlier and more flexible context for working through a conflict. But the more distributive the conflict is, the harder it is to maintain this separation. Therefore, we have a natural tendency to want to avoid this element of the conflict.

An unrealistic, premature, naive, or exclusive focus on the win-win or integrative potential of conflict does not move serious conflicts forward. Instead, we need to be able to help people face and work on the distributive elements, knowing that this is often what hard bargaining is about, without sacrificing our ability to work on the integrative aspects, knowing that these can ameliorate the conflict significantly.

## Belief Four: Interests Are In; Positions Are Out

We have built a great deal of our practice theory on the distinction between interests and positions, especially as Fisher and Ury articulated in *Getting to Yes* (1981). This distinction has been useful in teaching new mediators and providing alternative ways of thinking about negotiation and conflict to advocates, managers, and the general public. But we may have overdone our reliance on this. Often we have underestimated or misunderstood the power and value of positions in conflict, and we have too readily accepted the notion that if only people could talk about their interests, integrative outcomes would be possible.

Positions and interests are not opposites or mutually exclusive concepts, and I believe the distinction we have made between them is somewhat artificial. Almost any interest can be translated into a position and any position into interests. Two main characteristics separate the two: the manner in which they are communicated and the degree to which motivation is disclosed.

For example, if we are in a dispute over whether I am owed money for work done on a contract, I can take the position that you owe me X dollars for the hours I put in. You can then say that I delivered on only half of what I promised, so I should get only 1/2 X. We have both put forward positions. Alternatively, I can say that I have an interest that I be paid at the rate we agreed for the hours that I put in, and you can say you need to get the job done and cannot afford to pay more than agreed, and that half of the work still needs to be done. In the second go-round, we have essentially said the same thing as in the first, but in a nicer, more open-ended way. Rather than asking, demanding, proposing, or insisting, we have informed, revealed, and shared our concerns. But the basic message, although wrapped somewhat differently, is the same.

What is more important, perhaps, than presenting our needs in terms of positions or interests is how far we reveal our motivation and thinking. Do we indicate, for example, that we are worried about our reputation, that we have a cash flow problem, that we feel embarrassed that we have let things get to this point, or that we have other deadlines or pressures on us that are limiting our choices? The more we reveal about our thinking and the deeper the level of motivation we express, the more likely we are to discover the integrative potential in a situation. But at the same time, the more we discuss our underlying needs, the more vulnerable we may make ourselves as well.

Using the ideology and concept of interest-based negotiation, we are essentially committing ourselves to be softer in our approach and more explicit about our motivations. But in a genuinely distributional situation, where there are serious vulnerabilities and people feel tense, mistrustful, and angry, people are often not willing to risk this kind of disclosure and don't believe that the interest framework is very powerful.

Positions are often necessary and helpful to moving a negotiation forward. An artfully crafted position is often the best and most efficient way of defining the conflict or setting the stage for effective problem-solving activities. Positions can often be windows into what the conflict is about for participants, and by exploring the rationale behind a position, we often encourage a rich discussion of people's feelings, the way in which they are thinking about outcomes, their view of their choices, the range of options they might be willing to consider, the values they are bringing to bear, and the information that they feel is relevant. Without soliciting, welcoming, and occasionally helping people to craft positions, it can be very hard and even torturous to get at this information.

To be sure, positions can also mislead, create an artificially constricted focus, and lead to a certain amount of game playing. But we should not be so naive as to think that these problems are averted if we recast the tenor of the discussion to an exchange of interests. If positions are offered in a rigid take-it-or-leave-it demanding sort of way, constructive discussions are going to be harder to start. But the issue here is how the positions are presented more than the problem of positions versus interests. Consider for example, these two statements in the payment for services example:

> "You only did half the work; you promised to do it all; so
> you only get half the pay."

> "My understanding was that this entire job could be done
> for the amount we discussed. I think it makes sense for me
> to pay only for the work that is completed."

The difference between these statements is not in how much they are about interests versus positions but how rigid, accusatory, and demanding each of them is. This issue may be solved by exploring rationales and motives, cutting a deal, or coming up with a creative solution that meets both parties' needs. But whether it proceeds productively may have less to do with whether the focus is on interests or positions than with how the position is put forward.

We need to be ready to help disputants articulate their positions in an effective, powerful, and strategic way if we are going to engage with people on their own terms. If our response is simply to try to force-feed an interest-based formula, we are going to frustrate people and drive them to someone who is willing to help them with a more positional framework. This does not mean that we ought not help people figure out what is really important to them and to the others involved in a conflict or to think of a variety of ways to meet their needs beyond the one proposal they may be fixated on. But often we have to start by helping people formulate their initial positions. Interestingly, people are often a lot clearer about what their positions are than they are about the underlying interests that inform those positions. Until they have articulated their positions, and done so in a powerful and effective way, they may not be able to consider the "why" questions. Often they have to experience the positions they want to take in a tangible and sometimes emotional way before they can gain access to the motivation behind the position.

There are two other reasons that we should not be so quick to say that the essence of good conflict resolution is to avoid positions and focus on interests. One is that an exchange of positions is sometimes all that is necessary to resolve certain conflicts and avoid exacerbating a dispute. Disputants may in fact be able to settle a dispute by agreeing on an outcome, by compromising between different positions, but have profoundly different interests nonetheless.

A divorcing couple, for example, may be willing to agree on a parenting arrangement because each can live with it, but they may have profoundly different concerns about what they want a parenting schedule to accomplish for their children. Similarly, labor and management may have extremely different interests concerning the allocation of excess revenues to wage enhancement or stockholder dividends, but they may still be able to arrive at an acceptable compromise between their positions. They do not have to share their interests in order to do this. In fact, sometimes a simple compromise between positions avoids a potentially unproductive and divisive discussion about competing motivations or belief systems.

The second is that interests are not always benign or a suitable basis for constructive negotiations. What we find when we look at the full range of interests involved in conflict is not always rational, pleasant, pretty, or even legitimate. People may want revenge, to hurt others, to best someone else, or to win bragging rights about an outcome. The art of conflict can involve knowing how and when to put these suspect motivations on the table and when to let them be. A positional approach can be a means of allowing a conflict to proceed without having to confront some of these nasty interests. Of course, underneath the nasty interests are likely to be more constructive or universal interests, but these can be pretty abstract and difficult to access.

In one labor management mediation, I recall a shop steward (who had been to an interest-based bargaining workshop) saying, "We are being interest based at them, they are being positional at us, and we won't put up with that." In that statement are all the paradoxes and contradictions of trying to focus a conflict resolution approach around the difference between interests and positions.

Under the right circumstances, the tactic of transforming positions into interests can be effective, even powerful. But it is just a tactic, not the basis for a whole field of intervention or approach to conflict. Instead, we have to look at the motivational structure, the worldview, the power relations, and the fears that govern how people approach and avoid conflict. Our approach has to be nuanced, realistic, and powerful, and this means understanding the value of positions and the uses to which they may be put.

## Belief Five: Constructive Communication Is More Important Than Passionate Advocacy

We all want to believe that we can communicate effectively and constructively, but of course what we mean by *effective* and *constructive* is not always so clear. And being effective depends on what our goals are. In conflict resolution, we place a high value on reasonableness, open-mindedness, good listening, and respectful expression of our ideas. In fact, this is true not just of conflict resolution; it has become an important societal norm. Managers, business leaders, teachers, parents, children, in fact most of us, have been taught and have to some extent bought into the use of "I" messages, open-ended questions, active listening, reframing, validation, and so forth. Despite my undoubtedly mixed success in putting these into practice, I certainly believe in the value of these tools, and I teach them to new mediators.

Two things concern me about this. One is how much we have substituted formulaic rules of interaction for genuine and deeper communication that does not always follow such logical approaches. The other is that this may not leave room for passionate advocacy. Sometimes what we mean by constructive communication may be out of sync with effective communication.

Effective communication is not always polite and tactful. If in the name of being constructive, we are urging people to blunt their true opinions or feelings, we are not in the long run promoting more effective engagement in conflict. In fact, we are contributing to avoiding, minimizing, or making light of essential differences. In many conflict situations, the fundamental need that people have is to express strong feelings in strong ways. This does not always seem constructive, sensitive, or fair. It often involves expressions of anger, lots of "you" messages, and many positional and value-laden statements. When people are passionate about their beliefs, they want to give voice to these in a forceful, sometimes dramatic, and, we hope, effective way. Such a voice is not always tactful, constructive, or sensitive, but it is a voice that needs to be heard. We may have spent too much time creating formulas for communication and norms of interaction and not enough time figuring out how to help people express themselves passionately, forcefully, and powerfully or how to hear such expressions from others without shutting down or unwisely escalating a conflict.

Why don't we argue more about the things that really matter to us as a society? Why don't we argue about religion, abortion, gun control, care for the needy, how to approach and understand terrorism, sustainable development, race, or economic policy? This may seem odd since there are debates in the media, nonstop talk radio, and much public discourse about these issues. But these tend to be very formulaic or programmed and do not constitute genuine engagement or genuine argumentation.

How often, on an individual or small group level, do we really argue about these things—argue with people with whom we have profound disagreements? If we do argue, it is mostly with those we fundamentally agree with, or we quickly shy away from the discussion for fear that it will become unpleasant and maybe get out of hand. Instead we let talk radio and crafted television substitute for genuine debate.

I have not used the word *dialogue*, although I certainly support dialogue. But genuine dialogue is not possible if we are not willing to engage in argumentation about our most important issues. Argument is different from dialogue, at least by implication. In argument, we are willing to disagree passionately, thoroughly, and not always politely. We advocate our point of view, disagree with others, challenge people, and accept being challenged. We can do this in a way that shuts down communication or opens it up, that is fundamentally respectful of the people we disagree with or dehumanizing of them, that is open to the potential validity of other points of view or that excludes this as a possibility, that seeks to intimidate, even endanger, others or that invites them to be powerful themselves.

In other words, not all argumentation is the same, and some will clearly lead to harmful escalation or a retreat into avoidance. But if we are not willing to argue our most deeply held beliefs, then we inevitably cut ourselves off from those who have different points of view, and we cannot then engage in genuine dialogue. Ultimately, this will lead to a society that is segregated and divided. We are already seeing this in the pronounced political differences that are reflected geographically in the United States.

When we as conflict resolvers shy away from argumentation and focus too much on constructive communication and not enough on passionate advocacy, several problems emerge. One is that we end up reinforcing conflict-avoidant tendencies and promote the view that it is better to speak nicely than to risk stirring up emotions. This can easily guide us to the more superficial realms of conflict. Second, it separates us from people who feel passionately about a conflict, and this inevitably contributes to the skepticism and distrust that people sometimes feel about conflict resolution professionals.

A further problem with this belief is that it contributes to the notion that people cannot passionately advocate for what they believe in without endangering relationships, escalating conflict, and making things worse for themselves. We have focused so much on how to help people be constructive communicators that we have not developed the tools, concepts, and strength to help people in conflict be passionate advocates in an appropriate and effective way.

Perhaps the biggest problem is the way this value indirectly reinforces social injustice and inequality. If I am in a powerful position, I do not particularly need to be a passionate advocate; I can continue to exercise my privilege or meet my needs through quietly and politely using my advantage. But if I am disenfranchised or excluded from decision-making mechanisms, I may need to be very passionate, noisy, and demanding in order to get noticed. Gandhi was viewed as a rude, manipulative, and uncollaborative troublemaker by British colonial authorities. It took a lot of anger and passion, and not just constructive communication, to move a civil rights agenda forward in the United States. If we promote a norm of constructive communication in a way that makes it more difficult to be a passionate advocate (even if our rhetoric says we can do both), then we are inevitably reinforcing the powerful and putting an obstacle in the path of the oppressed.

As conflict resolvers, we have a number of important potential roles to play in reinforcing passionate advocacy. As neutrals, we can help encourage people to give voice to their views with passion and help them find ways of doing this that do not shut the door to future communication. As advocates, we can model effective ways of being passionate with dignity and wisdom and of articulating strongly held views and feelings without ever losing sight of the humanity of others.

Our attitudes about communication and passion are reinforced and closely related to the sixth nonproductive belief that conflict resolvers have: that respect trumps anger.

## Belief Six: Respect Trumps Anger

We advocate a norm that disputants should always show respect for each other. Often in mediation, we suggest a guideline that people treat each other with respect. There is nothing wrong with asking that people be civil in mediation and not use conflict resolution forums to attach, intimidate, or insult each other. But there are two problems with this. One is that we are often dealing with people who do not respect each other, and the other is that we often equate respect with not showing anger.

In the name of showing respect, we may fail to honor and allow space for the deep anger that people in conflict often experience. What does it mean to say to a Palestinian or an Israeli that they should respect each other? How can we tell a couple embroiled in a bitter divorce that they should evidence respect for each other? When people feel that they have discriminated against or harassed, or that they have been unfairly accused of such actions, what does it mean to show respect? The most we can hope for is an "as if" behavior. That is, we can suggest that people treat each other "as if" they respect each other, or that people engage according to certain behavioral norms that prevent them from being disrespectful.

But what is even more problematic is that in the name of respect, we fail to honor equally the anger, rage, hurt, and fear that people are often experiencing. Conflict resolution forums can create a sort of emotional straitjacket that sometimes allows people to discuss their feelings but seldom provides an opportunity to give genuine voice to them. Mediation or facilitated dialogues may not be the best opportunity for people to give expression to the full range of their feelings. But that means only that other arenas for the expression of conflict are needed.

As a result of this attitude, we give out tremendously mixed messages, which are not lost on people in conflict. On the one hand, we suggest that emotions are part of the picture, and we talk about providing an opportunity for people to vent. But on the other hand, by focusing our efforts on creating an interaction characterized by respectful communication, constructive dialogue, and collaborative problem solving, we imply that anger has only a limited and carefully circumscribed place at our table. This places us out of sync with many people in conflict and engenders a suspicion about our ability to genuinely understand them. This does not mean that we should give up our values about human interaction and the dignity of all people or allow unproductive and damaging interactions to occur when we bring people together. But it does mean that we have to think of ways to engage productively with people who are very angry and do not feel any respect for those with whom they are in conflict.

One of the most surprising expressions of emotion I encountered in my experience as a mediator occurred a number of years ago, when I was asked to work with two corporate entities that shared some infrastructure and were in a conflict about how these should be financed. What surprised me was not that there were negative feelings on each side but just how vitriolic and personal these had become. In a private meeting with the top decision makers of one of the organizations, a member of the board of directors launched into a tirade about the CEO of the other organization. She was called every name, every four-letter word that one could imagine (well, maybe not every—but a lot). The other board members just listened. I think they wanted to see what I would do. I am afraid my response was a bit lame. I said something insipid, like, "Boy, you are really pissed off aren't you?" This led to a slightly milder repeat of the tirade with a little bit of cynicism about just how clueless I was.

Eventually, I got this team to agree about what they were going to say, to focus on the agreement they wanted, and to tone down their rhetoric, at least in public. We reached an agreement on most of the immediate issues, but there remained some deeper and longer-standing issues that we decided not to address at that time.

Maybe that was the right decision: the corporations continue to work together with regard to this infrastructure (they really had little choice). But I wonder what would have happened if my way of thinking about this had been a little different—if instead of trying to contain and redirect this anger, I would have encouraged it? What might have occurred if I had said, "I want to hear more about why you are angry, and I want to work with you on how to convey these feelings effectively in this situation"?

## Belief Seven: Facilitative Mediation Means Minimal Substantive Influence

No doubt, mediators with a facilitative perspective (see Mayer, forthcoming) have a special kind of power because they do not take sides and do not present themselves as substantive experts. This allows us to encourage more confidential disclosure and promotes a focus on the process of the interaction. When we see ourselves as having a substantive role, we can easily lose sight of the power of creating the kind of dialogue in which parties work through their own conflict and come to their own resolution.

But there is a problem with this. Whether we carve out a substantive role for ourselves, whether we take an evaluative, facilitative, narrative, or transformative approach, we have an impact on the outcome because we have substantive influence. Parties know this, and I think most of us know it, but we do not always face the implications of this in our practice.

As mediators, we can have a direct or indirect influence over substance, and our impact can be conscious or unconscious, intentional or unintended, but we cannot have zero impact. Furthermore, parties want mediators to have an impact. They want help in analyzing the issues; understanding choices; knowing which items to link and which to keep separate; what alternatives are reasonable, practical, or within a normal range of outcomes; and how to craft creative solutions to difficult problems. What they do not want from mediators is to push the interest of one party at the expense of another or to manipulate the interaction to promote an outcome that is not in their interests.

Within this broad framework, considerable space exists for different styles of mediation. We may meet the parties' need for substantive assistance by asking artful questions, directing the conversation, suggesting linkages, guiding parties through an examination of the substantive issues, bringing substantive experts into a process, or simply helping parties clarify their own views. We can also do it by providing information, making recommendations, and bringing our own substantive expertise to bear much more directly. Even if our goal is simply to look for opportunities to encourage communication between parties, our choice of when to intervene and about what will be guided by our view of the substantive issues.

People want this kind of help, and they will not understand or believe us if we assert that our role is in the process realm, not the substantive one. This is a distinction that we have made too much of. Process and substance are inextricably linked. How we discuss something affects what we are talking about, and the substantive concerns we are facing greatly affect the process we employ to address them.

For many, the concept of process is a confusing one, and it is easy to see it as an absence of substance. Therefore, if we present ourselves and think of ourselves as being mostly focused on process, it can seem to many people as if we are light on substance, short on depth, and therefore not likely to be very helpful.

If we are going to help people embroiled in conflict, we have to work not just in one area or in the other; we have to help them across the complicated interface between process and substance, and we cannot do this if we always define our role in terms of an artificial distinction. In most conflicts, when people look for assistance, whether from a neutral, an advocate, or a coach, they want someone who is not simply a process expert but who knows something about the issues at hand.

Mediators are increasingly expected to specialize, and for good reason. They have usually had some broad areas of specialization—family, community, workplace, or environmental, for example. And while many of us have crossed over among these areas as our field has developed, this is less frequently the case. In fact, the reverse seems to be happening: more specialization is expected.

Parties want conflict resolvers to have very specific and relevant substantive background. Mediators and facilitators specialize in hydroelectric relicensing, allocation procedures among potentially responsible parties at Superfund sites, equal employment cases in federal facilities, estates and inheritance, transportation, wetlands, and so on. Sometimes we can be overly focused on the substantive aspects of a dispute just as we can be overly focused on process. The important work has to be done where these two sides of a conflict come together. But what parties do understand is that to be truly helpful in a conflict, conflict resolution professionals have to have a firm grasp of the substantive issues.

We are often asked to assist with conflicts in which we have little prior information, usually because we are experienced in the general type of issue or because of our conflict resolution experience. But we have to become familiar enough with the issues in a dispute to play a useful role when people tackle substantive questions. For me, that has been one of the joys of being in this work: getting an opportunity to delve into new and intriguing substantive areas, with the help of some wonderful coaching from experts to which I would not otherwise have been exposed.

As a field, we have improperly defined our role as process experts, even when we know that we have a substantive role to play. We have also become somewhat divided and even polarized about where we stand on this issue—that is what separates different schools of mediation to some extent. As a result, we have further narrowed the role we can play in conflict and the vision of our field that we have projected to the public. People want neither a mediator who is going to take over the responsibility for solving the problems they face nor someone who is unwilling to get down into the depths of the substantive issues involved or engage with them in struggling with the substantive complexities. They want help with substance, help with process, and help with the interaction between these. Although we are not generally hired simply because of our substantive expertise (although we are sometimes) and although the added value we bring beyond that of technical and legal experts arises from our understanding of communication, conflict, negotiation, consensus building, culture, and power, this does not mean that people expect or want us to keep our hands off substance.

In many ways, the problem we face in this respect comes from a false dichotomy between substance and process (and sometimes between substance, process, and emotions). Instead, we should understand these as different components or aspects of the same problem or conflict. We should accept that we have an impact on substance and process, and whether we consider ourselves experts or not, we should embrace that impact and use it wisely.

## Belief Eight: Good Relationships Are Our Goal, Adversaries Our Problem

We know that we cannot always change how people feel about each other or even how well they understand each other. Some mediators say that the realm of relationships is not their focus. Nonetheless, as a spoken or unspoken goal, most of us hope to build better, more constructive relationships among conflicting parties. Sometimes we see building better relationships as a road to solving a serious conflict (Northern Ireland), and sometimes we believe that reaching agreements about particularly toxic issues is important mainly because it will help lead to better relationships (a workplace grievance). Under the right circumstances, a focus on building better relationships is not only appropriate but essential, but this goal brings certain problems with it.

Our approach to building relationships is often to suppress conflict and disapprove of adversarial behavior. Most conflict resolvers will say that conflict itself is not the problem; the problem is how it is conducted. But often we then provide such an idealistic, narrow view of how conflict should be conducted that either we are not operating in the real world or we are giving an implied message that conflict should mostly be suppressed. Let's consider as an example four of the norms that we often promote in conflict:

- We should separate the people from the problem. That is, we should identify the problem in terms that separate it from whether we like or dislike, respect or disdain, believe or mistrust others. But when we are embroiled in conflict, the people and the issues often seem inseparable.

- We should not ascribe motives to others. We can use "I" messages and statements about behavior, but we should not say what we think is driving someone else's behavior, particularly if we think the motives are less than pure. But we usually have ideas about what others' motives really are, and the attributions we make about these often drive our reactions to them.

- We should look at multiple options in an attempt to build a win-win solution. Rather than push one option or position, we should be open to multiple approaches. But often in conflict, people are convinced that something really must happen or that only one approach is acceptable.

- We should use persuasion- and interest-based approaches rather than power- or rights-based approaches. Threatening retributive action, using pressure tactics, or arguing about who has the better legal case are things we usually discourage. Instead, we want people to base their efforts to move a conflict toward resolution on a reasonable and essentially mild-mannered discussion of what is the best way of maximizing mutual gain.

Many of these norms are reasonable, especially in the context of mediation, but their cumulative effect can easily be to suppress conflict and label the behavior of people who are champions or advocates for a particular side of a conflict as adversarial and therefore bad. What we mean by *adversarial* is twofold. We believe that people who are adversarial do not genuinely want to resolve a conflict in a mutually acceptable way and that they violate some norms of behavior that we promote in conflict. If instead we can understand that in many conflict situations, people really do believe that they are in a win-lose contest, that the distributive elements of a conflict seem far greater than the integrative, and that others are essentially to blame for the situation, then we can understand why adversarial behavior, if not necessarily "nice," is at least understandable and sometimes justified.

Under the right circumstances, we are all sometimes adversaries, and we should be. The challenge is to get past seeing adversaries or adversarial behavior as necessarily a problem, and instead view it as a sign of where people are in their progression through the process of conflict. If we are genuinely committed to working with conflict, then we have to accept that adversarial behavior (as distinct from oppressive or threatening behavior) is not bad or something to be suppressed but is something to be worked with—even if it is relationship threatening. This is very hard for many of us to swallow, because it violates our norms about interpersonal behavior, but it may be key to understanding what we have to learn to work with if we are going to be more effective in a broader range of conflict situations.

Of course, sometimes conflict should be suppressed or avoided because the cost of engaging is too great, the timing is wrong, the issue at hand does not lend itself to constructive engagement, or we simply are not in a personal place to take on a conflict. All individuals and groups do this, and this is often an intelligent and adaptive response to the challenges of conflict. The question we need to ask as conflict resolvers is when and how people should engage in conflict and when and how they should avoid it. Too often in the name of approaching conflict constructively, we suppress major elements and realities about the conflict. When we do this, we inevitably distance ourselves from the experience and needs of people who are embroiled in a dispute.

## Belief Nine: We Offer a Level Playing Field

In our attempt to provide a constructive forum within which disputants may interact, we work to develop a process that is fair and inviting. In so doing, we offer several guarantees or at least goals that are unrealistic: neutrality, confidentiality, equality, and safety. We often think about this in terms of "creating a level playing field" or "balancing power." These are all worthy aspirations, but they are unrealistic in practice, and disputants know this. We have already discussed neutrality, but let's consider the promise of confidentiality, equality, and safety.

Confidentiality is offered in an attempt to help people feel safer, open up communication, protect the impartiality of the third party, and promote a more creative and open-minded approach to problem solving. As a mediator, my ability to maintain confidentiality is an important tool, source of influence, and ethical commitment. Mediators have rightly worked very hard to defend confidentiality against efforts to erode it (such as the efforts leading up to the Uniform Mediation Act). I have gone to court four times in my career to defend efforts to subpoena mediators (each one of these defenses has been successful).

Nevertheless, confidentiality may often be a somewhat ephemeral commitment. For one thing, neutrals may be able to offer their own commitment to confidentiality, but they can never guarantee that of other participants.

Confidentiality is usually more about the timing and framing of information than its ultimate release; moreover, it is usually not about facts at all but about less tangible issues, such as bargaining ranges, attitudes, flexibility, bottom lines, intentions, and suspicions. Furthermore, just because confidentiality is offered does not mean that there are not consequences to sharing information or ideas in mediation.

For example, once someone has indicated to a mediator a willingness to settle for a certain amount of money, it becomes practically harder for that person to hold out too long for a different amount, even if the mediator absolutely guarantees confidentiality. Once someone shares in a confidential setting that he or she is intending to take a certain course of action, it is more difficult for him or her to deny this in a nonconfidential setting. In the end, what may be most important about a confidential setting is the opportunity to give people some control over the timing and manner in which to share information rather than offering an absolute guarantee of privacy. When such complete confidentiality is guaranteed, it is often not in the public interest, particularly when public issues are involved.

When we offer equality, a level playing field, or a balance of power, we are again promoting a worthwhile value but not a reality. We can control certain aspects of a process so that neither side is given a formal edge. For example, we can ensure that all parties are provided the same amount of time to present their views, that everyone can bring advocates, that certain types of pressure are not overtly or directly applied, and that a neutral will not formally take sides. But conflict resolution structures do not exist in a vacuum, and the realities of inequality that exist outside a conflict resolution process inevitably have something to do with what happens within it.

Furthermore, the nature of the process, though evenly applied, can interact with the dynamics of external power in such a way as to reinforce one party's power and diminish another's. For example, if I feel that I am under no time pressure to settle a dispute and believe I have many alternatives, I can use a mediation process to slow things down, obtain more information, appear flexible to many different alternatives, and in general strengthen my bargaining position. But if I feel my alternatives are very poor, my time limited, and my ability to articulate my needs in a rational and dispassionate way minimal, then the process of mediation may further disempower me.

When people talk of "balancing power," I never know what they mean. We cannot change the external power relationships, and any effort to change them would fly in the face of our commitment not to take sides. Furthermore, the idea that power is a tangible (not to speak of measurable) quantity that can be balanced seems to me to be a misleading assumption. Everyone in a conflict has some power, or there would be no conflict. How much power someone has is a complex mixture of personal, situational, and structural factors (see Mayer, 2000).

We run into problems when we offer more than we can deliver with respect to equity and power, especially since parties basically understand the nature of the situation. If we pretend to offer a level playing field to people with great differentials in power, we will be perceived as either naive or dishonest, or we will be leading people down a path that can be very dangerous for them. If we can acknowledge the true nature of the power dynamics and have the more modest goal of offering a choice of different approaches to engaging in a conflict that take these dynamics into account as best as possible, then we will appear less naive and be less prone to mislead disputants.

Safety seems like the bare minimum we ought to be able to offer in dispute resolution processes, but often we cannot even promise this, certainly not in an absolute sense. Peacemaking can be dangerous, as the lives of Anwar Sadat, Yitzhak Rabin, and Mohandas Gandhi demonstrate. But even in less dramatic circumstances, participation in conflict resolution efforts can be dangerous. Things are said that people remember, and sometimes, despite our desire to separate the people from the problem, the face-to-face and personal nature of voluntary resolution processes can do the opposite: identify individuals with a conflict or disagreement in a way that can stir up a variety of emotions and reactions. We can offer safeguards, but we cannot guarantee safety, and we need to remember that people are often taking genuine risks of a personal, practical, or psychological nature when they engage with us in conflict resolution efforts.

Holding out the hope for confidentiality, equality, and safety are different approaches to offering a level playing field. The intention is good and the values important, but the reality is something different.

We cannot fundamentally change the nature of the structural or interpersonal power relationships. This reality accounts for much of the strength but also the limits of conflict resolution processes. Because people do not usually have to relinquish their power to participate, they are sometimes more willing to enter into conflict resolution forums, but by the same token, whatever inequalities exist outside a process are likely to be reflected inside as well.

If we cannot offer a level playing field, what can we offer? We can offer an alternative or several alternatives that have certain advantages and some disadvantages that participants ought to evaluate. We can be as transparent as possible about the limits of all alternatives, including the ones we are most committed to ourselves. We can try to make our processes as confidential, equal, and safe as possible without being naive about what we can deliver in this regard. Above all, we can respect the reality parties face when they choose to take a chance by engaging in conflict resolution efforts.

## Belief Ten: Conflict Resolution Is a Process

When we write and talk about conflict resolution, we are almost always talking about process, as if the essence of what we have to offer is a process. Some of us argue that our substantive knowledge about a conflict is not particularly relevant because we operate in the world of process and that substance belongs to the disputants. This is a comforting notion because it frees us from responsibility for mastering substance, for attending to substantive nuances, and for the success of the substantive outcome. Furthermore, thinking of conflict resolution as a process helps simplify the complexity of our work. If conflict resolution (and therefore conflict) is a process, our job is to design and conduct this process. Therefore, much of what we write is about process, procedures, and process-based interventions.

But conflict resolution has to be more than a process, because conflict is more than just a process. Furthermore, the idea that we can separate substance from process (or theory from practice) is neither realistic nor helpful. Conflict is a system of interaction (see Chapter Six) that can involve multiple processes, the flow of energy, many different agents, different forms of communication, and many key events that can lead to a reorganization of the system. When we limit our thinking or our approach to intervention to a particular process or a particular role in a process, we play into a misunderstanding of the nature of the system with which we are working.

There are several ways in which we do this. We have already discussed our tendency to discount our substantive role, especially if we take a facilitative or transformative approach. If we take an evaluative approach, we may make the opposite mistake: we assume our approach is substantive, when in fact we are still prescribing an essentially procedural intervention. That is, we assume that a particular process, namely an evaluative one, is what people always need. This process involves a substantive and legal analysis, a discussion of likely outcomes, and a means of inducing parties to reach an agreement based on this analysis and discussion. I think evaluative approaches are less about assisting disputants to find the best or most realistic substantive solution and more about conducting a process that is intended to help them overcome certain procedural and psychological barriers to arriving at an agreement. In this sense, they are every much as fixated on process as a transformative or facilitative mediator is. This focus on process can easily lead us, no matter what our orientation is, to discount the many other aspects of the system of conflict that disputants need assistance with.

Furthermore, our whole tendency to identify our work by whether we take an evaluative, facilitative, narrative, or transformative approach is at best artificial and at worst rigid and even manipulative. Our work is as complex as the conflicts that we intervene in, and there is no single simple approach that is always appropriate or effective. Most conflicts require a multiplicity of different interventions, and most experienced conflict resolvers use these. An evaluative mediator without good facilitative skills is likely to be considerably less effective at intervening in a complex conflict. Even dedicated facilitative mediators use evaluative techniques at times. They might not tell parties how strong their case is should they adjudicate it, but they may well evaluate the pros and cons of different approaches to communication, framing of issues, or constructing a table.

Transformative mediation in my view is not really a different approach at all, despite the efforts of many of its adherents to claim a unique status for it. In fact, it is a particular kind of facilitative approach with an agenda about what ought to transpire in terms of interpersonal interactions. The tactical suggestions of facilitative mediators (Bush and Folger, 1994, 1996) can be very useful under the right circumstances, but they are neither unknown to other mediators nor universally appropriate.

The description of our different approaches to conflict in such procedurally oriented terms is one sign that we have fallen into the common mistake of understanding conflict and its resolution in a narrow and overly procedural way. Conflicts do not resolve themselves simply by using different or more productive procedures, although these can certainly make a difference. Similarly, the right substantive solution is not what is usually missing either. In fact, significant conflict is almost always a complicated interaction of substantive, procedural, psychological, cultural, historical, and cognitive factors. To assume that effective conflict intervention should always focus on any one of these factors is a mistake. At some level, I think we all know this, but we still persist in defining our work in terms of process.

What disputants need from conflict resolvers is more than process: they need understanding, engagement, creativity, strength, wisdom, strategic thinking, confrontation, patience, encouragement, humor, courage, and a host of other qualities that are not only about process or substance. Each of us brings a different set of personal and professional characteristics and skills to the table that helps people work their way through conflict as best they can. All of us use a variety of procedures, and none of us can completely rely on them. We know this, and so do the disputants with whom we work. When we put ourselves forward as playing primarily a process-oriented role, we greatly understate the complexity and value of what we can and do bring to people in conflict.

---

All of the beliefs that I have challenged in this chapter have merit, and the approaches they imply have their place. Many of the beliefs are simple representations of values that are worthwhile holding onto and tactics that are often worthwhile employing. But we have built a great deal of our practice and our field around the notion that these values or beliefs represent reality and that these tactics are the cornerstone of our profession. In doing so, we have often limited the potential role we can play with people in conflict, and we have also raised suspicions about how realistic we are about the real nature of conflict or the actual way people experience conflict.

By challenging these assumptions or beliefs, we can open up our own thinking about what we do. More important, we can begin to expand the role we can play in helping people engage in conflict in a productive and wise way. The more our beliefs and concepts match the reality that people face in conflict, the more open they will be to our help. If these concepts have been comforting and helpful on one level, they have been restrictive and misleading on another. To move our field forward, we have to give up or at least significantly modify some of the ways we have understood our work and approached conflict. In the short run, this may make our work more difficult, but in the long run, it is the only way we can break out of the limits we have imposed on ourselves and address conflicts in a richer and more profound way.

If the prospect of taking some chances and going through a difficult period of transition seems daunting, it should also seem familiar: it is what we ask our clients to do every time they participate in a significant resolution effort. And if the notion that the first step in change is to question the beliefs that we rely on and often comfort us, that too should not seem so unusual, because that is also the largest challenge people face in altering their approach to a conflict.

We do not have to abandon the values underlying these beliefs or many of the tactics that are implied by them, but we must demand of ourselves a level of inquiry and honesty that will not sustain a simple adherence to them either. We can and must become more sophisticated and realistic in how we approach conflict. The more we do this, the more we will genuinely have something of value to offer people in a wider range of conflict situations.

In order to understand the limits and potential of what conflict resolution practitioners have to offer to disputants, we have to consider the historical role of conflict resolution as a field of practice. We need to be aware of the tension between conflict resolution as a profession and as a social movement and the way in which conflict resolution processes can act as forces for social control or for social change. We consider these issues in the next chapter.

# 5

## Conflict Resolution and Society

Why have a field called conflict resolution (or alternative dispute resolution)? Is this something that exists for the good of the public, or is it mostly to provide a home for alienated refugees from other professional settings? In other words, does this field exist for the benefit of society or for its practitioners? Obviously, no field can exist without benefiting its practitioners in some way, but no field ought to exist solely for that purpose either. We should not be afraid to ask whether there is an important societal interest served by the existence of conflict resolution as a separate field of practice with its own professional organizations, credentialing procedures, academic programs, and identity.

We should also ask whether the right way to identify what we do is in terms of the resolution of conflict. There are certainly alternative identities we could choose—for example, change management, decision making, intergroup communication peace studies, collaborative problem solving, or negotiation. These are all terms that we occasionally use in our work or in our description of what we do, but the generic term we keep coming back to as a field is *conflict resolution* or *dispute resolution*. This identification is wrapped in with a great deal of assumptions, values, and specific frameworks. Is it a useful one to us as a field and to society at large?

In order to consider this, we need to think about the social role that conflict resolution as a field plays in society and the complicated interplay between conflict resolution as an avenue of social change and as a means of social control. We should also look at the difference between considering conflict resolution as a profession and as a social movement.

## Conflict Resolution: A Social Movement or a Profession?

There has always been a creative tension between the characterization of conflict resolution as a movement or a profession. Many of us have seen the growth of conflict resolution and its various applications as an effort to change something fundamental about how society does its business—how decisions are made, how people are involved in the issues that affect their lives, how participatory democracy can be achieved in a practical way, and in general how the public can be empowered. In a previous book, I wrote, "The work of conflict resolvers is key to the deepening of democracy and struggle for social justice in the world. Conflict resolvers are advocates and designers of practical democratic processes. And these processes are key to transforming the world we live in and to addressing fundamental issues of peace, democracy and social justice" (Mayer, 2000, p. 246).

### A Social Movement

Many key figures in the development of the conflict resolution movement have come from a social activist background (John Haynes, James Laue, Christopher Moore, and Albie Davis, for example). This was my route into conflict resolution work. For some of us, conflict resolution has provided an intellectual and vocational outlet for the impulses that led us to be activists at an earlier stage in our lives. Here was a way in which we could fulfill our desires to improve the world we live in, contend with major issues of social inequality, promote our values about peace and nonviolence, and make a living as well.

Looking for a way to live out one's social values in a practical way is a time-honored quest. Making a living helping people, contributing to a better world, and doing challenging and interesting work is a wonderful privilege, something many people search for.

The Quaker concept of "right livelihood" addresses this urge and this value. The potential that conflict resolution has offered as a means of accomplishing this is both an advantage and a danger to the growth of the field. The élan, excitement, and enthusiasm that the field has generated are in no small measure related to its appeal as a force for positive social change. Many practitioners are genuinely devoted to their work, not only because of the benefits that they see for clients, but because of a sense that they are part of a larger social movement. We have often equated building the field with creating social change.

This motivation has accounted in large part for the significant presence of unpaid volunteers in our field, particularly in the areas of community mediation, school-based conflict resolution, and restorative justice. Volunteers have played a major role in moving the field forward, extending services to traditionally underserved populations, and holding down the overall costs of conflict resolution programs. Many people who have been disenchanted with their profession of origin (particularly but not only law) because it has not provided a vehicle for actualizing their social change aspirations have been attracted to conflict resolution. The work we do has appeared particularly congruent with values about creating a more peaceful and less alienating world. This is a powerful motivator to conflict resolution practitioners.

But there is a danger here as well. The more our devotion to our work is based on our beliefs that we are part of a force for social change, the harder it is to look at the limitations of what we offer. Criticisms of our field and its relationship to social change can threaten our sense of identity, and therefore we have an urge to discount these. Furthermore, our belief in the larger impact of our work can encourage us to overlook the immediate needs of our clients or the people involved in the conflicts we are working on. It can also get in the way when we try to help people decide which approach to dealing with a conflict is most appropriate for them. When people decide not to use mediation or collaborative problem-solving processes, it can seem to us like a violation of a basic value. This makes it harder to discuss with potential participants their choices in a dispassionate (and therefore empowering) way.

## A Profession

The other side of this tension is the view of conflict resolution as a profession. The birth of conflict resolution as a modern field is also rooted in the dissatisfaction many professionals have had with the traditional way in which decisions have been made or conflicts dealt with in their work. Lawyers and psychotherapists were searching for a better way to handle divorce. Human resource managers and union representatives were looking for alternative ways to deal with grievances or equal employment disputes. Corporate counsels were looking for ways of cutting down on the costs of litigation. In many different arenas, there was a sense that an alternative was needed to more formal, rights-based processes. As the conflict resolution field grew, particularly the use of mediation and arbitration, a growing number of people wanted to add these tools to their professional tool box. Some saw this as an adjunct to existing professional roles, but as the use of these approaches gained traction, many began to see this as their primary professional identification, or at least as a very separate professional role.

With this professional orientation came a desire to professionalize the field. The more the field could be presented as a profession, the easier it would be to charge professional fees, get referrals from other professionals or from the courts, and establish the credentials that provide status and credibility. As the conflict resolution field developed, those interested in professionalizing it pushed for certification, professional organizations with different levels of membership, formalized standards for approving training programs, professional journals, practice standards, protective legislation, and the like. There has been a division of conflict resolution associations into those that are more prone to promote the social change agenda (National Association for Community Mediation, National Association for Mediation in Education, National Conference on Peacemaking and Conflict Resolution) and those with more of a professionalizing agenda (Academy of Family Mediators, Association of Family Conciliation Courts, Society of Professionals in Dispute Resolution, Alternative Dispute Resolution Section of the American Bar Association, and the Association for Conflict Resolution). The relations between these two types of organizations have mostly been friendly, but their missions and visions are very different, as is the tone of their conferences.

The movement for professionalizing has helped establish conflict resolution as an effective field of practice, earned an increasing legitimacy among other professionals and organizational leaders who are critical to ensuring a steady flow of cases, and created some baseline of training and professional development. Without this element, the field would be even more marginalized than it is, and there would be considerably fewer resources for conferences, publications, educational programs, policy initiatives, and quality assurance processes.

But there is a danger here too. There is artificiality to all the efforts at presenting the field as if it were a professional discipline. Although there are more people getting degrees in conflict resolution, most practitioners still come from a different field of origin, and the major source of their credibility to many disputants and referral sources still stems from their association with their first field. The biggest player in conflict resolution in the United States may well be the Alternative Dispute Resolution Section of the American Bar Association, made up primarily (but not entirely) of attorneys. The professional degrees that most practitioners put after their names are not conflict resolution degrees.

Furthermore, the amount and sophistication of training that most conflict resolution practitioners receive, or that the field requires, is minimal and does not match the requirements of almost any other professional field. The educational standard that has stuck for most credentialing purposes is the forty- to sixty-hour training, with a certain amount of case consultation or supervision added on. Despite considerable lip-service given to the idea that this is not enough, just a beginning really, this seems to be the standard that has been most widely used over quite a few years now. I do not believe that sixty hours of training makes someone a professional.

In many ways, conflict resolution is still aspiring to professional status, a pretend profession so to speak. One of the major American conflict resolution organizations, the Association for Conflict Resolution (ACR), of which I have been a board member, is still struggling to get established. It currently has about six thousand members, none of whom really needs to belong in order to pursue their work. The lack of substance to this professional enterprise lurks right beneath the surface of most of our consciousness and is why it's hard for many practitioners to commit themselves completely to conflict resolution as their major and sole profession.

Ironically, the professionalizers need the élan and energy provided by the social movement to maintain commitment and loyalty. This provides the all-important normative element to motivate the involvement of practitioners in the field even when they are not receiving the business from conflict resolution work that they need to sustain themselves. But the social movement elements need the professional push to provide credibility, legitimacy, and business. This provides the all-important utilitarian element for the field. So there is a certain creative synergy, even symbiosis, between these two elements.

But these two aspects of the field get in each other's way as well. The requirements of a profession for standards, quality control, credentialing, and training can exclude or marginalize the volunteers and community practitioners, who are more likely to be motivated by a social change agenda. But the more the field is focused on social change and community-based volunteers, the less likely it will be seen as a highly skilled profession justifying significant fees and the referral of highly complex issues. Put more bluntly, the social movement adherents can see the professionalizers as elitist, self-aggrandizing, and even reactionary, while those with a profession-alizing orientation can see the social movement elements as naive, ineffective, and even flaky.

One tangible manifestation of the differences in these orienta-tions arises when deciding where and how to hold professional con-ferences. Should they be held in the comfortable and relatively pricey hotels or convention centers that typically host professional conferences but probably exclude many community- or school-based conflict resolution practitioners? Or should they be held on college campuses or in other lower-cost facilities that might attract a more diverse participation but would not provide a professional ambience? Different organizations have chosen different answers, which reflect how they see themselves in terms of being a social movement or a profession.

The tension between these two thrusts of the conflict resolution field is sometimes creative, often divisive, and usually confusing. It's not going to go away, but we can do a better job in naming it, work-ing with it, being more creative about how we integrate these ele-ments, and understanding its implications. To confront the issues facing conflict resolution, we have to pay attention to these two very different but equally important elements of what we do.

But we also have to ask how well we are doing on either front. Are we effective as a force for social change? Can we be a profes-sion? As with any other field of practice, there are complicated forces guiding our development. Professions exist because they serve societal interests and meet individual needs. The interplay between this is always complex. Conflict resolution as a movement is about social change, but as a profession it is also about social control or at least social stability.

## A Brief History

Conflict resolution is as old as human society. When people have had to balance individual needs with communal needs, when they have had to cooperate to survive—in other words, always—conflict resolution has been necessary. Furthermore, there has always been a rights-based and an interest-based component, although the terms themselves are quite modern.

The biblical story of King Solomon and the two women claiming to be the mother of a child is a classic example of an attempt to solve what is posed as a rights-based problem through assessing people's underlying interests. Traditional societies generally have some community dispute resolution process, often based on the role of elders or clan leaders. Disputes have been resolved through reliance on normative structures embodied in tradition, communal practices, and, in more recent centuries, formalized structures of rules, laws, policies, and legal precedent.

At the same time, disputes have also been resolved by an understanding of the individual needs of participants and the particularities of the circumstances. To take another classic example from American literature, consider the moral dilemma of Huck Finn, which Mark Twain presents to such great effect. Huck believed that he was a bad a person because he liked Jim and was helping him despite the fact that this violated the norms and rules of the society he grew up in and the laws of the land. But his interests were in friendship, adventure, and someone he could rely on given his horrible experiences with his father. Using the rights-based framework of his time, he would never have done what he did, but his emotional reality—and inner values—allowed him to follow through on his strong sense of what was in everyone's interest in this particular situation. This balance between a rights- and interest-based framework continues to be one of the challenges and opportunities of conflict resolution practice.

## Formal and Informal Approaches to Conflict

Historically, most conflict has been resolved outside the formal legal or diplomatic system. This is still true today, but the informal structures that worked in the past have been less effective in handling social conflict as our society has become more complex, communal and familial networks less powerful, and people more mobile. For example, the community church (or synagogue or mosque) provided an institutional framework for the informal resolution of many community and intercommunity conflicts in the past. Respected elders or community leaders were often looked to as the arbiters of conflicts that individuals or groups could not resolve themselves.

Wise elders did not simply rule on the basis of their personal opinions or some rigid set of criteria, even when texts such as the Bible or the Talmud were important sources of normative standards or rules. Instead, they integrated the needs of the community, the needs of the individuals, the formal or informal norms or practices of the community, and their own personal wisdom. Of course, as is always the case, some of these informal resolvers were more effective and humane than others, and in many of these practices, there was a great differentiation between the rights of privileged groups (men, in-groups, favored clans) and those of subservient groups (slaves, outsiders, women).

More formal legal or other rule- and contract-based systems arose as more formal organizations developed and more complex social and commercial institutions required more predictability and guarantees of the enforceability of agreements. Furthermore, as communities grew, mobility increased, and competing interests intensified, the informal means of decision making proved less effective, and more formalized and rule-based systems grew. Also, as the nature of the state changed and the role of an inherited authority structure diminished, new forms of social control were required as well. This led to an institutionalization and depersonalization of conflict resolution processes, primarily through the development of the court and other adjudicatory systems.

The legal and related systems therefore grew and infiltrated more aspects of societal decision making and conflict resolution procedures. But this system has always been designed to promote and actualize only one aspect of the conflict resolution equation: the formal, rule-based, and normative elements. The need for individualization, attending to the specific circumstances, and allowing for the ongoing integrity and effectiveness of social relations in the face of conflict is not best dealt with by this more formal, institutionalized aspect of conflict resolution. It requires more informal and flexible structures that allow for creative problem solving, a focus on interests or needs, a particularization as opposed to a generalization of processes and outcomes. The counterweight to the growth and strength of rights-based processes has always been informal processes, usually based in community institutions such as churches, schools, and other communal groups (granges, service groups, voluntary associations, and so forth).

With the incredible leap in population, geographical mobility, suburbanization, and complex organizational structures (multinational corporations, huge government bureaucracies, large professional organizations, diverse and complicated religious groups) that we have experienced in the past century, the informal conflict resolution mechanisms have been inevitably weakened, thus forcing an increasing reliance on more formal mechanisms. Issues such as disputes over partnership arrangements, disagreements among neighbors, conflicts between doctors and patients, or fights about proposed locations of public facilities (such as homeless shelters or landfills) that would seldom have been taken to formal systems of dispute resolution in the past almost automatically go there now.

This shift in emphasis from informal to formal mechanisms has been dramatic. Some of this has been very fortunate because the informal systems often failed to protect the rights of the underpowered and in fact could easily contribute to the ongoing suppression of disadvantaged groups. But formal systems did not always protect them so well either, and the cumulative effect of this trend has created a cumbersome, often alienating, and sometimes terribly inefficient approach to conflict.

## The Birth of Conflict Resolution as a Field

One of the main responses to this trend toward a more rights-based focus has been the development of the modern conflict resolution field. If informal mechanisms for resolving conflict were gradually disappearing, then some more organized and institutional approach to bringing people together to solve their problems without having to resort to a rule-based system was inevitable. Out of this need, the modern conflict resolution field has developed.

When did our field begin? A variety of perspectives can be taken on this. Early in the twentieth century, labor mediation and arbitration began to take hold. The U.S. Conciliation Service was founded in 1918, the National Mediation Board in 1926, and the Federal Mediation and Conciliation Services (FMCS) in 1947. The first application of the term *alternative dispute resolution* to the formal work of the FMCS was in 1975 when it was asked to intervene in a land dispute between the Hopis and Navajos. The Community Relations Service of the U.S. Department of Justice was created by the Civil Rights Act of 1964.

But the real mushrooming of conflict resolution, alternative dispute resolution, and mediation as fields of practice with an individual identity occurred in the late 1970s and early 1980s fueled by a desire to find better ways for dealing with organizational, family, environmental, and community disputes.

There were several impetuses for this. The Law Enforcement Assistance Act of the late 1970s created a number of community mediation or neighborhood justice centers to promote community-based conflict resolution. Several foundations, most notably the Hewlett Foundation, but also the CS Mott, Pew, Ford, and many local foundations, began seeing conflict resolution as a field deserving of investment. These efforts arose in part out of an awareness that the courts and other formal structures were unable to contend with widespread community tensions, the escalation of divorce, and the emerging strength of the environmental movement. To some extent, this was also a reaction to the disruption of the 1960s and 1970s when the absence of effective societal and community-based responses to conflict was keenly felt.

So we can see that the modern conflict resolution field grew out of a long-term trend that created an imbalance between individualistic and specific approaches to conflict, on the one hand, and formal and rights-based approaches, on the other. Without a clear historical context, it is easy to view the field as a completely new development that will fundamentally change our way of approaching conflict rather than as part of a long-term historic dynamic in how we approach conflict.

Conflict resolution, mediation, arbitration, collaborative problem solving, public involvement, consensus decision making, participatory management, collective bargaining, and related concepts have entered our public discourse and consciousness. A new balance between formal and informal, rights-based and needs-based approaches to conflict may be taking place. But we may have over-promoted our field and viewed it as a completely unique and unprecedented development rather than in its proper historical context. As a result, we may have greatly exaggerated our potential to affect the way conflict has always been handled.

In many ways, conflict resolution has been absorbed into the rights-based system of social maintenance and control as much as it has provided a counterfoil to it, and we have become as much a part of stabilizing and maintaining existing approaches to conflict and decision making as we have been in altering them. Let's consider conflict resolution as a force for social control and social change further.

## Conflict Resolution as Social Control

While conflict resolvers like to think of the work we do as contributing to social justice, social change, and peace, if we are honest with ourselves, we also have to face the ways in which our work contributes to the maintenance of social order and social control. In so doing, conflict resolution can be part of a process of maintaining social inequality and supporting exploitative practices. How? Conflict resolution provides an effective form of social control in four primary ways:

- By privatizing disputes, thereby isolating disputants and undercutting the policy change process

- By reinforcing certain structural sources of inequality (and thereby failing to protect the unempowered)

- By providing a means of displacing or engaging energy that might otherwise be directed toward social change efforts

- By defining issues in terms of system maintenance rather than system change

## Privatizing the Issue

Privatizing occurs in a number of ways. Most mediated settlements are private, and many are nondisclosable. They do not become part of a public record that can be used as both precedent and a means of evaluating the cumulative impact of these settlements on social policy or on the relationship between different parts of an organization or community.

For example, what is the cumulative result of the private settlement of sexual harassment complaints if 90 percent of these result in minor reprimands, some form of apology and monitoring, and otherwise business as usual? Does this in the long run result in the protection of workers from harassment, in confronting the underlying attitudes and structures that promote harassment, or in changing organizational culture? Or does this end up instead in contributing to a climate that allows exploitative relationships to continue, albeit with a slightly changed set of norms, but without providing genuine protection for victims? Similarly, if violations of toxic discharge policies are handled primarily through settlement processes, is the overall impact on a watershed or urban environment adequately monitored, and is the end result a cleaner and healthier environment?

Another contribution and result of privatizing conflicts is that parties with similar problems are kept separate. Individual grievances may be settled in a way that addresses individual needs, but not in a way that addresses the collective concerns or allows individuals the reinforcement of participating with others in the conflict process. This makes it harder to discern when there is a pattern that needs to be addressed or to obtain the systemic response that may be necessary to address the root of the problem.

The revelations about the extent of molestation that has occurred within the structure of the Catholic Church provide a dramatic example of what can happen when structures are in place that keep individual complainants separate from each other. Until the wall of privacy and isolation started to break down in this situation, no real change could occur. To my knowledge, no formal ADR efforts were employed before the dispute erupted into the public, but the whole process was characterized by very private settlement efforts, and these private and unscrutinized responses allowed the church to avoid looking at the systemic issue.

## Reinforcing Inequality

We should not expect conflict resolution processes to change major sources of social inequality (although we have sometimes held out the promise that we could do this). If women are disadvantaged by the way in which child support guidelines are written and enforced, it is unlikely that mediation itself will change this. If institutional racism is allowed to flourish in universities and corporations, conflict resolution procedures will not by themselves counteract this problem, which is so deeply embedded in our social structure and history. At best, conflict resolution can allow these problems to be aired, can be part of a process of gradually changing our awareness of these issues, and can ameliorate some of the worst individual effects.

But conflict resolution procedures should not make the inequalities worse, and sometimes they do. Consider these three examples:

In the XYZ Corporation, there has been a string of grievances about gender-based inequalities in pay and promotion practices. In accordance with the company's grievance procedure, almost all of these were settled through mediation or private settlement. In each of these individual cases, the company representatives knew exactly what the range of previous settlements and settlement offers had been, but none of the individual grievants had any information about this at all, putting them at a severe negotiating disadvantage.

A district court in an urban setting routinely refers all child custody disputes to mediation. Lawyers are allowed to advise their clients before any settlement is finalized, but many clients, particularly poorer ones, either cannot afford a lawyer or do not feel they can delay the settlement process. Although there is a policy that calls for screening for domestic violence, there are not adequate funds to do this in a thorough and systematic way. As a result, women enter into mediation without adequate representation and are often forced to negotiate with abusive spouses. Were these mediation programs not in place, might they be more likely to seek legal assistance and protection?

A state department of environmental quality has a process for conducting facilitated discussions that includes community members, environmental groups, and industry whenever there is a request for a variance on emissions or the location of a new toxic waste facility. The companies involved are very wealthy and have a full-time staff of legal and technical experts assigned to these processes. The environmental groups are represented by volunteers with limited amounts of time and resources.

These are not isolated examples. Although there are policies that could and sometimes are put in place to correct these problems, there are also many circumstances in which such practices continue. In this way, what is already a situation of structural inequity can be exacerbated, weaker parties can be further disempowered, and the conflict resolution field can contribute to the maintenance of social inequality.

## Displacing Energy

Social change efforts require considerable amounts of focused and wisely expended energy. Movements build up over time when the cumulative impact of exploitative social policy and structures becomes increasingly intolerable. When this discontent is collectively experienced and focused on change, amazing results can occur, but it is easy to throw this process off by providing opportunities for this energy to be discharged in small increments and directing the collective energy for change toward settlement efforts or minor change rather than organizing and advocating around the larger issues. This is an old tactic, but one that the conflict resolution field is almost ideally suited for.

As in the third example above, the limited resources of advocacy groups can easily be occupied by policy dialogue, collaborative problem-solving activities, individual negotiations, and a host of elaborately constructed and time-consuming public input processes. An important part of our work as conflict resolvers is to design and conduct these processes. And while virtually all of the conflict resolvers I have worked with are highly attuned to this dynamic and committed to designing and conducting these processes with integrity, they cannot fundamentally alter the structure of what occurs. We are oriented to encouraging dialogue, problem solving, and communication. At the right point in the development of a movement, these are appropriate and wise courses of action for activists representing all sides of an issue. At the wrong time, they are a distraction and a drain on energy, and it is not always clear when the right and the wrong times are.

Activists are put in an awkward position by what conflict resolvers do on occasion. To refuse to participate, especially on the grounds of the energy required, seems to violate commonly held norms about problem solving and communication. And we don't help when we try to encourage them, usually through quite legitimate means, to participate in what are often very demanding processes, the results of which may be a good solution to a specific problem but not necessarily a significant contribution to a larger social issue.

## Defining the Issue

A more subtle but particularly significant way in which conflict resolution procedures act as agents for social control is to define issues in terms of systems maintenance rather than change. Conflict resolution forums are about resolving conflict and therefore narrowing the scope of the issues rather than taking conflict to a higher level so that more fundamental problems can be confronted. For example, efforts to resolve disputes about the allocation of limited water among agriculture, municipal and industrial users, recreational needs, and environmental requirements (such as the preservation of habitat for endangered species) generally look at very specific decisions made about particular watersheds.

The problem dealt with is how to tinker with water allocation to allow for different climatic conditions and local changes. The fundamental question of whether the laws and policies regarding the use of water are outmoded given changing values and social realities—and perhaps also given a changing climate—is not taken up in these forums in a serious way and probably could not be. So the consciousness that arises out of discussions about this issue is one of reform to maintain the system rather than of challenge to the system itself (whether the system should be fundamentally changed or not).

Similarly, disputes between workers and management are dealt with either through a collective focus on the terms of a contract or an individual focus on the specific needs of individual workers and managers. But the fundamental nature of the relationship between workers and management—between those who own an enterprise and those who work in it, the major difference in benefits and incentives at different ends of the pay scale, and the amount of resources devoted to the upper end of the economic spectrum versus the lower end—is not addressed. While these issues might be raised, the thrust of conflict resolution procedures is to narrow the focus and narrow the terms of the debate rather than broaden them.

## Are We Part of the Problem?

None of these elements of social control occurs because of nefarious intentions on the part of conflict resolution practitioners and generally not on the part of those who hire and fund them either. These are all a result of the structure, focus, and philosophy of what we do. We try to remain neutral, we try to resolve conflicts, we try to prevent escalation, and we try to keep relationships intact. But if broad social change is desired, then advocacy is needed more than neutrality, conflict needs to be deepened—and often escalated—and good relationships are probably not appropriate as a central focus.

This field is inevitably going to be a force for social control and social stability at times. When that is appropriate, that is fine, but when it is not, we can be part of the very problems that many of us are motivated to struggle against and that we look to conflict resolution as a means of addressing.

I have considered the ways in which we contribute to social control independent of looking at how we are funded and where our financial interests lie. But how we are funded definitely affects the impact of what we do (Mayer, 2002). Professions are not funded by society to change the basic social structure itself, although if that structure is changing, professions can play a role in guiding that change. We are no exception.

The source of most of our funding is such that if we saw our role as helping disputants address the deeper issues in a conflict, to collectivize their agendas, to define problems in a more profound way, or to marshal their energies for a more concerted change effort, much of our work as neutrals would dry up. For example, as committed to being neutral and empowering as we may be, mediators who work repeatedly for the same company know that if one disputant is dissatisfied with their service, that is too bad, but if the company itself is, a major loss of income can ensue.

We don't like to think of ourselves as agents of social control, but we cannot really understand our circumstances or the situation we find ourselves in if we do not look at this reality and understand what it means for us. At the same time, we also should understand the ways in which we might be a force for social change as well.

## Conflict Resolution and Social Change

Just as conflict resolution is at times a mechanism for social control, it is also a force for social change, though not as directly or unambiguously as many of us want or have hoped and argued it would be. In challenging some of the assertions and directions of the field, it is important not to overlook its genuine contributions in this regard.

Whether we view conflict resolution as a genuine force for change depends to a large extent on our views about democracy and change. If deepening democracy on a communal and institutional level, and thereby allowing people to have more control over their lives, is necessary for social change, so is conflict resolution. If bringing ever more decisions to the field of democratic interaction and decision making contributes to social change, then conflict resolution is essential.

### Deepening Democracy

Democracy is a cumbersome and often inefficient process. It is weakened when democratic forums for dealing with social problems break down or appear to stagnate and as a result decision making is taken out of the hands of democratic institutions and thrown into the courts or other hierarchical structures. Bringing people together in a respectful and democratic forum to contend with major issues has always been scary and risky, and there are always many forces aligned against doing this. Even when it has not been scary, it has often been tiresome, exhausting, and frustrating. Effective conflict resolution and collaborative problem-solving procedures can help this critical participatory element of democracy work. By empowering democratic decision-making processes, we empower groups and people, and they then are better able to engage in active social change efforts.

In essence, we are talking about helping to give people more of a voice and more control over their own lives. Some may define this as important social change in and of itself, but in any case, it is an essential aspect of social change work. Thus far, we have primarily played a design- and process-oriented role. That is, we have not mainly viewed ourselves as having a contribution to make as advocates, advisers, or substantive experts but as designers and facilitators of effective processes. By creating effective forums for interactions, we are in essence saying that given the opportunity to have a voice, people will know how to use it effectively to promote the concerns that are important to them and that this is the way in which constructive change can come about.

At our best, we also pay attention to ensuring that not just one set of voices is heard, but very diverse voices, including many who are ordinarily excluded from the table. By creating practices and structures that allow for a diversity of voices, we promote the engagement of those who are often left out or marginalized in decision-making processes, and in so doing we contribute to social change. I will consider issues of diversity further below.

## Confronting Hierarchical Institutions

Sometimes conflict resolution practices can be seen as a counterfoil to hierarchical and elitist social institutions. That is, the alternative to conflict resolution in many circumstances is to turn key decisions over to those who are empowered to act in a hierarchical way and whose power comes from the authority of their position rather than from the cumulative powers of those they are working with. Hierarchical structures tend to be conservative, nondiverse, and not particularly creative or forward looking. Examples are the courts, legislative bodies, boards of directors, and hierarchies in public and private institutions. The more effective the conflict resolution mechanisms are in an arena, the less likely these hierarchies are to dominate the decision-making process.

Embedded in this discussion is an assumption that the values that conflict resolution promotes are contributive to social change effort. Built into what we do is the presumption that people should make the decisions that govern their lives and are capable of doing so effectively and with wisdom. We promote open communication, flexibility in decision making, finding creative and individually crafted solutions to difficult problems, a respect for diversity, and a belief in the importance of expressing the full range of beliefs and emotions that inform a problem.

## Providing Optimism

Perhaps optimism about facing seemingly intractable problems is the most important value (or attitude) we bring. Pessimism is a great force for inaction, optimism for change, and if we are not optimistic about people's potential to solve difficult problems, then we are not likely to be very happy or effective in our work. Of course, optimism is not the same as being naive or unrealistic.

I believe that effective social, personal, organizational, and communal change requires that we know when and how to raise conflict effectively and wisely and when and how to solve it as well. If early in many of our careers we were more oriented toward raising conflict in dramatic (but not always very wise) ways, later many of us focused on the resolution side of the equation. Both are necessary. To the extent that conflict resolvers promote genuine resolution of significant social issues, they promote social change. To the extent that they suppress raising these issues in a powerful and meaningful way, they suppress social change. We are at the time in the development of our field when we can, should, and indeed must embrace both sides of this equation.

## Diversity and Conflict Resolution

As with other elements of our field's relationship to society, our record on diversity in the practice of conflict resolution is full of good intentions and some positive outcomes, but also considerable ambiguity and at best mixed results.

The ostensible and oft-repeated value of the field is to promote diversity, be welcoming of diversity, and be sensitive to diversity in all aspects of what we do. A former director of a national conflict resolution organization used to refer to the commitment to diversity as "our prime directive." Active efforts to encourage a greater diversification of the field have been made by setting up diversity task forces, offering scholarships, engaging in proactive recruitment efforts, examining ways in which our organizations and professional gatherings can be more welcoming of diverse voices, and attending to the diversity of presenters at national conferences.

Yet in many ways we remain a primarily white, middle-class, English-speaking field. The conferences of the more professionally oriented (as opposed to social change oriented) organizations are not particularly diverse. Recruitment of people of color as professional mediators and trainers has had mixed results, and many of those who have entered the field have expressed a feeling that they do not feel particularly welcome or understood by the profession. Some of this, of course, is the result of being solidly located in a larger society that is struggling with issues of diversity, racism, and exclusion. But nevertheless, there are unique issues and problems that our field is experiencing in this regard.

### Our Own Assumptions

The field of conflict resolution is built around certain normative assumptions that are rooted in a very particular social context that is not necessarily inviting to people from diverse backgrounds. We value neutrality, professionalism, objectivity, linearity in communication, direct dealing about concerns and issues (but not necessarily the expression of emotions), confidentiality, and objective rights-based standards of fairness.

These values or norms may not appeal to people from backgrounds in which respect and credibility are created through affiliation rather than training and objectivity, where nonlinear approaches to communication are considered more effective and inviting, where feelings may be very directly expressed or very hidden, and where fairness can be determined only in an interactive structure (through what emerges from an interaction between people rather than through reference to an objective set of rules and regulations). The bottom line is that our forms of intervention, the conceptual frameworks we bring to our work, and the roles we carve out for ourselves are much less universal than we might think and are therefore not nearly as conducive to our values about diversity as we might wish.

## Talking About Racism, Sexism, Ethnocentrism, and Homophobia

Then there is the problem of even talking about racism, sexism, ethnocentrism, and homophobia. We don't do this very well as a society, and we don't do this well as a field either. We conflict resolution professionals hold ourselves out as having the skills and commitment to helping others talk about very difficult issues, such as race and sexual orientation, and so we certainly ought to be able to talk about these ourselves. But as in so many other institutions in North America, we find it easier to work on socially acceptable formulations of the issue rather than raise the most difficult questions and deal with the most controversial and potentially hurtful beliefs and stereotypes. For example, I suspect that all of us who have mediated employment disputes have encountered some of the following hidden attitudes about race:

> "The only reason she got hired [or has not been fired] is that everyone here is afraid of being called a racist."

"Anytime I raise a concern about performance, I am treated as if I am a clueless white male. Just because someone is black does not mean that there are no consequences for incompetence."

"If I ever raise any issue of race around here, people act as if I am trying to hide behind the color of my skin. People have no clue just how white this place is or how hard I had to work to get in the door."

"People act as if the only reason I have this job is because I am a person of color."

What have we done with these attitudes when we have run across them? Maybe on occasion, we play a role in helping people discuss these ideas in a constructive and genuine way, but we often end up working with people on rules about what they can say without fear of consequences rather than helping them express and work through the more difficult but usually unstated underlying attitudes.

Not only do we fail to do this with our clients; when issues about diversity arise within our own field or organizations, we often fail to take them on courageously, openly, and frankly. When racial or gender tensions arise, the nature of our own dialogue seems to change, to become more guarded, careful, and circumspect. The heavier the feelings are, the more we seem to resort to almost choreographed interchanges about respect for diversity, without really revealing the underlying beliefs of concerns that people may have.

Several years ago, I attended a professional conference in which a number of African Americans, youth in particular (but not only), took offense when Bill Ury presented the work he had done in preparation for writing his book *The Third Side*. Bill is an anthropologist, and he had studied how conflict has been handled by people of color from various parts of the world, including clans from Papua New Guinea and Aboriginals from Australia. He treated the practices of these groups and the insights he had received with great respect, but still it seemed to many an example of cultural insensitivity. Here was a white man who was studying people of color and then using this to promote his own ideas, which he was presenting to an audience including many people of color. This is a classical anthropologist's dilemma. The situation was exacerbated by the fact that he was the third white male in a row to deliver a keynote address. This was, of course, not Bill's fault, and he participated in a number of discussions with African American youth to discuss their concerns and his work, which I believe were very productive.

But it was interesting to note the overall nature of the discussions around these issues that took place at this conference and afterward. In general, many of the conversations were tense, sometimes convoluted, and in an interesting way, somewhat patronizing. That is, for the most part, the white response was to try to listen, understand, and accept the concerns— even if they had a hard time completely understanding them. But everyone seemed reluctant to assert arguments for why it might be legitimate to try to learn from the historical conflict resolution practices of diverse cultures around the world and how useful the work of anthropologists can be. The essential white response seemed to be to avoid the discussion or to agree with all the concerns and criticisms raised by people of color. It seems that when issues of race or gender arise, whites—white males, in particular—often adopt a defensive posture. We listen, agree with as much as we possibly can, and are very careful not to raise any of our own concerns or thoughts that might be viewed as insensitive to issues of diversity. This is not how to get at the real problems of diversity or how to create a genuinely diverse field.

What would have happened, for example, if we had been able to really argue the pros and cons of dominant culture anthropologists' studying minority societies? It might have been tense and at times painful, but it would have been productive and interesting. I might have argued that we have learned a lot from the work of Bill Ury and other anthropologists who have studied conflict in diverse societies, and that just because someone is white does not mean he or she should not be able to do this. Others may have argued that I was completely clueless about how marginalized people of color feel to be presented as objects of such research. We could have had at it about these issues, and it might have led in the end to a greater feeling of deeper unity instead of a sense of surface calm but underlying alienation.

## Individualizing a Societal Problem

Another problem in taking on diversity issues is that most of the models we teach and practice tend to individualize the problem (see the previous discussion about conflict resolution as social control). As a result, issues of race, gender, culture, and sexual orientation get translated in our practice into issues between individuals, or at most small groups, rather than being viewed as systemic or institutional problems. Furthermore, we look for rather immediate behavioral resolutions to these issues rather than attack the underlying attitudinal and structural basis of the problem.

In practice, this means that individuals may often receive assistance in getting past their immediate problems with one another, but organizations are seldom forced to face the culture and structures that continue to marginalize certain groups of people. It may be unfair to expect our field to be able to change patterns of interaction that are so deeply routed in society, but we should be willing to face the ways in which we contribute to the perpetuation of these patterns.

A related question is, How can we be neutral in the face of injustice? Our very commitment to a process rather than goal orientation and our consequent reliance on the neutral role has limited the extent to which people from diverse backgrounds have been able to trust us or see us as allies in their struggle to be fully equal and empowered members of society.

Our commitment as a field to diversity is important, and many of our interventions are structured in a way to ensure that new voices are continually being added to the decision-making table—voices that have been traditionally marginalized. This is an important contribution of our field to diversity, and it is largely why we have not been written off as irrelevant or useless by diversity activists. Furthermore, the alternative arenas for dealing with conflict are, if anything, less friendly to diverse groups.

But this should not be an excuse for ignoring our own ambiguous record in dealing with diversity. The dilemma of diversity will continue to be acute for our field. While conflict resolution espouses values of diversity and seeks to broaden participation in decision making, it also contributes to the feeling of isolation and disempowerment that many diverse groups experience.

## The Essential Value of Social Conflict

At the root of much of what we are talking about is the simple reality that societies and communities need conflict. In his classic work, *The Functions of Social Conflict* (1956), Louis Coser offers an analysis of the many ways in which social conflict is essential to social cohesion and interaction. We depend on conflict to bring together otherwise isolated groups, work through potentially divisive issues (such as issues of diversity), provide a release for pent-up frustrations and energies, focus on important problems, experience people whom we would otherwise ignore, break down barriers, and in many other ways as well. Societies, communities, families, and groups that have no conflict are not usually very healthy. Their basis of unity is probably fragile, and there are likely to be many issues that are not dealt with in a forthright and timely manner.

Most of us accept this analysis, which is often repeated to the point of being a cliché. But accepting the idea and truly embracing the reality are two different things, especially since conflict almost always has its destructive and demoralizing side as well. If we truly see the value of conflict in our social and interpersonal lives, then we have to confront the role of conflict resolution processes in suppressing or at least damping down conflict. When the time comes for conflict to be resolved or deescalated, then we should be in a place to assist with that, but we do a disservice if we fail to appreciate the value and necessity of conflict and therefore focus too quickly and readily on amelioration and resolution.

## The Limit of Resolution and the Power of Engagement

Conflict is necessary to society, organizations, individuals, and communities. A world without conflict would be a lifeless, soulless place. Organizations that suppress conflict are often rigid and incapable of adapting to changing conditions and new challenges. Societies that suppress conflict are not healthy, not democratic, and seldom safe. Families without conflict are often abusive and harsh.

In other words, our freedom, sense of autonomy and independence, and sense of community and connectedness are all wrapped up in our ability to engage in conflict effectively and wisely. But conflict can also be destructive and debilitating, and we often avoid conflict for good reasons. When conflict is not readily solved, individuals, organizations, and societies tend to resort to undemocratic, divisive, and hierarchical approaches to its suppression or resolution. Organizations that ostensibly are committed to participatory management can become hierarchical and even punitive if genuine differences about important issues, such as retrenchment or relocation, are aired. When public policy dialogues do not readily produce consensus on important issues (snowmobiling in Yellowstone, allocation of limited water among competing uses, location of public housing facilities in neighborhoods, gun control, protesting parameters outside abortion clinics), then policymakers are quick to resort to more traditional, hierarchical, and politicized approaches. More recently, it has seemed that international treaties or forums for dialogue are useful only if they produce the exact results desired by the powerful players (specifically the United States) involved with them. When this is not the case, those with power exert their control directly and unambiguously.

### More Than Resolution

Let's go back to the question that began this chapter: Should there be a conflict resolution field? All that I have discussed suggests the need to promote and develop effective approaches to working with and engaging in conflict. But this does not necessarily mean resolving conflict, and certainly not that we should always operate from a neutral stance.

If we are going to be effective in helping people deal with conflict, we have to shift our focus fundamentally. We have to become committed to assisting people at all stages of the conflict process, and we can't participate at an earlier stage of the process simply with the idea of moving people toward resolution. We have to learn how to help people and groups be effective and wise wherever in the process they find themselves.

At almost every phase of the conflict process, we can offer help in a number of ways:

- Understanding the nature of the conflict
- Figuring out what the underlying needs of all participants are
- Identifying alternatives for how to proceed
- Framing concerns and issues in a powerful way
- Making sense of the power dynamics
- Looking at meaningful approaches to communication
- Separating the personal from the structural aspects of conflict
- Raising conflict in a way that is powerful yet does not preclude later communication and problem solving
- Understanding the cultural dimensions
- Considering the different types of outside assistance that might be useful
- Providing that assistance as appropriate
- Helping people have a voice

If we can open ourselves up to the many different ways we can help people participate in conflict effectively and wisely at all the different stages of the process, we can play a much more powerful role in conflict. We will be able to enrich both the professional side of our work and the social change aspect. We will be better able to tackle issues of diversity and genuinely honor the functions that conflict plays while ameliorating its most destructive elements.

## The Conflict Engagement Field

To do this, we have to change our paradigm fundamentally. We have to stop thinking of ourselves as a profession of conflict resolution and start viewing ourselves as a profession of conflict engagement. That means that our job is to help people engage in conflict in a powerful, meaningful, wise, and honest way.

All the core values we bring to resolution, we can also bring to engagement. All the skills we need as third-party neutral conflict resolution specialists, we will need as conflict engagement practitioners, whether we operate from a neutral stance or not.

In order to do this, we need to understand the power of engagement, rethink the various conflict roles we may choose to play, and learn from other conflict specialists such as coaches, organizers, diplomats, and advocates. Advocacy in particular offers a particular challenge because to many of us, it seems anathema to how we see ourselves and what we think we are all about. But if we can embrace advocacy and add that to the set of roles that we play, then we can move beyond the confines of conflict resolution and enter into the larger context of conflict engagement.

This is a big challenge, but it is a wonderful and exciting opportunity as well. This is how we can face the limitations and shortcomings we have experienced while appreciating the genuine contributions we have made. This is the way in which we can grow and develop our work to the point where we can have an impact on the most important conflicts of our time in a far more profound way than we have so far. It won't be easy, but it will in some ways be natural.

In Part Two of this book, I explore the concept of conflict engagement more fully and look at the roles and processes we can use to fulfill this potential.

# PART TWO

# From Resolution
# to Engagement

# 6

# The Power of Engagement

Resolving conflict is often the most effective way of avoiding it, and avoidance may be the number one problem we face in handling conflict constructively. Of course, a genuine and thorough resolution of all issues involved is a worthwhile goal, but few resolutions of difficult conflict actually achieve this. We are always faced with the challenge of deciding what level of resolution to seek, how to determine what the real issues are, and how to know when genuine progress has been made. As mediators or facilitators, for example, we are always considering how deeply to probe, how much dirty laundry to air, and how much to delve into the emotional and attitudinal dimensions of conflict, as well as its behavioral or substantive aspects. Disputants and their advocates have to figure this out as well.

When we consider the entire trajectory of conflict, from its onset through its conclusion, and the full spectrum of the roles we could be playing, we can see that the concept of conflict resolution is limiting. We can play roles that range from advisers, to mediators, to decision makers, to process designers. We can help people initiate conflict, and we can help them resolve it. We can assist people when their primary task is to get their issues noticed—to raise the level of conflict—and we can help them handle conflict and conduct themselves through the course of a conflict, well before the situation is ripe for resolution. And, of course, we can assist people in recognizing and using the opportunities for genuine resolution when these arise.

If we embrace this whole trajectory and the multiplicity of ways in which we can assist people throughout the course of conflict, we can begin to think of ourselves as conflict specialists, and we can think of our task as helping people to engage in conflict powerfully and wisely. Engaging in conflict is our consistent and overriding purpose. While engaging includes conflict resolution since that is an appropriate goal and focus at the right point in the trajectory of conflict, it does not assume that to be the goal. Rather, engagement is about helping people be effective in addressing conflict at whatever point in its progression they may be, whether their need is to prevent it, identify it, escalate it, manage it, deescalate it, resolve it, or heal from its impacts. Rothman (1997) discusses the importance of "creative engagement in deep and persistent conflict," which he defines as occurring "when all sides can give voice to their essential concerns and can hear and  recognize the essential concerns of the other side as well" (p. 8).

In this chapter, I discuss the concept of engaging in conflict. What does it mean? Why focus on engagement rather than resolution? What makes conflict productive, and how can conflict be viewed as an adaptive system? In what specific ways do people need assistance with engaging? By understanding the concept of engagement better, we can get a better handle on what our focus as a field and as conflict practitioners should be. We start by considering the problems with an exclusively resolution-oriented focus.

## The Resolution Trap

By automatically thinking in terms of resolution, we inevitably drift toward a shallower and more behavioral definition of the issues because those are the ones that are usually the most easily available to resolution processes. But by doing so, we inevitably avoid some of the deeper and more poignant aspects of conflict—the elements that often keep people at odds, in turmoil, and dissatisfied. Often, addressing these would require encountering a considerable amount of pain, fear, or anger or making some very difficult choices.

We avoid conflict in this way all the time—as individuals, groups, and communities. For example, couples argue about chores, money, free time, or parenting rather than deal with their growing unhappiness with their lack of intimacy. And business teams grapple with work assignments and office space rather than face concerns about incompetent job performance or plummeting morale. As a society, we struggle about the fine points of affirmative action rather than face the destructive long-term effect of institutional racism and discrimination.

If we reach an agreement about the smaller issues, we achieve a temporary respite from having to deal with the larger ones. But in the long run, real concerns are not addressed, significant problems remain, and the long-term pattern of alienation or dissatisfaction is allowed to continue. Often people come to us because they don't want to deal with these more perplexing or frightening issues. Instead, they want a relatively painless, usually quick, and sometimes cosmetic resolution to easier problems, which can help them avoid facing their more profound issues. Sometimes it is best to avoid this deeper level, but if over time, these concerns are not dealt with by a community, an organization, or a marriage, they erode the structure of the relationship and the effectiveness of the system.

By offering people a service that is primarily defined along the lines of resolution, we are playing into this tendency, and as a field we pay the consequences. When a conflict is brought to us, we define our tasks in terms of steps toward resolution, and we instinctively focus on the part of the conflict that is amenable to resolution efforts. In this way, we can easily play into the conflict-avoidant tendencies that we all experience, and we can also play into the hands of those who have an interest in maintaining the status quo.

We all want to be helpful to others, and that has been an important motivator for engaging in conflict resolution work. We don't want to see people in pain or to leave a conflict in an unresolved and perhaps escalating state. If we can ease some immediate and nagging pain, that is particularly satisfying to those of us who are motivated by helping impulses. But that is also why people are suspicious of conflict resolvers and why we are not used except within tight boundaries. People often sense that only superficial resolution is possible through our efforts. None of this is to say that resolution services are not sometimes exactly what people want or that they are not often very beneficial; rather, it is that our constant and systematic focus on resolution reinforces the natural and universal tendencies to avoid conflict.

When disputants successfully take on the most challenging aspects of the conflicts they face, they are almost always stronger and more powerful as a result. But engaging in conflict in this way is difficult, at times dangerous, and always unpredictable (Cloke, 2000). Effective engagement is challenging but empowering. We have a role to play in helping disputants with this challenge, and it is a role that inevitably takes us beyond a resolution focus.

## What Is Conflict Engagement?

Engaging in conflict means accepting the challenges of a conflict, whatever its type or stage of development may be, with courage and wisdom and without automatically assuming that resolution is an appropriate goal. Effective engagement requires finding the right level of depth at which to engage. It also means being fully aware of the many different ways we could choose to avoid conflict, including trying to resolve it prematurely.

Certain conflict resolution roles are more appropriate for some phases of conflict than for others (for example, see Curle, 1971). Negotiation and mediation generally imply trying to explore the potential of reaching resolution. Conciliation or restorative justice processes generally involve some type of healing or working on relationships. Community organizing and advocacy approaches are oriented to changing the power dynamics and structure of interaction and helping people find a voice so that they can raise their issues to the level of effective conflict. Therefore, engagement implies considering a multiplicity of levels to work at and roles to play in conflict. This is challenging for conflict resolution professionals because we usually market ourselves from the perspective of one or two roles.

## Finding the Right Level

What further confuses the concept of engagement is that each party to a conflict may desire or need a different approach to engagement. Those who do not want a conflict to grow or a fundamental practice to be challenged may want to prevent, suppress, or quickly resolve a conflict. Those who wish or need a more fundamental change may desire a conflict to escalate and take root. Consider this community conflict:

> A middle-class community was upset about a community public health clinic that was being expanded and moved to their neighborhood. Although the existing facility was located only two blocks away, this felt like yet another intrusion into an area already containing more than its share of social services. Leadership of the clinic voiced a commitment to work with the neighbors to address their concerns, but also expressed a belief that their resistance was probably related to the high numbers of minority clients who used the clinic. Neighborhood leaders articulated concerns about traffic, parking, substance abuse (the clinic had a number of substance abuse treatment programs), and intimidating conditions their children would face at public transportation facilities that both adolescents on their way to school and clinic patients used.
>
> A series of public forums was convened, and a small working group of neighborhood representatives, clinic staff, and city officials was also formed to look at these issues. Through these processes, a number of agreements were arrived at and commitments made. Policies regarding substance abusers who were "under the influence," oversight of particular clinic programs, design considerations for parking and traffic flow, clinic size, and

ongoing communication with neighbors were all discussed, and commitments from the clinic were elicited.

Based on the success of these negotiations in addressing many of the concerns that the neighbors raised, the city approved a permit that incorporated these new agreements into its terms. Nonetheless, many neighbors felt extremely skeptical and resistant to signing off on any agreement. Suits were threatened (and some were filed, although they did not go anywhere), and many neighbors insisted that they "had never really been heard or acknowledged," that they were being painted as "enemies of the poor," that their concerns had never been taken seriously, and that "we may not get our way, but we are not willing to give up simply because we are fighting an uphill battle." They appreciated the efforts of the facilitators to organize a forum for discussion, but they did not believe that the clinic or the city would ever really listen to them—despite the fact that the clinic's plans and operations were significantly altered as a result of these discussions.

This is a typical example of how muddy it can get to consider what "effective engagement at an appropriate level of depth" means. The decision about clinic location was representative of much broader issues concerning the ways in which the neighbors felt they were being treated by the city government.

Specifically, they felt that because they were a less established, and in their view less powerful, neighborhood, an unfair proportion of undesirable facilities was being located there, and furthermore they felt that they had no genuine voice in city decision making. To get at their real concerns, they needed to deepen and expand this conflict, whereas the city and the clinic wanted to make sure that this did not expand into a major confrontation about values and neighborhood relations, so they wanted to prevent or quickly resolve any conflict that might arise.

For the most part, the city and clinic met their goals, and this is partly because the design of the process was behavioral and solution oriented. The neighbors did get some of their needs met, in particular their concerns about the specific impact of the clinic, but at the deeper level, their issues were not only never addressed, they were never given an effective forum for presenting them. Their more fundamental need (at least for a substantial number of neighbors) was for conflict escalation. Had a process been established to allow the city and the neighbors to look beyond the clinic, issues about the disproportionate location of public services in their neighborhood, the difficulty in obtaining a response from the city to neighborhood concerns, and their overall sense that they were being treated like second-class citizens would have at least been discussed.

By framing their concerns in terms of the impact of this specific facility, the neighbors contributed to the narrower focus of the discussion. One of the ways in which a conflict engagement approach might have helped them would have been by strategizing how they could increase their ability to raise their more fundamental issues—knowing that these might not be solved quickly or easily—while also accepting the proffered forum for dealing with the specific concerns about the clinic. Without engaging this conflict on a deeper level, there was no way for the neighbors to address their more fundamental concerns. If the deeper concerns of the neighborhood had been articulated more forcefully, there might have been a two-part process initiated: one addressing the immediate issue of the clinic, the other dealing with the neighborhood's overall relationship with the city.

## Understanding the Developmental Tasks of Conflict

Conflict is as varied and unpredictable as human relations. There are no set stages or established progressions for conflict. By referring to conflict as a trajectory, we roughly imply that there is a period of rising conflict and a period of diminishing conflicts and some discernable point between the two that is a point of crisis or dénouement. But as with all other metaphors, there are truth and inaccuracy here.

Another metaphor might be to view conflict as a river that has its calm moments and its rapids; sometimes it even has treacherous waterfalls that require avoidance at all costs. We can enter and exit this river at many different points, and just because we have made it through one challenging rapids and reached a calm stretch does not mean that another set is not around the next bend.

My point is not to find the perfect metaphor, but to avoid a misleading or limiting one. We use the metaphor of stages or steps to describe complicated processes, as if they are linear events, and that having accomplished one step, we are now ready to go on to the next.

I prefer two other metaphors for understanding the nature of conflict. One is that of a complex adaptive system, something akin to a living organism, which I discuss later in this chapter. The other is of a developmental process.

In other words, we can look at conflict as requiring a series of developmental tasks. They can be accomplished in different ways and in different orders, but at some point they need to be accomplished if a conflict is to be addressed effectively. The role of the conflict specialist is to help people engage with these tasks in a powerful and productive way. Let's consider several of these tasks:

- *Awareness*—becoming aware that there is something we are in conflict about or someone we are in conflict with. This can be a clear and rationally described awareness or an inchoate or experiential one. Interestingly, many people do not become aware of a conflict until they are well into the process—sometimes at the end of it.

- *Articulation*—giving voice to the existence of the conflict in some way. This too can be done directly and clearly, or it can be indirect and through actions more than words. This also means creating a story that explains the conflict to oneself and usually to others. This story can include positions, interests, values, frames of reference, metaphors, characterization of participants, a narrative of what happened, and all the other elements of a conflict drama. When we give voice to the existence of a conflict, we define and characterize it.

- *Mobilization*—mobilizing resources to assist in carrying on the conflict and bringing it to a level of intensity and action where participants want it to be. This can involve mobilizing our internal resources (such as our will, determination, clarity, energy) and external resources (allies, legal arguments, finances, organization).

- *Activation*—taking the action steps that bring about a response to further a goal. This can range from a direct communication with someone else to war. Usually when we describe conflict, we are talking about all the different ways in which conflict has been activated. Activation can be escalatory (raising the awareness and intensity of conflict) or deescalatory (taking conflict to a lower level of intensity). Both are often happening at once.

- *Connection*—finding a way of interacting with others with whom we are in conflict. This can be accomplished through negotiation, but it can occur in many other ways as well: through public actions, court fights, political struggles, private discussions, third parties, and many other ways. If we have not succeeded in connecting in some way with the others involved in conflict, we are probably not in a very powerful place.

- *Need satisfaction*. We engage in conflict to try to satisfy certain needs, but these needs may change through the course of a conflict. For example, an essential early need may be for voice and legitimacy, but at some point, we may be more interested in peace and security. Until we have reached the point where our needs can best be satisfied through deescalation or agreements, then we are probably not looking for a quick resolution.

- *Release*. At some point, we want the energy occupied by a conflict to be freed up, at least in part. We may be ready to give up the conflict, resolve it, or change our stance within it.

- *Process selection*. Disputants need a process by which to accomplish all the other tasks. We often think of our role as a process-oriented role, and that is certainly one of the tasks that people need help with, but it is not the only one. Often this involves designing processes, sometimes it means entering into existing ones, and sometimes it means continuing with an existing process in an effective way.

Prevention, management, resolution, or healing functions might be involved in each of these developmental steps. Conflict engagement as an approach is not committed to any one of those functions but implies helping people accomplish whichever of these tasks they are struggling with. As conflict specialists, we can do a great deal to assist with each. From within this broad concept of what we do, there are many particular strategies or actions we might take or roles we might play, but they are subservient to the larger goal of effective engagement.

One way of looking at the conflict specialist's job is through the lens of these developmental tasks. Our task is to understand which of the tasks disputants are most in need of assistance with and then to consider how we can help—what roles we should be playing and what strategies we should be employing. By looking at conflict in this way, we can escape the trap of automatically assuming our job is to take people through a predetermined linear process toward an inevitable end of resolution. Instead, we are helping disputants deal with the particular challenge to engagement that they are experiencing at any given time.

## Engaging or Transforming?

By arguing for an orientation to conflict that promotes engagement rather than resolution as a goal, I am making a somewhat similar point to what Bush and Folger have said in *The Promise of Mediation* (1994). In this influential book, they argue that mediation has the potential to transform disputants but that this potential is often squandered by an automatic and unwise assumption that outcomes and resolutions ought to be the focus of mediators. But if we consider the concept of engagement and transformation more deeply, we will see that they are very different concepts and the underlying approach of engagement versus transformation is really very different. The goal of engagement is to help people enter into conflict at whatever phase they are in and to work with them on accomplishing the developmental tasks of conflict with which they are strug-

Visit our website at
www.yogajournal.com

# BUSINESS REPLY MAIL

FIRST-CLASS MAIL    PERMIT NO. 1403    BOULDER CO

POSTAGE WILL BE PAID BY ADDRESSEE

**yoga** JOURNAL

PO BOX 51151
BOULDER CO    80323-1151

gling. The goal of a transformative approach is to change disputants in some significant way through the conflict experience.

I believe effective conflict interventions can result in the transformation of individuals and groups, but I do not think that there is any way to take this on as a primary goal of a conflict specialist without imposing our values and purposes on disputants. Conflict is probably a necessary force for transformation, and transformation of some kind is often necessary to deal with conflict. By focusing on helping people engage in conflict fully and courageously, we probably increase the likelihood that the conflict experience will have a significant impact on disputants and may even transform them in some ways. But that is at most a secondary benefit. If we take that on as a primary goal, then we will in fact interfere with our ability to help people engage in conflict because we will have a goal that is very different and potentially contradictory to their needs from conflict.

In fact, I think Bush and Folger's view of transformation is actually quite narrow and fails to address the potential for the social transformation of conflict, the alteration of how conflict is conducted within and among cultures, societies, communities, and organizations. This concept is eloquently developed by John Paul Lederach among others (see Lederach, 1995, 2003; Kriesberg, Northrup, and Thorson, 1989). Their vision is less restricted to an interpersonal context and does not impose the same agenda on disputants that Bush and Folger's approach does. In Lederach's view, we can help people transform their relationship to conflict through our intervention, but the most appropriate route to do this is through an elicitive approach, in which we help disputants articulate their own ideas and approaches to conflict and then assist them in carrying these forward. I believe this is a much more profound view of transformation, and one that is more akin to the ideas that I am discussing in this chapter.

I hope that as conflict specialists we do not prevent constructive transformation from occurring (destructive transformation—witness the Middle East—also occurs), and that we are sometimes even the agents or catalysts for transformation. But I also believe that people and conflicts transform themselves as they are ready to and when circumstances allow. The concept of engagement is some-what different from even this broader view of transformation, al-though it shares many of the same values.

I believe that our most appropriate approach to maximizing the potential gains people can realize from conflict is to focus on helping them engage successfully in the various development tasks of conflict. If we do this well, we will increase the possibility that they can trans-form themselves when they are ready and that they will resolve con-flict as appropriate. Engagement is in some sense a more modest goal for conflict specialists, but it may actually be a more challenging and important goal as well.

This is not an abstract distinction. There are in fact practical ramifications to this stance. Empowerment and recognition, to use the key goals that Bush and Folger discuss, are appropriate under the right circumstances, but not all circumstances. When there is a disconnect between what disputants need in order to engage ef-fectively and what we are trying to offer them because of our own values about conflict and transformation, then our goals, laudable though they may be, can get in the way of constructive engage-ment. We have to make sure that our own hopes for transformation or social change do not take over from disputants' sense of their own needs and goals.

Conflict engagement is both an organizing principle and a goal. It is what our work should be all about. When we can help people be fully engaged in conflict in a constructive, powerful, and effective way, we have accomplished something important. By taking this on as our purpose, we avoid the twin traps of focusing on premature and shallow outcomes or on a personal change agenda that might appeal to us but is not the reason disputants seek our services. Addressing the developmental needs of people in conflict can organize our approach to our work, help us stay in tune to our clients' needs, and define a path to participating in a far wider range of conflicts.

One challenge in helping people engage in conflict is to develop an understanding of what constitutes constructive, effective, and wise engagement. If we are going to help people engage in conflict, what are the principles of engagement we are going to promote? This raises the question of how can we define constructive engagement.

## What Makes Conflict Engagement Constructive

Conflict is often incredibly destructive and should be avoided, but it is also necessary for social cohesion, social change, and personal growth. Our challenge is to help people engage in conflict in a productive and constructive way. This raises the question of what is a productive way of engaging in conflict, what makes conflict constructive rather than destructive, how conflict can be growth producing rather than disabling, and how it can be adaptive rather than dysfunctional.

Certain characteristics of how we engage in conflict, whether as disputants or intervenors, are both causes and indicators of a constructive approach, no matter what part of the process is occurring:

- *Congruence with our values*. None of us can be very effective in conflict over time if we are in violation of our own basic values. We can violate more superficial values about politeness, language, tone of voice, or even listening. But we cannot violate our core values about human dignity, truth, human life, or equality if we are going to engage in conflict effectively. People violate these values, and often gain a short-term upper hand in this way. But in the long run, this disempowers them and makes it considerably more difficult to address their real issues. People are more powerful when they are acting in accordance with their most fundamental values and beliefs, whatever they are.

- *Authenticity of voice*. When all those involved in conflict have found an effective and authentic voice, that is a way of speaking to their issues and needs in a way that addresses their most significant concerns and reflects their sense of how they see themselves in relationship to the conflict, then they are most likely to be able to carry on conflict effectively. People sometimes put on masks or take on roles that are not congruent with who they are, and this makes it harder for them to speak to what is really important to them or to be heard by others in the way they intend and need to be heard.

• *Addressing the right issue.* When disputants are talking about the right issue and hearing the issues of most concern to others, they can be the most effective in conflict—even if that does not lead to resolution. This does not always mean speaking to the nice or polite issue. If a conflict in a workplace is in fact about the attempts of some to maintain positions of privilege based on ethnicity or gender, then it is far better to hear this and address the real issue than to work instead on a surrogate issue, such as seniority or job security. The right issue is subjective, changing, and hard to define, but finding it is critical to effective conflict engagement.

• *Getting to the right level of depth.* Issues and needs can be addressed at an overly superficial or overly deep level. Finding the level where an issue lives for people is part of the art of all forms of effective conflict engagement and perhaps all interpersonal relations: too shallow, and we are avoiding the genuine conflict; too deep, and we are wallowing in the mire.

• *Involving the right people.* The right issue at the right depth addressed to the wrong people or to the wrong range of participants is a prescription for frustration. For divorcing parents to argue about custody arrangements for teenagers without the involving the teens is not likely to be very productive. Community activists who are attacking a local governmental representative for what is a national policy do not often accomplish much.

• *Appropriate time frames.* Taking too short a view of a conflict or interaction can result in a failure to consider the real consequences of our action. Taking too long a view can lead us to feel that nothing we do will make a real difference. Historical context is important but not determinative. To look at a conflict from a variety of time frames and to be informed but not disabled by history are critical to effective engagement

• *Allowing for change.* A fundamental ameliorating factor to deadlocked conflict is the idea that people change, relationships change, and circumstances change. We should never act in a way that assumes that the people we are in conflict with cannot change, that we cannot change, or that our relationship cannot change. A principle of nonviolence is that all of our adversaries are our potential allies, and this is a principle that we can adopt in all conflict situations. By allowing for the potential of change, we can avoid precluding the possibility of change. This does not mean being naive or taking unwise risks, but it does mean not letting our pessimism or negativity become a self-fulfilling prophesy.

• *Attending to both the distributive and integrative dimensions of conflict.* Most conflicts, perhaps all, have an element that calls for creativity in understanding how conflictants can meet each other's needs and expand the available benefits to be distributed. This is often referred to as the integrative dimension of conflict (Thomas, 1983; Walton and McKersie, 1980). Conflicts also have an aspect that demands making the hard decisions about dividing up benefits when there is not enough to go around and people want more than they can get (the distributive dimension). If we fail to pay attention to the first, we fail to explore the potential for cooperation and leave a lot of unrealized value on the table. If we fail to attend to the latter, we are not being realistic about the hard choices that have to be made and the need for people to take difficult steps to protect their own interests.

• *Fundamental safety.* Engaging constructively in conflict is very hard and may not be possible if we don't feel we are fundamentally safe. Of course, we frequently engage in conflict from a fundamentally unsafe position, usually because we have no other choice. However, constructive engagement is much more likely if basic needs for safety can be addressed.

• *Grounded optimism.* It's easier said than done, perhaps, but when people are optimistic about their own ability to engage in conflict or the long-term likelihood that a conflict experience can lead to positive results, they can engage more effectively, more powerfully, and at the same time with more respect for the needs of others. Of course, ungrounded or baseless optimism is not real and therefore not effective.

- *Uncertainty.* If we are sure we are right, sure that we know what will happen over time, sure of our arguments and evaluation of others, sure that virtue is on our side, then we are not only harder to deal with, more rigid, and less appealing, we are also less effective in the long run. Uncertainty does not mean lack of clarity, determination, or consistency. Rather, it is the characteristic that gives us flexibility and, to some extent, humanity. Furthermore, given the nature of human interaction, uncertainty is realistic. We can't know what is going to happen. All the preparation and analysis in the world will not guarantee an outcome, particularly in the highly fluid context of intense conflict. So if we are not uncertain, we are not facing reality.

## Helping People Fight

Let's consider one particularly challenging part of the engagement process: helping people fight. Tempting as it might be to add the word *fairly* at the end of that sentence, that would take our focus off the fight part and onto the containment or management part of the task.

Sometimes fighting and escalation are necessary. People are prone to two key kinds of problems when fighting is necessary: they avoid the fight, or they fail to fight effectively. Conflict specialists sometimes have to help people face the necessity of escalating a conflict in order to meet their needs. Keeping in mind the first principle of constructive engagement, value congruence, we should consider why we might want to help people fight and how to do it.

In the early 1960s, I was active in the civil rights movement in the North and the South. Something that I have often thought about, given my commitment to nonviolent social change, is the impact on national and state policy of the riots in American cities and the rise of the Black Panthers with their implied or outright threat of violence. How much change would have occurred without the threat of social disruption and violence that these forces represented? As necessary and influential as they were, would the work of the Southern Christian Leadership Conference, the Conference on Racial Equality, the Student Nonviolent Coordinating Committee, or the NAACP have had the same impact were it not for the threat of violence and escalation that hovered over the times? Does this mean that the riots in the end were a force for social good? There was much accomplished, of course, before the rise of the Black Panthers, but would the changes that the civil rights movement achieved have gone nearly as far as they did without the disruption and even the chaos represented by these more militant groups?

These are not easily answered questions, but they point out that without at least the threat of escalation, or some other powerful BATNA (best alternative to a negotiated agreement), disputants are less likely to be effective in conflict. Sometimes we have to help people face the need to raise the ante, escalate a conflict, or threaten negative consequences in order to help engage in a conflict effectively. I am not promoting violence or the threat of violence here, just pointing out that without the possibility that a conflict may escalate, change may be impossible.

## The Value of Fighting

It may be that strikes are a ridiculous way to get to a new contract or address conflicts between labor and management, both with a strong interest in a profitable, efficient, and productive workplace. However, without the threat of striking or some similarly powerful action, it is hard for workers to have a genuine voice at the table. But the threat of strikes is not credible if they do not occasionally occur.

Therein lies a real dilemma for our field. If we always are helping people avoid strikes or similar job actions and never helping either management or labor prepare to deal in a powerful way with a breakdown in negotiations, then we are helping with only one side of an equation that necessarily requires both sides. Labor and management have to do all they can to negotiate solid agreements, but if they do not prepare for the possibility of a breakdown in negotiation, they are making themselves very vulnerable and undercutting their own potential power.

In their comprehensive and insightful book about negotiation, *The Manager as Negotiator,* Lax and Sebenius (1986) discuss the tension between creating value and claiming value (the integrative and distributive dimensions). They point out that the more we focus on claiming value (getting the most for ourselves), the harder it is to discover the potential for joint gain and the more likely it is that a conflict will escalate. But the more we focus on creating value (enlarging the amount of value available to all), the easier it is to make oneself vulnerable to exploitation by others who are focused on claiming value.

To turn the Einstein quote on its head, we often have no choice but to prepare for war and peace at the same time. By preparing for war, that is, by developing the capacity to fight, to take a distributional approach to conflict if necessary, we make it clear to others (and to ourselves) that a more cooperative approach may be desirable. But we also have to prepare for and work toward a cooperative relationship, or we can get swept up in the momentum of confrontation. So if we are unable or unwilling to help people fight, to help with the distributive dimension, to assist with claiming value, then we will often also forgo the opportunity to help people consider how to create value—to work on the integrative dimension or to consider win-win possibilities. Preparing for peace is important. Being willing to escalate is often important as well.

## How to Assist with a Fight

How can we assist people to fight, from the vantage of our expertise and values as conflict specialists? In the next chapter, I discuss the roles we can play; here I focus on the skills and concepts that we offer. We can assist people to fight by working with them in four fundamental ways:

- Help them develop the legitimate power they can bring to the conflict—and prepare to deal with the power that is likely to be directed at them.

- Help them consider rights-based approaches to accomplishing their objectives.

- Help them understand the array of interests involved in a conflict and what these suggest for how to develop an effective conflict strategy.

- Help them examine their own values and those of others in a conflict to consider how a fight can be carried out in keeping with the system of values in play.

We bring other assets as well: understanding communication, the cultural context, historical factors, and the system within which a conflict is playing out. But our particular value may be in helping people consider the interplay of power, rights, and interests within the context of our own values.

## Conflict as a Complex Adaptive System

If we are to help people successfully engage, we have to face an important aspect of conflict: its unpredictability. As much as we might like to think that we can choose the optimal approach to handling a conflict through analysis, planning, and the application of our wisdom and experience, there probably is no such thing as one optimal approach. We can't predict with certainty how conflict will evolve, what the impact of a particular intervention will be, or what the long-term outcome will be. To understand this point, we only have to look at some of the many well-intentioned efforts, conducted by wise and well-informed people, that ended badly. The considerable efforts made during the last year of the Clinton administration to achieve a breakthrough in the Middle East and the many different initiatives to deal with North Korea are two examples that come to mind. This unpredictability can be disconcerting, but it opens up some important insights about what we can do as a field to help people engage in conflict.

## Conflict as a System

To start, we have to understand conflict as a system of interaction; like all other systems, a change in any one part of it can lead to a realignment of the whole. This means that we need to understand that the direct and immediate conflict we observe may not necessarily be the most productive place to intervene or even the genuine source of the conflict. An ongoing conflict between a special education teacher and a regular classroom teacher may be best handled between the two of them, or the issue may actually be a reflection of a lack of clear leadership by the principal or an overall atmosphere of stress caused by poor school scores on standardized tests.

Where to intervene becomes an important question, but not one that can be answered with certainty. One question we can ask, however, is what simple change is most likely to stimulate the larger system to reorganize in a productive way. This cannot be answered authoritatively either, but it points our thinking in directions that are both broader and more focused—broader because we look beyond the direct conflict toward the larger context, more focused because we do not have to intervene in every problem that exists and instead have to look for that key change that can cause a system reorganization.

## Conflict as an Adaptive System

But conflict can also be viewed as a particular type of system—a complex adaptive system. In adopting this view, we think of conflict as a system of interaction that is constantly evolving and adapting to new inputs in ways that we cannot fully understand, predict, or control, but can watch with an idea of trying to enter something new into the system to see how this alters the nature of the interaction. This is the concept of nucleation: the idea that a small change can have large effects through how it causes a system to reorganize.

In order to understand the impact of viewing conflict as a complex system, we need to distinguish it from a complicated system. Jones and Hughes (2003) contrast a complicated system, such as a computer network or a jetliner, with a complex adaptive system such as the human brain, an ecosystem, or a community conflict. A complicated system can be understood through linear and analytical processes. That is, we can break it down into its component parts, analyze them, and thereby understand the system. Furthermore, we can assume that a given input will produce the same output under similar circumstances. But this is not true of a complex adaptive system, because this system is constantly reorganizing and adapting itself to any new input, such as the intervention of a mediator.

When we try to analyze conflict as if it is a complicated system, we might look at the needs of all the individuals, the past relationships, the relative power, the legal framework, and thereby feel we can construct an approach that is going to produce predictable and consistent results. But when we look at it as a complex system, we realize that we can't really break it apart in this way; instead, we have to enter into it and in a sense join with it. This makes true neutrality, objectivity, and objective standards of fairness impossible.

For example, Jones and Hughes say:

First we must recognize the invalidity of the concepts of neutrality and impartiality and, in their place, recognize that mediators are coparticipants in the conflict who bring their own unspoken and often unrecognized biases to the conflict. . . .

As mediators, we must also embrace our own existence in the mediation as feeling beings with thoughts and share that realization with disputants. Only then can we begin to constructively engage conflict and individuals in conflict, and thus begin the incredible search for new understandings about conflict [pp. 492–493].

Taking the more linear and straightforward approach to understanding and intervening often helps us choose a direction in the middle of what feels like a chaotic system. This can be comforting and on occasion effective. But as any experienced mediator knows, what is a brilliant intervention in one situation will be a total flop in a different conflict, no matter how similar the circumstances appear to be.

Conflict is chaotic—or, more accurately, complex and adaptive. When we think of conflict as a complex system, akin to organic systems that have a great capacity to adapt to different stimuli, new situations, and unpredictable events, we can understand that there is no one best approach or specific set of steps that can be counted on to guide people through the turmoil. We then have to fall back on a very valuable but challenging asset, our ability to tolerate high levels of uncertainty, and to help others tolerate this as well. When we try to help people engage in conflict, we know we are helping them enter into a very uncertain and unpredictable system of interactions and that our guidance may help make their experience more productive or not. (For an interesting application of complex adaptive systems to consensus-building forms, see Innes and Booher, 1999.)

## The Value of Complexity

This uncertainty, unpredictability, and complexity make conflict engagement especially important. Disputants know that conflict is unpredictable, that no one knows for sure what will happen, that to enter into a conflict system (which they are probably already part of) will take them on a journey that they cannot map out. Anyone who pretends otherwise and acts as if conflict can be predicted or determined is not going to be a credible resource to disputants. But if we acknowledge the uncertainty of the process, the limits on how much can be controlled, and we are still comfortable with the value of what we bring, people will resonate to this.

Anyone who approaches people deeply embroiled in conflict—a dysfunctional couple, an embattled community, or Palestinians and

Israelis—with a process that they guarantee will improve the situation is probably fooling themselves and no one else. That does not mean that we cannot be useful, because we can. But we can do so only if we are clear about the unpredictability of the process, the systemic nature of the interaction, and the importance of looking for those few key actions that at the right time can help the system reorganize effectively. We can offer our conceptual and interactive tools—they are the source of our added value—but we should never think of these as enough to predict or control the course of a conflict.

The value of thinking about engagement as our primary focus in the complex system of conflict is the recognition that we are helping people take a more conscious and intentional role in the ongoing system of interaction, while acknowledging that the outcome is unpredictable and resolution is only one possible goal or end point. This does not mean that we are never resolution focused. It may be that our most important task is to press people to resolve a particular issue in order to foment a reorganization in the pattern of interactions. But it is hard to know what the specific impacts of our interventions will be. It is equally hard to predict which of the many ways in which we try to help people in conflict will have a significant beneficial effect.

Consider this example of unintended—and beneficial—consequences:

> After months of fierce and unproductive interactions, the management and union negotiation teams decided to seek out the services of a mediator to try to change the way they were working together. Their last contract negotiations had been disastrous, leading to a strike that almost did the company in. But changing how they interacted was not so easy. Despite having received some training in interest-based bargaining and committing to a new approach to negotiations, discussions between them continued to be bitter and recriminatory.
>
> I participated as a trainer-facilitator in a three-day retreat. During this time, many different interchanges and discussions

took place. We reviewed the history of the last negotiations and their hopes and fears about the next, and a number of commitments were made to do things differently. I don't think anyone, myself included, thought anything was really going to change—until two things happened.

In a conflict simulation exercise, one of the union people thought he was being double-crossed by a member of the management negotiating team, only to find out that it was another member of his own team that had made the decision that felt unfair to him. This was only a simulation, but it seemed to have a profound impact on him. He could immediately sense the difference in how he reacted to the behavior when it came from management versus when it came from a fellow union member, and this caused him to reconsider his entire approach to management.

Toward the end of the time together, one of the leaders of the union made an offer concerning a concrete way of doing things differently that the union viewed as a major concession. Management instinctively went through a process of reactive devaluation: if it came from the union, it must be manipulative. I said to the management team in a private meeting that offers like the one they had just received could be viewed as a glass that is half empty or half full, and which half they decided to relate to was significant. I also suggested that this was a time in which taking a risk and offering an olive branch might have an enormous impact, and this might not be an opportunity they would have so quickly again. This mixed metaphor—the olive branch to the half-full glass—became the frame for a discussion that led to an exchange of concessions and seemed to lead to a significant improvement in the relationship.

What I did not know until several years later was that the simulation and the glass–olive branch metaphor were used very effectively and productively throughout the whole contract negotiations and for several years after. This was not an intervention that could have been planned or an impact that could have been foretold. But the exercise serendipitously crystallized a lot of the issues this conflict system was struggling with, and the exchange of procedural concessions became a metaphor for a new way of relating as well.

When the system is primed for change, many things can stimulate a systems reorganization, but you can't plan it. The lens of complex adaptive systems is a powerful one to use in understanding conflict and helping people engage in it. We help people by offering our best advice, insights, and skills, but we do so knowing that we too are entering into this adaptive system, which will adapt to our intervention in unpredictable but potentially constructive ways.

## From Avoidance to Engagement

Avoiding conflict is a powerful instinct and one that should often be honored. Some of the best and worst decisions we make in life are around when to avoid and when to engage in conflict.

No matter how hard we try to handle a conflict effectively and productively, there are times when nothing we can do will lead to productive ends. Moreover, it is sometimes unsafe to take on a conflict. Although no one wants to face the dilemma of women in abusive relationships by suggesting that sometimes they had best stay put, there are also plenty of women who tried to leave and did not survive the effort. One of the more prevalent norms of our field suggests that virtually all conflicts can be handled productively and therefore ought to be faced. But conflict cannot always be engaged in effectively or safely. We have an obligation to face this very unpleasant fact and to know that we cannot necessarily predict what will happen if people move from avoidance to engagement.

But avoidance as a general pattern of handling conflict is also destructive and sometimes lethal. Women who are not willing to confront their abusers are often doomed to a downward and ultimately lethal spiral of interactions. One of the most important functions we can provide, therefore, is to assist people in assessing when and how to avoid or engage in conflict and to try to help them find a path for successful engagement. We can do this by providing assistance with all elements of the engagement process: awareness, articulation, activation, mobilization, connection, need satisfaction, release, or process selection.

## Deciding to Engage

Exactly how we help people decide between avoidance and engagement depends on our specific role and how and when we are brought into a situation. Following are some of the specific ways in which we can help people decide to take the step from avoidance to engagement and to do so in an effective way:

• *Naming the conflict.* This is related to both awareness and articulation. When people label an interaction as a conflict and identify its nature in some way, they have taken a significant step past avoidance. A named conflict is much less likely to be avoided than an implied one. The moment we say, "We have a conflict . . . ," some further step is almost always necessitated. How we help people name it is critical too—implying the who, what, and why of a conflict and also whether further action might be fruitful. For example, if one parent says to the other, "I don't like the way you discipline our children," the implication is that the dispute is between the two of them about how to set limits. If, however, the parent says, "I don't think you know the first thing about parenting and I don't trust you alone with the children," a much broader problem is implied, perhaps necessitating the involvement of other people. Working with the parent to name the existence of a conflict and identify its nature is an important first step to helping him or her decide to engage.

• *Considering the costs and benefits of engagement and avoidance.* Helping people consider the costs and benefits of engagement and avoidance with an open mind about which direction to go in can both help them decide about engaging and actually set the grounds for an effective process of engagement. But it can also help them let go of a situation they decide that they had better avoid. One parent may be better off letting the other discipline a child differently given the relative costs and benefits (the child's interests are a different matter), but this may mean that they have to let this issue go.

Of course, this is not about an entirely rational calculus, and the emotional messages people are receiving as well as their instincts are important information for them as well. Nonetheless, surfacing people's concerns about this and helping them think it through is very important to people who are on the verge of taking what may be a perilous journey.

• *Discussing various approaches to engagement.* People often get locked into an unproductive pattern in conflict—or fear that they will and therefore avoid the conflict entirely—because they have only one model of how to engage. They may believe the only choice when facing a looming conflict is between a fight-or-flight response. But there are many approaches to engaging, and one of the ways we can help people is to consider a range of possibilities.

Conflict can be entered into in a gradual and nuanced way or with voices raised and fists clenched. If our goal is not necessarily to resolve, contain, deescalate, or in some other way manage a conflict, but to help people figure out whether and how to engage in it powerfully and effectively, then we face a very different task. Maybe the parent in the above example should sit down directly with his or her spouse, or maybe a report should be filed, a child therapist contacted, an intermediary used, and so forth. We are often unavailable to people at this critical point in the process when a decision about engagement or avoidance must be made, and we therefore miss one of the most powerful opportunities to have an impact on the course of the conflict.

• *Rehearsing engagement.* I think most of us have used someone at some point in our life to rehearse or at least talk through an upcoming charged interaction—whether positive or negative. This is a type of assistance that most or us could use more often. How often do managers have a chance to practice how they are going to raise a difficult issue with an employee (say, suspicion of alcoholism), or a public official to respond to hostile questions from an audience, or a community organizer to confront a government representative for insensitivity to his or her concerns? Often, when practice is available, it comes from public relations consultants, legal advocates, or other managers. Conflict practitioners have a special angle on this that can be useful—and one that can be as much oriented to raising the level of conflict as resolving it.

• *Finding an appropriate forum or agent for raising issues.* Sometimes the lack of an appropriate forum or agent for raising an issue or engaging in a conflict stymies people who want to take the step into engagement. Forums can range from private meetings to facilitated dialogues to public confrontation, and the forum chosen is very important in determining the nature of the engagement. Helping people find or providing a forum for engagement can be critical.

Whatever critics of the United Nations may say, it is an important and often productive arena for raising a conflict. In designing dispute systems for organizations, the designation of a safe person or mechanism (such as an ombudsman) for airing a conflict is usually critical. Citizens often are limited (or think they are) to unproductive forums for taking their issues to government, such as the open comment portion of city council or planning board meetings. One of the functions we can serve is designing, creating, and improving such mechanisms or, alternatively, helping people locate and consider different forums or individuals to assist in raising an issue and engaging a conflict.

• *Raising the conflict directly.* Depending on our role, we can sometimes raise a conflict—that is, we can be the ones to assert that a conflict exists and work is needed on it. Sometimes we do this from a neutral position, but we can also do this as coaches, consultants, and advocates.

• *Discussing issues of timing.* To avoid or to engage is not a once and forever decision. We can help sequence engagement—that is, work with disputants on when to raise which issue and at what level.

- *Bringing the conflicting parties together.* Sometimes our role will be to bring parties together, not necessarily as mediators or facilitators—but also as conveners, process designers, providers of "good offices," and negotiators as well. Whatever role we play, the act of bringing disputants together to talk—sometimes to fight, sometimes to seek resolution—can be a significant contribution to helping people engage. As a manager, I have sometimes heard separately from two employees that they had a problem with each other that they want me to resolve. Sometimes as a manager, my job has been to provide resolution, but at other times, the best thing I can do is to sit people down, with or without my presence, state the usually obvious fact that they are in conflict with each other, and ask them to work on it. Sometimes I have had a role to play as facilitator, at other times as arbiter, but most often the main contribution I have made is the simple act of bringing them together and stating the obvious.

- *Providing safeguards for engagement.* Because engagement is sometimes dangerous, one way we can assist people is to put safeguards in place that can mitigate some of the danger. Are there equivalents to peacekeepers or restraining orders that we can put in place as conflict specialists? I believe so, and I think this is an area ripe for the development of new services. For example, we can provide

- Interaction observers
- Ground rules for interaction
- Distance technologies
- "Good offices"
- Group settings
- Time-out mechanisms for conflictual interactions
- Cool-down activities and periods
- Debriefing mechanisms
- Agreed-on consequences for the violation of boundaries

There are two essentially inescapable dilemmas that conflict professionals face in assisting with the transition to engagement. One is that engagement often occurs in an entirely chaotic and unplanned way. People have avoided a conflict or decided to handle it in a very low-key manner, but then something is said or done that elicits a response (such as losing one's temper), and for better or worse engagement has occurred. The second has to do with the dynamics of avoidance. The more individuals or groups are in an avoidance mode, the less likely they are to reach out to anyone for assistance in deciding whether and how to engage. This is similar to the problems faced by any preventative program—whether it is in the arena of mental health, medicine, special education, or conflict.

As a field, we have not seriously addressed issues of prevention, and when we have, we have sometimes equated prevention with avoidance. Prevention is as much about helping people decide whether and how to engage in conflict before it has spun out of control as it is about preventing conflict from arising to begin with—especially since conflict is often a healthy response to social and interpersonal problems. We can be more available to disputants during this critical phase of the conflict process if we do not limit our thinking to the conflict resolution task. As system designers, we can build in consultation and early intervention programs. As consultants to groups or organizations, we can be available to help people consider whether to engage. As trainers, we can help people identify the potential conflicts in their organizations or their lives. As coaches, we can work with individuals on whether and how to move to engagement. We can offer our services in such a way that people can consult with us at a very early point in a conflict process. Of course, no matter how attentive we are to being available at the point where people decide whether or how to engage and no matter how hard we work at removing the barriers of structure and self-concept that make it less likely people will use our services at this time, people's avoidance tendencies will keep many away until a conflict has fully erupted.

## Engagement as an Ongoing Activity

These modes of assistance are not necessarily new to us. If we are going to work in conflict, we will have to help people decide whether, when, with whom, and how to engage. But if we do this from the new standpoint of a conflict specialist and not necessarily as conflict resolvers, we do this in a different manner and spirit. We do not assume that engagement is necessarily connected to resolution. We recognize that engagement is potentially dangerous. We are willing to help people consider how to engage with different values or goals than win-win. We are clear that conflict is a complex system of interaction and that powerful engagement approaches can sometimes lead to good resolutions, but that conflict is unpredictable.

Working from an engagement perspective involves more than simply taking people from avoidance to engagement. We need to find ways of helping them through an interaction process that can be quick or lengthy. While we may be asked to assist with a very particular part of this process, we may also need to play a role over time. If we are going to work on very serious and difficult problems, we are not going to be able to come in with a single wonderful intervention and fix things. The more serious the conflict is and the more intractable it is, the less we should think of ourselves involved in time-limited ways. People who have made a difference in major conflict situations have normally been involved in one way or another for many years.

The ways in which we help people move from avoidance to engagement are also appropriate for assisting with the ongoing demands of engagement. We can help with awareness, articulation, activation, mobilization, connection, need satisfaction, release, or process selection throughout an engagement effort. We can help people work on all the elements of constructive conflict: achieving value congruence, authentic voice, dealing with the right issue, at a productive level of depth, with the right people, using appropriate time frames, allowing for change, working along both the integrative and distributive dimension, attending to fundamental safety, grounded optimism, and creative uncertainty. We can also help people fight productively. We have a powerful role to play throughout the engagement process, and I believe we have a great deal of value to add because of our understanding of conflict and conflict interactions.

We sometimes will have access to a conflict, for financial, structural, or other reasons, at only one or two key points. In that case, we should attend to the particular developmental requirements of the conflict at that point. But our overall understanding of what is needed should be framed by an understanding of the ongoing nature and demands of engagement. When we enter into a conflict will be determined to some extent by how we market our services and what response we receive from our client base. I discuss the business of conflict engagement in the final chapter.

## From Engagement to Resolution

In this chapter, I have emphasized our role as engagement specialist with particular emphasis on how to understand conflict from this perspective and the ways in which we can help people engage successfully in conflict. Because I am trying to provide an alternative way of looking at what we do that takes us beyond focusing on the resolution of conflict, I have not examined that part of what we do. After all, that is what our field has focused on for over thirty years.

I end this chapter with a clear acknowledgment that helping people move to the resolution aspect of conflict is also a critical role for conflict specialists, and one that we will continue to play. I don't believe we will reach our potential as a field by ignoring or underselling the importance of this. Instead, I believe we will build out from this important element of our work; in particular, we will expand from our original roles as mediators, facilitators, dispute system designers, and trainers.

Our dilemma will be how to continue offering the valuable contributions that we have historically made, how to retain the market base that has allowed our field to develop to the extent that it has, but how at the same time to expand the boundaries of our work in some fairly fundamental ways. The challenge of helping people engage in conflict is not so much that we have to develop a whole new set of skills or even conceptual frameworks but instead that we have to open up our thinking about our purpose, function, and role.

No matter how we proceed, however, we will always have a critical role in helping disputants resolve conflict. We will do this by using all the tools we have always used: communication, problem solving, negotiation, rapport building, forum creation, facilitation, mediation, system design, convening, interest-based bargaining, and so forth. We have worked very hard to develop these skills, and it is on that foundation that we will build a larger, more vital field.

One of the crucial ways we can help is by identifying when a resolution focus is appropriate and how to take the first steps in that direction. We can also help people identify the potential forums and the resolution strategies disputants might use and consider the range of resolution options that might be available. We have not given adequate thought to how to identify when a conflict is really ripe for resolution, that is, when it has matured to that point.

I have sometimes thought of conflict resolution as a dramatic process, with the mediator as stage manager or director. Our job is to help the drama develop so that plot unfolds in an effective and powerful way, the players emerge as rich and understandable characters, and the scene or context unfolds as the climax approaches. At this crucial moment, the conflict has reached its richest point and we are ready for the dénouement of resolution. At that point, the energy can change, and a critical exchange can occur. The role of the conflict specialist is to provide the best opportunity for this to happen in an effective way.

Where this metaphor breaks down for me is that the drama does not end after resolution; in most important conflicts, it continues to unfold in different ways. In general, our work is not over with a resolution, although depending on our role in a specific conflict, our particular involvement may or may not continue. In fact, resolution can come at almost any stage of a conflict engagement process, including the preengagement phase.

Sometimes our role will be to help people resist a premature resolution. At other times, it will be to help them use resolution as an opportunity to continue to engage in conflict more effectively (many of the most important international conflict resolution efforts have been about helping to find alternative routes for engagement, such as the Northern Ireland peace accords). And sometimes resolution will be the signal and the means for disengaging from conflict, for release. As conflict specialists, we will have a varied and multifaceted role to play in resolution, as well as in all aspects of conflict.

There is a looming question that I have touched on throughout the book but have not directly explored. If we are not only third-party neutral conflict resolution professionals, who are we? What role can we play? How will this role be different from that of traditional advocates such as lawyers and union organizers? Is there a market for us in this way? How do we really do this? I address these issues in the next two chapters.

# 7

## The Conflict Specialist

If we are not just mediators, facilitators, arbitrators, or dispute system designers, then who are we? I believe we can move forward as a field only by adopting a new way of thinking about our fundamental identity as a field and as practitioners within that field. I don't think that this new identity is going to emerge because of this or any other book; rather, circumstances will demand and opportunities will promote it. The specific ways in which we characterize ourselves will develop as the roles we play develop. Whatever label we select now could well evolve into an entirely different term as we become increasingly clear about exactly what we do and understand the implications of these different names for how the public views us.

I have suggested that we think of ourselves as conflict specialists (or conflict engagement specialists) for two reasons. One is that I believe our focus will need to be on the entire conflict process, not simply on how to resolve conflict. The other is that we need to think of ourselves as a profession in terms that imply role flexibility. In Chapter Six, I discussed how we might assist disputants in engaging in conflict throughout its entire course rather than focusing primarily on how to help them move toward resolution. In this chapter, I focus on the broad variety of roles that we might play under the rubric of being conflict specialists.

I am not implying that any one of us will fulfill all the potential roles I discuss in this chapter. As in many other fields, we will have subspecialties, and most of us will focus on one or two specific areas of practice. So although individuals may function primarily as a facilitator, coach, mediator, or dispute system designer, we will need to view these specialties as part of a larger field of practice that encompasses many different roles.

Some of these roles are easy for us as a field to accept. We already see ourselves as mediators, facilitators, arbitrators, ombudspersons, or trainers. (*Ombudsman* is a Swedish word with no gender implications. But in English, it sounds as if it does, so I will use *ombudsperson*.) Some of the roles are newer but not significantly out of keeping with our current self-image, such as coach, system designer, or on-line process manager. As a field, we have been fairly creative about adapting, combining, and redefining our more traditional roles within the general framework of third-party neutrals. Although we have sometimes had difficulty in figuring out how to combine decision-making or advisory roles (arbitrator, evaluator, fact finder) with process-oriented roles (mediator, facilitator), we have given this challenge a great deal of attention (see, for example, Barris and others, 2001), and many of us provide advisory or evaluative mediation or med-arb services (and sometimes arb-med).

Where the concept of role flexibility becomes more challenging is when we are asked to look beyond neutrality to roles in which we are clearly in the business of promoting the interests of one side of a conflict. We have not usually viewed the role of advocate, negotiator, organizer, or strategist as part of our calling. Although many of us have taught negotiation and we see an understanding of negotiation as key to the skill set that mediators and other neutrals need to acquire, when we have actually worked as negotiators or advisers for one side in a dispute, we have not generally viewed ourselves as conflict resolvers.

Because embracing advocacy as part of the conflict field and seeing advocacy as an aspect of what conflict specialists have to offer is perhaps the most challenging aspect of taking on a new self-view, the following chapter focuses specifically on that role. In this chapter, I discuss advocacy as one component of the overall conflict specialist role. What is key here is to understand the range of roles that conflict specialists can play and how these can work together and build on one another to constitute a coherent field of practice.

## The Expanding Role of the Conflict Specialist

Why should we take on roles that challenge our identity and public image? We will lose some clarity of function, and how to market and contract for these new roles remains unclear. Furthermore, many in our field will resist the idea. Despite these obstacles, the needs of our clients and the reality of how conflict is conducted require this of us if we are to expand the impact of our work, survive as an independent field of practice, and become more relevant to how conflict is resolved.

Conflict for the most part is not conducted or resolved by third-party neutrals; it is resolved by disputants themselves with the assistance of their advocates, advisers, and allies. Conflict resolution professionals have been helpful, as we have seen, in a fairly narrow range of circumstances and cultural contexts. Outside this range, the help disputants want and genuinely trust is not neutral, process oriented, or facilitative. They want the kind of help that is very hard to provide from the vantage point of being a third party.

When disputants do not view resolution as their immediate goal, they are especially reluctant to pull in third parties. If we want to be part of the work that needs to be done on major conflicts and want to meet the needs of disputants as they see them, then we will have to be willing to take on the challenge of expanding our role definition and being able to join the ranks of "home team" advocates, advisers, and allies.

### Client Demand for New Roles

Joining the disputant's team will not simply be a matter of our choice. I believe this is what our clients will increasingly ask and sometimes even demand of us. Our challenge will be whether we can be creative in filling these roles and astute in marketing them. The opportunities will come our way because of the needs of disputants. We can adapt to these demands or stay locked within our narrower definition of our roles, in which case disputants will continue to go elsewhere to get the advice and assistance that they require.

Consider, for example, these three situations:

A police department is facing multiple suits for police misconduct, most arising from one of the poorest neighborhoods in the city, and as a result, there is a call for an investigation of police hiring, training, and supervisory procedures, including a call for an external review board. The leadership of the police feels this is a problem in police relations with this neighborhood and wants to meet with neighborhood representatives, but feels that representatives of other parts of the city should also participate. The neighborhood's representatives will not meet with the police unless they agree to the principle of a review board, with at least two representatives from their neighborhood. The police department is unwilling to agree to this, believing that the larger community is supportive of the department and would not approve of a review board. There have been numerous public input meetings, task forces on police-community relationships, and incident investigations, but these problems have continued.

A union with a strong history of activism and a record of winning highly favorable contracts within a large manufacturing sector is now facing the economic deterioration of that sector due to new technologies and increasing international competition. A more cooperative stance with management would be desirable, but a rival union is campaigning to become the new bargaining agent for many of the older union's largest shops, citing the existing union's "coziness with management." Any effort to reach a negotiated or mediated deal with management that recognizes the need for a different kind of contract is ammunition for the rival union. The union needs to find a way of working with management, holding its own against the rival union, and protecting the interests of its members. Going to a mediator for help could well reinforce the argument that the union is more willing to compromise than to fight, yet without some accommodations to management, chances are great that large units will close down or relocate.

For the past twenty years (some would say a lot longer), an ethnic group located in a resource-rich province of a developing nation has struggled against discriminatory practices of the government, which is dominated by a different ethnic group. Over the years, there have been repression, acts of sabotage, contested elections, international mediation, the courageous work of a number of relief and development workers, and many other efforts to address the tension and growing violence in the region. Yet the situation appears to be deteriorating. This is a time when things could turn better or worse. Both the government and the leaders of the ethnic minority are under pressure from more militant groups, who see them as overly compromising, and both would like to find ways of calming the situation and paving the way for more cooperative relations. Yet both sides feel that an attempt to reach a signed agreement would fail and would play into the hands of the more militant groups.

In each of these situations, there is a clear need for assistance in dealing with the conflict. Depending on our background and the focus of our work, we might be contacted about any of these situations. One role we might choose to play is as intermediaries or neutrals attempting to bring the contending parties together to discuss how to proceed or to design a process for bringing the disputants together. But in each of these situations, there is reason to question whether that is the most valuable role we could fulfill and even whether the effort to intervene as a neutral might not make the situation worse.

If we see our task as helping people engage in conflict, there are two key questions to ask:

- Which of the tasks of engagement are the key players struggling with?

- From what vantage point can we best assist them?

In each of these situations, we could at least argue that the third-party neutral role is neither feasible nor likely to be productive at the point in time described. While those conducting these conflicts will be the ones to work toward deescalation and resolution, and while they need assistance and may well be open to it, they may be suspicious or resistant to the services of a third-party neutral. If we are open to the possibility of playing a variety of roles, the likelihood of our being of value to the disputants may be much greater.

Mediators, facilitators, and arbitrators don't resolve disputes. They don't change the nature of a conflict. They don't escalate or deescalate disputes. Conflict resolvers instead provide a service or assistance to the people who do those things—who determine the direction of a dispute and have the challenge of engaging productively: the disputants themselves. Our role and our goal should be to help disputants engage productively.

As in so much of what we do, the power of what we have to offer is in the limits of what we try to accomplish and our flexibility in how we pursue our purpose. That is, by understanding that our purpose is to assist disputants as they engage in the conflict process, but not necessarily to resolve a dispute or change a relationship, we pose a limited goal. By being willing to approach these goals from a variety of roles, we can adapt to the specific needs of disputants. The very limit and focus of what we try to offer, combined with the flexibility we take in how we offer it, is what can make our services potentially more useful and widely acceptable to disputants.

## Conflict Specialist Roles and Skills

There are three broad categories of roles that we can play as conflict specialists:

- The ally roles—roles in which we assist particular parties to engage more effectively. These are normally nonneutral roles (advocate, organizer, strategist, coach).

- The third-party roles—roles in which we assist conflicting parties to engage more effectively. These are usually neutral roles (facilitator, mediator, fact finder, evaluator, arbitrator).

- The system roles—roles in which we try to have an impact on the system and culture within which a conflict takes place. These are potentially neutral or nonneutral roles (process designer, case manager, trainer, researcher, system adviser).

Each of these roles requires certain common skills, and each demands particular skills as well. Conflict specialists, regardless of the particular role they choose to play (for a discussion of the essence of what conflict resolvers bring to a conflict see Chapter One) need some common skills:

- Understanding the dynamics of conflict, including the emotional, attitudinal, and behavioral dimensions, the structural and personal aspects of conflict, and the interplay between power rights and interests

- Understanding the conflict engagement process

- Ability to discern the different level of needs of the major disputants and the alternatives available for them to meet those needs

- Good communication skills

- Ability to look at both the integrative and distributive dimensions of conflict

- Ability to understand conflict as a system

- Awareness of cultural and gender dynamics

- Understanding of or ability to grasp the substantive, procedural, and psychological issues quickly

- Ability to take both a long-term and immediate view of the conflict

Many of these are in large part conceptual skills, and the specific competencies necessary to use them depend on the role and circumstances within which the conflict specialist operates. There is a lot of transferability of these skills from one role to another, but clearly not everyone who is an effective mediator will necessarily be a competent advocate or coach, or vice versa.

For many years, those of us who have trained mediators have seen people with a background in counseling or as legal advocates enter our programs, assuming that if they were competent in those roles, they would also be effective as mediators, only to learn that the function and therefore the skill base is very different. Yet good experience as a counselor or lawyer is valuable to those who want to be mediators, as long as they understand that they can't simply bring their approach in one arena into the other and be successful. Similarly, as we expand the roles we play in conflict, we can use the skills, concepts, and experience we have in new roles, but we also have to learn new approaches, tactics, and ways of thinking.

Let's now look further at the range of conflict specialist roles.

## The Conflict Ally: Advocate, Organizer, Strategist, Coach

Ally roles demand that we put ourselves squarely on the side of a particular disputant (or on the side of a particular group of disputants) if we are to be effective. When we offer ourselves in these roles, we are saying to one party or set of parties that we will help them be effective in this conflict. We may encourage them to think about how to meet the needs of the other side and to look at the integrative potential of a conflict, but we are doing this because we think it will help them meet their own needs as they understand them.

People will engage us to play these roles because they can see our potential to help them through a conflict. They will shy away from us if they think we will not be genuinely committed to help-ing achieve their goals, think we are naive about conflict, believe we are putting our own values and agenda ahead of their needs, or do not believe we have something of real value to offer. But we often have something to offer in these nonneutral roles, and we should not be afraid of them.

This does not mean that we have to give up our values or our beliefs about the importance of handling conflict in a humane way with an appreciation for the dignity and rights of all participants. What it does mean is that we believe we can hold these values and still provide assistance to one side of a dispute in service of its own goals, knowing that in the long run, constructive engagement is part of achieving a more just and peaceful world.

There are many specific ways in which we can be an ally to a particular party to a dispute. We consider the advocate, organizer, strategist, and coach.

## The Advocate

I will consider this more fully in the next chapter since it is such a major shift in roles. Suffice it to say that this may be the hardest role for those of us with a history in conflict resolution to embrace. Many of us have seen our approach as an antidote to the role of the zealous advocate, particularly the overly aggressive lawyer with a single-minded devotion to his or her client's rights, regardless of the impact on others. But this is also the role that people turn to first and most frequently when they enter into conflict. Our goal as advocates is to help people engage effectively and powerfully in conflict. If we disagree with their goals, we cannot be effective ad-vocates over time.

The problem with how advocates traditionally function is not that their first concern is meeting their clients' needs; it is that they take a narrow, short-term, and overly rights-based view of what those needs are. Many see their goal as achieving for their clients the maximum benefits they have a legal or contractual right to get.

This view can exclude taking into account the many interests their clients may have that cannot be addressed by a court, administrative tribunal, or some other rights-based forum. A wise advocate will help people achieve their goals with the perspective of the full range of needs their clients have, an understanding of the power of integrative solutions, a long-term view, and a clear sense of what a client's real alternatives are. In this way, an advocate can help people engage in conflict effectively, pursue their needs intelligently, and avoid some of the pitfalls of a purely distributive or rights-based approach to advocacy. (See, for example, Kronman, 1993, and Sebenius, 2001.)

The particular function of advocacy that distinguishes it from some of the other ally roles is that the advocate in some way provides a voice for the disputant. There are many different ways of doing this, from speaking up for the disputant in a public forum to representing him or her in an adjudicatory process, to acting as the spokesperson in a negotiation.

The idea that advocacy is a key conflict resolution role is not a new one. Early in the development of the modern conflict resolution field, Laue and Cormick (1978) argued that the negotiation of power inequities was essential to the resolution of conflict, and therefore conflict resolvers needed to find ways to empower marginal groups. Laue and Cormick proposed a number of roles for conflict resolvers to take in order to accomplish this, including activist, advocate, mediator, researcher, and enforcer.

So how is this different from what good lawyers do for their clients? Lawyers are in many ways conflict specialists. The more they view themselves as part of the conflict field, the stronger the field will be. But while we traditionally associate advocacy with legal representation, there are many other types of advocates as well, such as union representatives, diplomats, community organizers, victim advocates, patient rights representatives, real estate agents, and tax experts. We can learn a great deal from these advocates, and we can offer something as well.

## The Organizer

We do not think of organizers as players in conflict the same way we might of advocates, coaches, or negotiators. But under many circumstances, organizers are key to enabling successful conflict engagement. Without effective union organizers, workers are in no position to contend with management around issues relating to benefits, working conditions, or systemic problems, even if they can engage on individual grievances. Community organizers allow neighbors to speak effectively to local government. Political organizers enable citizens' groups to have a voice with government at all levels. The power of the civil rights, environmental, and women's movements would not have been unleashed without effective organizers.

Organization comes in many forms and involves multiple tasks, from developing and servicing structures for people to come together to discuss and promote their concerns, to helping people define the issues about which they are concerned and develop approaches to raising those issues in an effective and powerful way, to obtaining the resources to allow a group to function. One classic description of community organization defines it as "a process by which a community identifies its needs or objectives, orders (or ranks) these needs or objectives, finds the resources (internal and/or external) to deal with these needs or objectives, takes action in respect to them, and in so doing extends and develops cooperative and collaborative attitudes and practices in the community" (Ross, 1967, p. 40).

Other approaches may emphasize empowering a community, allowing groups to confront power structures in a more effective way, or changing the nature of the political relationships between the government and the people being organized (Alinsky, 1946; Osterman, 2003). Effective organization has a strategic element, an educational element, and a support role, and it usually involves a lot of hard practical work (creating phone trees, contacting people, writing brochures, and so forth). Whatever particular definition or approach one takes to organizing, it is always about helping to bring people together to discuss their issues and promote their interests in a more effective way.

Organizers work on all sides of issues (prolife, prochoice; for affirmative action, against it; protecting endangered species, challenging the Endangered Species Act) and in many arenas. They are key players in allowing a conflict to develop and have a lot to do with whether a conflict process unfolds in a constructive manner. Organizers play an essential role in articulating issues, framing the story of a dispute, defining the parties, and developing an engagement strategy. The best organizers understand the nature of conflict and take a long-term view to understanding the interests of their constituents.

As conflict specialists, we can learn a great deal from organizers about what constitutes an effective way of defining a dispute, using positions to articulate the key needs that people experience, helping people decide to engage in conflict, and speaking to disputants in a way that resonates with their own experience. We can offer organizers strategies for engaging in a conflict without precluding the possibility for effective communication with other parties. We can help them understand and articulate the key interests of both their own constituency and those with whom they are in conflict. We can assist in dealing with conflict among their constituents. If organizers are expert at helping people with the tasks of awareness, articulation, mobilization, and activation, conflict specialists can help them focus as well on connection, need satisfaction, release, and process selection. We can help to ensure that the organizing process occurs with a view to what constitutes effective engagement.

Can conflict specialists be organizers? Are organizers conflict specialists? Or are these two different roles that can work closely together under the right circumstances? Since neither role is defined in an exact way, the answer to these questions differs depending on the circumstances. In some circumstances, these two roles will meld together, and in others, they will be very distinct. If a community is upset about an issue but has not organized a coherent approach to responding, we may well play an important role in organizing that community. In other circumstances, we may work with organizers to help them be more effective. Sometimes our role will blur this distinction:

> During the mid-1990s, my colleague Susan Wildau and I were involved for several years in a project to promote ethnic cooperation in Bulgaria, We partnered with a Bulgarian nongovernmental organization, the Foundation for Negotiation and Conflict Resolution, and with several local organizations as well. Our goal was to help promote projects and structures that would bring together different ethnic groups to work on issues of mutual concern (Mayer, Wildau, and Valchev, 1995).
>
> At one point, we were asked to visit a very poor Roma neighborhood in a small city with a history of ethnic tensions in order to hear the concerns of this community about relations with the municipal government. The plan was to tour the neighborhood with the local "headman and headwoman" and talk with a small group of residents, representatives from the city's social welfare agency, and some local colleagues.
>
> When we arrived at the small plaza around which the neighborhood was organized, we found the entire neighborhood in turmoil. The day before, a confrontation had occurred between neighborhood youth and police, and a Roma teenager had been shot dead. The neighborhood was extremely angry and tense, and there was a heated debate as to whether we should go on the tour at all. We knew that this decision had to be made by the people in the neighborhood, and although there was a certain risk, the neighbors were expecting this visit, and to cancel could have added fuel to the fire.
>
> In the end, the headman and headwoman suggested we do an abbreviated walk through the neighborhood, followed by a brief meeting in the local coffee house. The walk was incredibly intense. At least a hundred people, perhaps many more, joined us as we proceeded around the neighborhood, and they

were upset—not with us but with some of the municipal employees with us. People screamed all sorts of complaints at us (they were probably not at all clear about who we were or why we were there) about how they had been neglected, mistreated, and discriminated against. Two complaints were repeated often: that social welfare officials had no idea who really needed assistance so they assumed that everyone, particularly Romas, cheated, and that they had no effective means of communicating their concerns to municipal officials. Several people were especially upset that social benefits would not be given to them if they had gold or silver fillings on the grounds that if they could afford these, they did not need assistance. (I was skeptical about this claim, but I later confirmed that this indeed was the policy.)

As our walk progressed, the numbers grew, and the intensity deepened. Something had to be done to channel this energy, or it could turn destructive. So on the spot, we arranged to make a local classroom available for a meeting among community representatives, municipal staff, and our project staff. At this meeting, a structure was created by which the community designated two representatives to the welfare agency to discuss their concerns and provide an ongoing link with the agency.

Somewhat to our surprise, this structure seemed to work quite well, and in a modified form it continues to this day. This was not the end of the community's problems with the agency or the municipality, but it did provide a structure, which had been missing, for the community to engage with the agency. Our local colleagues continue to work with the community and help them maintain some form of local organization.

This was just one example of many in this project where we thought our role was essentially as catalysts and where, with our local colleagues, we served as organizers, advisers, trainers, and facilitators, and our success was measured by the degree to which different communities could engage in an effective process. In order for us to be effective and, even more important, for our local colleagues to be successful in promoting multicultural cooperation and understanding, we all needed to bring to bear our skills and experience as both conflict resolvers and organizers. Where one role stopped and the other began was neither clear nor particularly important. Both were needed.

## The Strategist

Almost all roles that we play involve strategizing in some way, but sometimes that is our designated role. In some ways, this role can be thought of more generally as that of an adviser, but our task here is specifically to help disputants develop a strategy for how to approach a conflict. We are in some ways acting as substantive experts on conflict when we serve in this role.

In each of the three examples of conflicts described at the beginning of this chapter, the role of strategist may have been the most useful one we could play. What does a conflict strategist do? This is a generic enough concept to incorporate many specific activities, but four seem key:

- *Conduct conflict analyses*. We help understand and point out the dynamics of the conflict. This includes the nature of the interests, power, relationship dynamics, values, cultural variable, historical factors, communication issues, and structural variables that have an impact on the conflict. What is key here is not just the act of analyzing a conflict but the work we do to make the insights of this analysis useful to the particular disputant group with which we are working. If we were operating from a neutral perspective, we might think of this as a situation assessment.
- *Identify the pros and cons of alternative approaches to engagement*. People facing conflict almost always have a range of choices, including capitulation, avoidance, rights-based activities, power

moves, interest-based dialogue, and choosing whom to contact. As strategists, we can help disputants understand their choices and the implications of each. We can then help them make a choice.

- *Plan how to pursue a strategic approach.* Whatever approach is selected, we can assist disputants in planning how to carry out this approach. For example, if the choice is between participating as a stakeholder in a negotiation process and continuing to work to mobilize resources and support without participating, we can first help look at the pros and cons of each approach and then help a disputant plan how to engage in whichever approach is selected.

- *Assess how an engagement process is going and how to modify it.* Strategies in conflict should never be set in stone. Because conflict is an adaptive system, it is important to be prepared to adapt strategies. One of the ways we can help disputants is by assisting them in remaining flexible and avoiding getting trapped in a nonproductive approach.

To some extent, we have to engage in all four of these tasks at once or at least periodically throughout our work in a conflict. Analysis is an ongoing activity. Weighing strategic choices never really stops, nor does figuring out how to apply a particular approach, and it is always a challenge to remain flexible and adaptive.

One interesting aspect of the strategist role is that it may be the one that disputants in the most serious of conflicts are most open to. Of all the roles we might play, this leaves the most decision making, control, and flexibility in the hands of the disputants. We are providing a potentially powerful service to disputants, but what they do with it is up to them.

## The Coach

Coaching seems to be the newest rage in human services. There are personal coaches, executive coaches, leadership coaches, lifestyle coaches, fitness coaches, and, sure enough, conflict coaches. Courses on coaching abound, many of them primarily on-line. Look at the business section of most bookstores, and you will find a growing number of books on coaching (see, for example, Auerbach, 2001; Goldsmith, 2000; Hudson, 1999; O'Neal, 2000). In some ways, this phenomenon is reminiscent of what happened with mediation in the mid-1980s.

Just because there is a faddish element to all this does not mean that there is not also substance, and at the very least a significant need that is being tapped. *Coaching* is another term that means different things to different people, but the common ground seems to be a focus on helping individuals achieve their personal goals and perform to their potential. I think it is interesting to consider why this concept, essentially borrowed from the world of sports, has taken hold at this time. What is it about this metaphor that captures something that people feel to be of value to them? Coaching as a metaphor implies a number of important functions:

• The coach helps improve someone's performance but does not take on any direct role in the primary activity itself. In conflict, this means that we work to help people be more effective in conflict, but the responsibility for successful engagement remains entirely with the person being coached.

• A coach works with individuals not just on a specific situation but on their overall skill development. As coaches, we not only help people handle particular conflicts; we also help them work on improving their overall conflict engagement skills.

• An effective coach is a motivator. Coaches know how to give suggestions, critical feedback, and encouragement in such a way that people are motivated to try harder, push themselves, take some risks, and get excited about the challenges they are facing. Helping people face conflict with confidence and even excitement is enormously helpful to those who are reticent about engaging.

• A good coach zeroes in on the one or two things that someone can do to improve his or her performance. If we are offered fifteen ways in which we can improve our skiing, golf swing, or tennis serve, we probably are not going to change much about what we do.

But when we are told the *one thing* that we can work on that will make a difference, then we can see dramatic change. For example, it may be that getting a manager to focus on listening for the interests that employees express when they are upset can change this person's entire approach to conflict.

• Coaches encourage practice. We don't think of practicing as a regular part of preparing ourselves for conflict. In our initial training and perhaps in continuing education programs, we may participate in simulations, but the coaching metaphor suggests a much more regular and even routinized approach to practice—to developing our conflict muscles, as it were. We can prepare for a negotiation, for example, by practicing what we will say, anticipating what we might hear, and role-playing the exchanges that we might anticipate.

• Coaches help us learn from our mistakes and failures, as well as our successes. Although celebrating effective conflict experiences is important, so is learning from the mistakes or problems we have encountered. We don't often have tapes of the game to review during the week, although we sometimes do, but we can revisit with a coach what happened, why we made the moves we did, what we were thinking, what response we received, and what we can learn from the experience. Coaches can help with this. (For a good description of how this can work with mediators, see Lang and Taylor, 2000.)

All of us have acted as coaches in one way or another, and some of us have taken this on as an explicit role in conflict (Noble, 2001). We have played this role for negotiators, mediators, disputants, managers, organizers, facilitators, and others. We may have called ourselves consultants, advisers, clinical supervisors, teachers, or just peers. Sometimes we may have acted as neutrals and provided coaching to all sides to a dispute, and at other times, we may have worked with just one party. We may have done this from the vantage point of having managerial responsibility for someone (a new employee), or we may be completely outside the accountability structure. The coach role can overlap with other conflict specialist roles as well, but what distinguishes it is its primary focus on helping people develop their competence to engage in conflict effectively.

As with just about everything we do, there are multiple potential focuses, approaches, and styles for coaching. I think we can think of conflict coaching as occurring along three dimensions (see Figure 7.1).

One dimension describes our focus, ranging from a more individualized to a more systemic focus. For example, in working with a manager on the conflicts she may be experiencing, we could focus on internal issues in handling conflict, interpersonal relationships, how to handle conflict within a group, or the system of conflict that the manager may be functioning within or setting up. Although coaches move across all these levels, one important aspect of effective coaching is maintaining a useful and relevant focus during each coaching opportunity.

Another dimension describes the approach taken to the coaching process. At one end of this dimension is a more directive or even confrontational approach (the Vince Lombardi School of Coaching), and at the other end is a more elicitive approach (the Phil Jackson School). As in most other areas of our work, a certain flexibility or range of approaches makes sense, but it does not necessarily work to try to be directive and elicitive at the same time. Most approaches to leadership coaching promote a more elicitive approach, but different people respond to different types of inputs under different circumstances.

The third dimension describes at what level of depth we think we should be working. These parallel the dimensions of conflict I have previously described (Mayer, 2000). Coaches can work on the conflict behavior, the emotional component, the cognitive structures or attitudes supporting or interfering with effective engagement, or the way in which these three aspects are integrated. Employing a behavioral approach will encourage the disputants to work on what they actually do in conflict and how they respond to the behavior of others. Working along the emotional dimension involves helping

## FIGURE 7.1. Dimensions of Coaching

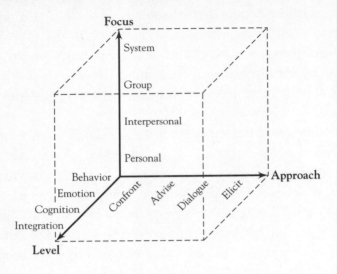

people understand, manage, and use their own emotional reactions to a conflict, as well as those of other disputants. An attitudinal or cognitive focus entails working on how disputants understand a conflict, the stories they tell about it, the metaphors they use, and the concepts that either limit or open up their thinking.

Coaches work along all dimensions, and exactly how they choose to function is an interplay among the circumstances under which they have been brought in, the specific role they have been asked to play, and the interaction that occurs during the coaching process itself. What makes the coaching process so interesting is that at any point, the work can occur at different places along each of the three dimensions.

For example, as a coach, I may take an elicitive approach to a discussion of a behavioral problem relating to a group conflict. Upon observing how appropriate and helpful this approach seems to be, I can shift to a more confrontational approach to an interpersonal problem, which we look at from an emotional perspective. Consider the following shift that I made in the middle of a coaching session with a public official:

Tony was the head of a large division in a state natural resource agency and had been working with a local government on how to deal with the threat to animal habitat created by a proposal to build a new water pipeline. Local residents at two public meetings and in the local newspaper had severely attacked the state agency for getting in the way of the city's legitimate needs to protect its water supply, for putting "bureaucratic red tape before people," and the like. From the agency's point of view, the approach that the city favored, which was the cheapest, would seriously disrupt an important wildlife habitat, and it refused to license the project without a complete (and expensive) Environmental Impact Statement. This led to a threatened suit and countersuit. As a result, and at the behest of a judge who would have to hear the suits, the city and state agreed to try to negotiate an approach to this issue. I was engaged by Tony to work with him in the negotiations.

Progress was being made in the negotiations when a member of the city negotiation team was quoted in the newspaper about some of the ideas being discussed and labeled these the "state's proposal." At their next meeting, city councilors leveled considerable criticism against the substance and process of the negotiations. The council directed the staff to suspend the negotiations and to hold a public meeting to solicit input about the "state's proposal."

The next week, I met with Tony and a couple of his staff to discuss this situation. Tony felt sandbagged by the city, and before we could go very far, we needed to work on the emotional aspect of this issue. We then took up the question of whether he should attend the public meeting. Here the focus was clearly behavioral and systemic. What would be the message to the community if Tony attended? What would be the danger of setting himself up for another series of attacks? Should a lower-level employee go instead? Should there be a press release? If Tony or another staff member did go, should they be observers, answer questions, or make a presentation?

After we played out a number of scenarios, Tony and his staff decided that the wisest course would be to send one of Tony's staff but for him to stay away since he represented the policymaking level of the agency. Although this alternative appeared to make sense, Tony did not seem happy. He was squirming in his chair, sounding pessimistic, and did not seem very present in the discussion.

I looked at Tony and said, "Something about this is not right. You are not happy with this approach." Tony then talked about his responsibility to play a more active role and his belief that this was an opportunity to make a case directly to the citizens. He did not think that they would be satisfied by anything he had to say, but he felt that he would be shirking his duty if he ducked out of this meeting. So we discussed what kind of presentation he might make, how it could be framed in a way that the community could hear his message, and what he would do if he was subjected to personal attacks. He decided he would go, and he would make a presentation. We then talked about how he might repair some of his relationships with the city negotiators.

Tony went to the meeting, made his presentation with spirit, humor, and dignity, and was attacked by the community, but in a considerably less personal or hostile way than previously. He ended up feeling that he had not shrunk from the challenge, had given it his best shot, had not made things worse, and may have set the stage for more constructive discussions later. The process continues.

In this example, we can see how effectiveness in conflict coaching requires being able to move along each of the three dimensions of coaching and the varying needs coaches can fulfill as they work with disputants. My role here was as a background player, and my contract with Tony was to help him be effective in representing the state through this conflict. The art of coaching involves discerning the many ways in which we can fulfill this function.

All of these ally roles are subject to great variation and overlap, and we can identify other roles that fit within the general category of assistance to one side in a conflict. To the extent that we are in an advisory role, we probably do not have to stretch ourselves as much to make the leap from our work as third-party neutrals, but to the extent that we actively take part in helping a disputant promote his or her own interests, whether at the expense of another party or not, we are likely to feel less comfortable. Are we violating our codes of conduct? Does working for one side of a conflict in one situation preclude our ability to be neutrals in another? What are the protections on our confidentiality? I will discuss some of this in Chapter Nine when I consider the business and logistics of being a conflict specialist.

Although I believe we will be increasingly called to fulfill ally roles in conflict, we will also continue to be in demand as third parties as well. Let's now consider that more familiar role.

## The Third Party

Of all the roles the conflict specialist can play, the role of third party needs the least discussion for conflict resolution practitioners. This is our bailiwick, the area in which we have developed our thinking and our intervention tools most thoroughly. We work as third parties, and whether we are always strictly neutral, we generally see our commitment as serving the needs of all parties to a dispute, and often the system within which the dispute takes place as well, rather than promoting the interests of just one party. We serve as mediators, conveners, facilitators, arbitrators, conciliators, and other related roles, and we do so in a wide variety of contexts.

Nevertheless, there are two important questions to consider for our purposes here. First, how can we think more broadly about the role of the third party in conflict engagement? To what extent is the third-party role structurally inconsistent with assisting with those aspects of the conflict engagement process that are not directed toward resolution? Second, to what extent is it compatible for a conflict specialist to act as both a third party and a professional ally in similar but different conflicts?

## Conflict Engagement and the Third Party

To what extent does the third-party role necessarily imply a resolution orientation, a focus on deescalation, or a tendency to deal with narrower and more superficial issues? Or to put it differently, can third parties play a role in helping people intensify conflict, broaden the scope of a dispute, and delve into deeper and more contentious issues? Third parties can and do help people engage in conflict, but it is hard to do this from the perspective of being mediators, arbitrators, or process facilitators. Marriage therapists are in a sense third-party neutrals whose challenge is often to get couples to engage on a deeper level. Referees are third parties whose task is to allow people to fight, but to keep the fight within reasonable and acceptable bounds.

We can play comparable roles. We can help to design and facilitate public meetings to encourage the most deeply held issues to surface. We can help create and conduct the processes within which people can discuss their most profound differences, their personal animosity, their value differences, and their anger.

One of the first experiences I had as a facilitator (in what was probably a nascent form of victim-offender mediation) involved bringing together a man and woman who had been domestic partners to discuss an incident in which the man pushed the woman out of his house while she was naked. Both had support systems with them during this meeting, and the commitment my cofacilitator and I were asked to make was to allow everyone to share their deepest concerns and feelings about the situation. In another circumstance, I was asked to facilitate a meeting in which adult siblings said good-bye to each other, intending never to see each other again. In both situations, some very hard and painful words were said, and in both, the outcome allowed the people involved to end this relationship (at least for that moment in time) with dignity and with a sense that they had communicated what they needed to in order to move on with their lives.

Probably most of us who work as mediators and facilitators have been asked to take on the role of guiding people through a difficult discussion with no real anticipation or goal of reaching a resolution, and sometimes with the specific goal of raising a conflict to a deeper level. We can do this if we confront and contain our own conflict-avoidant tendencies, if we have the courage, in Ken Cloke's words, to "mediate dangerously" (Cloke, 2000). But the special challenge we face is that we are usually brought into a conflict at least to contain it, if not to resolve it:

> In 1993, amid a public outcry about wolf control policies, the governor of Alaska, Walter Hickel, convened the Alaska Wolf Summit, a week-long meeting of over 150 stakeholders, 250 invited observers, and 5,000 members of the general public. This took place in January in a hockey arena in Fairbanks. (The joke of the week was that the ground rules were "no high sticking, no body checking.") My partner, Christopher Moore, and I were asked to facilitate this event, which was clearly an opportunity for many people to fight, argue, posture, and escalate. Any serious attempt to reach resolution on the fundamental issues would have been unlikely at best and even dangerous given the strength of the feeling about it. A few years later, a state employee involved in planning this meeting told me, "The real reason we brought you guys up here was to make sure that no one got killed. You accomplished that purpose very well."

In looking back at that effort, it seems clear to me that our purpose really should have been explicitly to help people engage in conflict with each other, but we were very conscious that we had been brought up there to contain the conflict, not to deepen it or expand it. As a result, our thinking was almost instinctively along the lines of how we could reach some principles of agreement, deescalate the angry feelings, and bridge the gap. Those are not unworthy goals, and no doubt some positive movement occurred, but a far more realistic goal would have been to help people engage in constructive conflict and, when necessary, to fight. That might not have played well with the state officials who contacted us, but in the end, despite a different view of our role, this is in fact what occurred. In the long term, this open, almost cathartic airing of the issues helped to change the nature of the engagement over this issue. To this date, the conflict continues and will no doubt do so for a long time.

If we can overcome our own presumptions about our role, our own conflict-avoidant tendencies, and the hope of certain parties to a conflict that we can help it go away, our skills as facilitators, mediators, and process designers can lend themselves very well to the conflict engagement role. To be sure, these are big ifs, but the more we can do this, the more we can help people who are embroiled in destructive conflict.

## Being an Ally and Being a Third Party

Being both an ally and a third party is nothing new to us. Many mediators also practice as lawyers, counselors, expert advisers, or other ally roles. The challenge is role clarification from the outset and then maintaining a boundary among those roles. If I am going to be someone's counselor, I cannot also be this person's mediator. If I have mediated a dispute between two parties, I cannot later represent that party in a matter related to that dispute (some would say on any matter, but that is easier said in large cities than practiced in small communities). We have established fairly clear codes of ethics and standards of practice governing this wall. But there are specific challenges in combining ally and third-party roles under the rubric of conflict specialist.

When conflicts come to us, it will not always be clear to either the disputants or to us what role is the most appropriate or useful for us to play. Can we enter into a conversation and assessment with a client about what his or her needs really are while maintaining our flexibility to move into either an ally role or a third-party role? Will we have already compromised our potential for neutrality by working with one side to determine what role we should play? Might we have a personal interest in occupying one type of role that will cloud our ability to make these judgments?

The answer to all of these is yes: we can maintain our flexibility, there is a threat to our neutrality, and we might have a personal interest. But as with so many other situations we deal with (assessing family cases for domestic violence, advising a company on its dispute system and providing mediation of specific grievances, doing a situation assessment of a public dispute that can lead to a further role for us in an ongoing process), a purist approach in the end serves no one. We will have to work to refine certain role boundary safeguards while maintaining the role flexibility that disputes call for. Transparency will be a key tool in helping us with this. We will need to be clear with the disputants just what role we are in, why we have chosen it, what has gone on before in terms of our contact with other disputants, and what process we will use to change our role.

As time goes on, we will learn which boundaries we will have to keep sacrosanct (for example, not to act as a coach for a party to a dispute we are currently mediating unless we act as everyone's coach) and which we can be more flexible about (how we can conduct a situation assessment and then act as an internal mediator for one side). We can predict how some of this may turn out, but we cannot be certain; the evolution of the field will be an adaptive process. An attempt to be overly prescriptive about this now will hamstring our development as a field and will not protect or benefit the public.

A second problem that we have also previously faced is that of our own conflicting interests (or the appearance of such). If I act as an advocate, coach, organizer, or some other type of ally for disputants on one side of a set of issues (say, management, environmentalists, or neighborhoods), have I developed an interest in promoting their causes that will make it harder for me to act credibly as a third party? If I am coach to a number of managers as they prepare to deal with workplace grievances, can I be a credible mediator for grievances—even with a different set of parties? Of course, this can lead to a potential conflict of interest, but we already have had to deal with this problem as well. As I discussed in Chapter Five, if we repeatedly act as mediators or arbitrators for a company in conflicts with its employees or customers, then we have probably developed an interest in pleasing the company enough so that it will continue to use our services, and this can contaminate our neutrality in any given case.

I don't believe the danger of contamination itself should stop us from pursuing greater role flexibility, but some safeguards should be put in place. We need to expand our standards of practice to cover these concerns. We need to do our best to be transparent about our various roles with our clients. The more we occupy potentially conflicting roles, the more important it will be to establish a clear agreement about our role. Furthermore, we need help from others in reviewing how we are doing this—from our own allies, from peer review groups, from the profession itself. Perhaps most important, we will need to learn from the mistakes we will inevitably make.

Knowing that we have a choice to make about whether we want to play a third-party role underscores the importance of following through on our commitment to neutrality when we do make it. Whether there is such a thing as pure neutrality or not, we know, and our clients know, that when we commit to being neutral, we are committing to not intentionally promoting one party's interests at the expense of another. When we choose to play that role, we must truly honor it, and the fact that we have a choice and decision to make about whether to put ourselves forward as a third-party neutral should only emphasize how important that commitment is. Ironically, seeing that we have an option to play nonneutral roles may also make it easier for us to maintain the essential commitment implied when we do take on a third-party role.

Third-party neutrals can play an important role in helping people engage in conflict, despite the specific obstacles they face in this respect. We already take on this challenge, and increasingly we will be called to do this. We do not have to take on roles that we feel are incompatible with our fundamental mission and work. Some of the need for role flexibility can be accomplished by networking, referral, and teamwork among different conflict specialists, each of whom individually maintains more role specificity. The more we take on the challenge of an expanded role for conflict practitioners, the more dilemmas we will face. But by engaging with these dilemmas rather than running from them, we can develop our field and increase our value to disputants considerably.

## System Roles

When we act to serve a system rather than functioning as either allies or third parties, we play a different role—one that can help transform the nature of conflict, but is focused on the functioning of a system rather than the resolution of any particular conflict. In these roles, our commitment is to creating a successful system of conflict engagement. The most familiar of these roles is that of the ombudsperson, but the program evaluator, trainer, system adviser, process designer, and case manager are also essentially system roles. Although these roles can be fulfilled in many ways, they often are neither neutral nor ally functions. Rather, they are in a sense bridging roles; that is, they span the gap between third-party services and ally roles.

These roles are essential to helping a system promote a culture of constructive conflict. An ombudsperson may or may not choose to act as an advocate, a go-between, a case manager, or an intake and referral source for organizational conflict. The interesting thing about this role is how varied it is. The overall purpose of the ombudsperson is to help ensure that people who have a complaint or a conflict can get it addressed effectively and respectfully. The researcher or program evaluator may not seem to be a conflict resolution role, but systems need systematic feedback in order to function well, and that is why the evaluator and researcher can also be considered important conflict roles. Evaluators and researchers are in a sense fact finders taken to a systemic level and with a more disciplined approach.

All of the system roles have in common that they are at least in part intended to ensure that an organization, agency, or program allows for effective conflict processes. Some system roles are focused on design and creation of approaches to conflict (process design, dispute system design, and system adviser). Some are oriented toward system maintenance and operation (ombudsperson, case manager, conflict program administrator) and some to system feedback and review (research, evaluation, and system consultant).

These are familiar roles to conflict resolution practitioners, although we don't always think of them in terms of their specific impact on conflict, particularly the research and evaluation role. But we do see them as part of the general work we do. It would not stretch us at all to incorporate them into our work in terms of altering our professional self-concept. The Association for Conflict Resolution has both an ombudsperson section and a research section.

## Incorporating Conflict Engagement in System Roles

Where we do need to challenge our thinking is to view system roles as conflict engagement roles. When we refer to dispute system design, we are usually talking about how to set up processes to prevent, contain, manage, or resolve conflict, not to help people engage in it. We tend to speak of integrated conflict management systems, not integrated conflict systems. After all, why would an organization hire people or fund programs to help raise or deepen conflict? But if we genuinely accept the notion that in the long run, it is healthier for organizations, individuals, communities, and society to welcome the full expression of the conflicts that exist and to guide this expression in constructive directions, then each of these roles should take as its responsibility to help a system become more effective at encouraging constructive engagement in conflict.

Systems designers should consider processes that will encourage people and groups to raise their conflicts in a meaningful way and will support them in staying with the conflict until it is dealt with at an appropriate level of depth and intensity. Ombudsperson functions should include efforts to encourage conflict expression. Researchers and evaluators should be looking at whether programs actually encourage people to raise conflict and engage in conflict. The over-all measure of a system's health is not just whether conflicts are resolved quickly, efficiently, and without having to resort to adjudicatory processes. The system should be one in which individual and group conflicts can be raised in a powerful manner. It's not easy to accomplish this. Systems resist engaging in conflict just as individuals do, and when conflict arises, they resist engaging in conflict when such engagement is likely to threaten some aspect of their equilibrium. But systems that are not organized to accept and deal with conflict are less adaptable to changing circumstances and therefore more vulnerable to conflict in the long run. System roles face many of the same development issues that other conflict roles do in dealing with avoidance and engagement.

I have always been suspicious of mediation programs that claimed a success rate in the high 90 percent range because I have wondered what price was being paid for those results and how they defined success. In general, I don't think that 90 percent of the cases that come to mediation should be settled, because in at least 10 percent of the cases in most arenas of conflict, the type of agreement that can be achieved in mediation is not in the interest of at least one of the parties. Similarly, I think it is a sign of a healthy organization if the rate of grievances filed is not excessive (one organization that I worked with had a greater number of grievances waiting to be dealt with than there were employees). But I don't think a healthy organization is one in which there are no grievances or in which all that are filed are settled at the lowest level. Organizations, particularly large ones, are likely to have enough sources of friction to warrant a certain number of grievances, and the absence of grievances is likely a sign that conflict is being suppressed rather than dealt with.

What we need to think about with regard to system roles is how to keep a focus on promoting a healthy atmosphere for conflict engagement. Ultimately, this is essential for the health of organizations, families, groups, communities, and societies.

## Integrating Roles

The challenge for each of us as conflict specialists will be to decide which mix of roles we can effectively fulfill and in what arenas of conflict. We also need to answer many practical questions about marketing, ethical constraints, role clarification, funding, and so forth, some of which I will address in Chapter Nine, but these are secondary to our becoming clear about our own comfort level, skill, and understanding of the different aspects of the conflict specialist role. Most of us as individuals and as conflict resolution organizations already fulfill a mix of roles, so the question is not whether we can play multiple roles. Instead, the issue facing us is how to stretch our thinking about our essential task and the range of ways in which we can fulfill this task.

Some of us will be comfortable experimenting, adopting, and adapting ally or system roles into our service offerings, and some may gravitate specifically toward those roles. Others may feel that their work needs to exist primarily within the third-party framework. Some of us will be constrained to a certain set of roles by the setting within which we work (a court mediation program, a government ADR office, a corporate ombudsperson team). Others will be constrained by our client base or our own comfort level and self-definition.

What is important in the end is less what any one of us chose to do, but what the mix of roles the field as a whole can offer to the public will be, and how these different offerings can build on, coordinate with, and learn from each other. Most of us will choose to take on new roles and new approaches carefully, experimentally, and incrementally. How each of us responds to the challenge and opportunities offered by the crisis in conflict resolution will vary tremendously. But the challenges and opportunities are real, and I believe they will become clearer in the next few years. In the end, the most important question is how we as a field collectively respond rather than how any given individual and program responds.

---

In this chapter, I have explored the general role of conflict specialist, some of its specific manifestations, and some of the challenges we face in taking on this identity. We now look at the one aspect of this new role that may be the most troubling to conflict resolution practitioners but also may open the most new doors for us as well: the role of the advocate.

# 8

## Embracing Advocacy

Aside from the disputants themselves, those most likely to resolve serious conflict are advocates. They are also the ones most likely to help raise conflict, assist people in conducting conflict, and help organize systems of conflict engagement and resolution. When people are stuck, confused, afraid, or outraged in conflict, they are most likely to turn to advocates of some kind for assistance. If these conflicts have a significant legal dimension, lawyers are likely to be chosen. In workplace disputes, human resource managers, union representatives, or equal employment opportunity officials may be used. In public policy disputes, lobbyists, organizers, public relations staff, or substantive experts may be engaged. In international relations, diplomats function as advocates for the interests of the country or international organization they represent. In many areas of commerce, we turn to people whose job is at least in part to be effective advocates, such as real estate agents or car brokers.

Advocates are essential to the functioning of conflict. Good advocates are skilled in conflict engagement: raising conflict, negotiating, and resolving conflict. If there is a conflict engagement profession in existence, it is under the aegis of an advocacy field such as law or diplomacy.

I find it curious, therefore, that for the most part, the conflict resolution field has not seen advocacy as part of its bailiwick. Why?

Substantial numbers of conflict resolution practitioners have come from an advocacy background of some kind—attorneys, for example. Many of those have wanted to leave advocacy behind or at least add a different kind of service to their work. We have tended to equate advocacy with all that we do not like about how people approach conflict. We associate advocacy with an adversarial approach, with positional negotiation, with "playing hardball," with escalatory tactics, and with a distributional orientation to negotiation. To be sure, one of the reasons people turn to advocates is for assistance with the most unpleasant aspects of conflict. That is all the more reason that they are a key to effective conflict engagement and resolution. And an effective advocate can help with more than just the combative elements of conflict.

The conflict field will be healthier and more respected if advocates believe that they can have a home in it. Furthermore, advocates have a great deal to teach those who see their primary purpose as resolving conflict and their primary role as third parties. Conversely, those of us who have worked for many years in the third-party role have a great deal to offer to advocates. We also have something important to bring to advocacy when we choose to take on this role in conflict.

There are many reasons that we should offer advocates a professional home (perhaps one among several) and that they should want to take us up on this offer. There are also many reasons that conflict specialists should offer their particular perspective and skills in the advocacy role. Embracing advocacy means providing a professional home for advocates. It also means developing the mechanisms and concepts that can assist experienced conflict practitioners to work as advocates while maintaining the perspective of being a conflict specialist. In this chapter, I discuss the reasons for embracing advocacy and consider in particular just what advocates and other types of conflict specialists can offer each other.

There are many obstacles to embracing advocacy in this way. Advocates already have professional homes. They don't necessarily view themselves as conflict specialists. Furthermore, for those with a third-party practice to take on an advocacy function will require rethinking our approach to the business aspects of our work. Embracing advocacy as a conflict specialist function will not be easy. Three things will need to happen to make advocacy a part of our work and our field:

- We will have to become clear about how advocates are conflict specialists and what they have to bring to our field.
- Professional advocates will need to see the conflict field as having something practical and positive to offer them.
- We will have to consider what it means to "bring advocates into our field" and how to identify the distinguishing features of our approach to advocacy.

Let's explore each of these questions.

## Advocates as Conflict Specialists

Advocacy is a very broad concept, and everyone is at times an advocate. Advocacy is a life skill, much like conflict resolution, mediation, negotiation, problem solving, and listening. For the most part, we don't identify ourselves as advocates when we take on this role; we usually have some other primary identification, such as diplomat, agent (real estate, union, sports, for example), or lawyer (although in some languages, the words for *lawyer* and *advocate* are essentially the same, as the French word *avocat*). But there is a specific function and set of skills that being an advocate implies, no matter what the formal role designation.

### What an Advocate Is

"An advocate is the representative of one particular interest in actual or potential conflict with others, and it is not his duty to define the collective well-being of those involved or to determine how it can be achieved. The advocate's job, as most people see it, is simply to get as much as he can for his client" (Kronman, 1993, p. 147).

Three key features are involved in an advocate's job: representation, empowerment, and substantive focus. Advocates represent a person, group, or organization in relationship to another individual, group, or organization. They take on some of the responsibility for promoting their clients' interests with these other parties, and they do this to some extent independent of their own views about these interests. They may be representing these interests directly to those whom their clients are in potential conflict with (as in a negotiation or confrontation) or to decision makers who are arbiters of some sort (judges, legislative bodies, executives).

Essential to the representative functioning is a commitment to advancing client interests. To the extent that these can be promoted by searching for a way to advance everyone's interests, that is well within the advocate's function, but the moment the goal of advancing the interests of the whole (win-win) overtakes the commitment to advance the particular interests of the client, the representative function is compromised.

Advocacy is about empowerment because an unspoken assumption of this role is that clients need the assistance of advocates to attain the power, leverage, voice, and wisdom to advance their interests. When clients do not need some form of empowerment, they usually do not need advocacy. The dilemma this often puts advocates in is how to provide effective representation in a way that is also empowering. When advocates simply take over from clients, they can be profoundly disempowering of them.

While it may be possible to envision someone who is a professional advocate in the role of promoting the entire set of interests of a potential client, most often an advocate is hired to promote a particular set of interests related to a specific substantive focus. A lawyer promotes the interests of a client with regard to legal issues. A union business agent promotes the interests of the union's members with regard to workplace issues and collective bargaining. A real estate agent is an advocate in the purchase and sale of a piece of property. People select different advocates for different purposes, and this focus means that disputants expect advocates to have a certain amount of substantive expertise in the area in which they are working.

Each of these core aspects of advocacy requires slightly different skills, and the dilemmas an advocate faces can often be explained by the sometimes complicated interplay among them. For example, as a representative, advocates' primary role is to promote their own clients' interests. But there are almost always contradictions within these interests or between different goals. Clients want to get the most money they can out of a transaction, maintain good relationships with others, allow for long-term as well as short-term benefits, feel positive about themselves, solidify a contract, keep their options open, and so forth. Clients often want to be told what they can reasonably expect as an outcome, and then they want the advocate to work for more.

The advocate's role is not necessarily to decide for clients what their goals or expectations ought to be or what their key interests are. That would be profoundly disempowering. But it is hard to be an effective representative when there are contradictory interests and unrealistic expectations, so advocates are often in the position of helping and sometimes pressuring their clients to choose among conflicting goals. They are also often in the position of delivering difficult messages about what can and can't be accomplished. Furthermore, by focusing too narrowly on one substantive area (say, financial), advocates can actually undermine clients' goals in other areas (say, relational). Effective advocates, while maintaining the clarity of their own focus, need to remain sensitive to the diverse and often contradictory interests of their clients.

The role of the advocate can be complicated, tricky, and not at all as straightforward as it might seem. And being an advocate requires a set of skills, many of which advocates are not taught or even tuned into. Specific kinds of advocacy require specific skills (legal, litigation, financial analysis, public speaking, debating, drafting, cross cultural, and so forth), but there are some more generic skills that advocates almost always need. Effective advocates almost always need analytic-strategic, communication, problem-solving, counseling, and negotiating skills. Let's consider each of these.

***The Advocate as Conflict Analyst and Strategist.*** A good advocate can analyze the nature of the situation, the system within which a conflict is occurring, the needs and concerns of the different key players, the relative power of each, the forces affecting the system, and the fundamental choices available to their clients. This almost always necessitates a fundamental understanding of the substantive and technical issues involved in a conflict or interaction. It also means understanding the dynamics of conflict and conflict resolution.

Advocates also need strategic skills. Full-ahead direct advocacy of all the interests a client may have is often neither effective nor even possible. Which approaches to take to whom about which issues and when are questions that advocates should always be considering. Working with their clients to decide when to raise an issue, which arguments to make, when to make concessions, when to make further requests, or how to mobilize their resources is key to the ability of advocates to assist clients.

Advocates have to use these skills both to develop their own advocacy strategies and help their clients understand their choices and the implications of the different ways they might choose to engage in conflict. Advocates are never acting in just a representational role. They are always to some extent acting as counselors, advisers, educators, and strategists. Key to assisting clients therefore is the strength of their analytic capacities and their ability to use these to help their clients become more strategic participants in a conflict process.

***The Advocate as Communicator.*** Effective advocates need three essential communication skills. First, they need to be very good listeners. Advocates must first be good listeners to their own clients.

When they have not heard what their clients are trying to communicate about their goals or fears, they are not going to be able to represent them very well. One of the most frequent problems in effective advocacy occurs when an advocate brings to a conflict his or her own set of assumptions about what a client needs and imposes these on the client—often with the acquiescence of an underempowered client who perhaps thinks that he or she should have the same priorities as the advocate:

> Sharon was the mother of two young children, one of whom was diagnosed with attention deficit disorder. She had not worked since the children were born and before that had been a sales clerk in a department store. She and Ted (a computer consultant) separated about one year before our meeting, and although Ted was very involved with the two children, he had never committed to a specific schedule of involvement, arranging things on a week-to-week basis. So although he was very present in their lives, Sharon never felt she had a specific schedule she could count on.
>
> In consultation with her lawyer, she expressed a great deal of fear about her financial future, which her lawyer responded to by focusing on how she might obtain maximum spousal and child support arrangements. What he did not hear, and what Sharon did not clearly express, was that her fear about money was mostly related to a sense that she was going to be alone in rearing the children, would not be able to return to work, and would be especially burdened with total responsibility for a very difficult child. A reasonable monetary settlement was important to her, but far more essential was a clear arrangement about parenting responsibilities and commitments. By asking for the most possible support, the lawyer was in a sense suggesting a much more minimal role for Ted than Sharon was hoping for.

Variations on this interaction are probably fairly common. Two problems may be going on here. One is that the lawyer and client have not established a very effective approach to their own communication. The other is that the lawyer may be substituting his or her evaluation of what should be important to the client for the client's own evaluation. Whether the lawyer is in some sense correct or not about what would best serve the client's long-term interests, this is ultimately the client's decision to make and to live with.

Advocates also need to be effective at listening to what others are saying—adversaries, other advocates, decision makers, other advisers. Advocates who can hear what others are saying are better able to understand the real nature of the conflict, options for how to pursue it, and the arguments or proposals that will have the most impact.

A second communication skill that advocates need is an ability to frame messages, proposals, arguments, issues, and information they have to deliver in a way that moves a conflict forward productively. Effective framing is not primarily about glibness or facility with a diplomatic turn of phrase. It is about how to present an idea or piece of information in a way that others will hear the essential meaning. How people frame what they have to say is often key to how a conflict moves forward. This is sometimes about making an issue seem less toxic, more open to negotiation, more amenable to resolution. But sometimes it is about presenting an issue in a way so that people realize its seriousness, its importance, and the commitment that others have to it. At other times, framing an issue means presenting it in a context that sheds a different light on it. Effective framing is key to effective advocacy.

The third essential communication skill is the ability to raise difficult issues. People often go to advocates because they do not know how to raise a difficult issue in a powerful way, particularly if they are concerned with maintaining relationships or protecting themselves from retaliation. Raising the level of conflict and helping people break through avoidance in a way that is ultimately in keeping with the long-term interests of one's clients is a key function and skill of advocates.

*The Advocate as Problem Solver.*   Advocates need to be creative problem solvers. This means being able to see their way through to a substantive solution to a client's problem. It may also involve being creative about strategy, tactics, and intermediate problems that clients face in carrying out a conflict. A good solution to a conflict requires creative problem-solving ability, but so does the development of a good strategic approach to a conflict amid conflicting choices and demands, even when no ultimate solution is in sight.

Perhaps even more important, advocates have to be tuned into how they can encourage their clients to be effective problem solvers. They need to conduct their advocacy in a way that does not interfere with the ability of their clients to search for creative solutions, maintain flexibility, and seize opportunities for moving a conflict forward in a productive way. This gets back to the challenge of taking on both the representational and the empowering aspects of advocacy.

*The Advocate as Counselor.*   Effective advocates also need to be competent as coaches and counselors. Advocates are often called on to provide emotional support to their clients to help them cope with the challenges of engaging in a conflict or negotiation. They provide coaching about how their clients should handle themselves during a conflict. Advocates often must sustain clients through a difficult process, but they also need to help them consider when the cost of pursuing a conflict may be too high, and in that case they need to help their clients let go of a conflict or an issue with grace and dignity.

The requirements of providing effective counseling can at times cause role conflict. Being a zealous advocate, an effective negotiator, and a counselor are very different functions, and the more one is focused on one aspect of the advocacy role, the harder it may be to fulfill another. Divorce attorneys are sometimes called on to play an almost therapeutic role with distraught clients, but this is neither their training nor their essential function. Yet if they do not support their clients through difficult negotiations, then their more direct advocacy work may be less effective. Real estate agents need to provide similar support to their clients. Union representatives often have to provide counseling to their constituents who are worried about job security. If advocates are not able to help their clients in this manner or see to it that they obtain this assistance in some manner, then all of their other advocacy skills may have come to naught since their clients might not be able to sustain an effective engagement process.

*The Advocate as Negotiator.* Another basic skill area for advocates is in negotiation. Advocates are often hired specifically to act as agents in a negotiation process, and being an effective negotiator is essential to the advocacy role. This raises a question that has been debated and researched quite extensively: What are the characteristics of an effective negotiator? The most significant and frequent challenge to negotiators that most negotiation researchers identify in one way or another is how to deal effectively with both the distributional and integrative elements of the process. (See, for example, Lax and Sebenius, 1986; Raiffa, 1982; Mnooken, Peppet, and Tulumello, 2000; Schneider, 2002; and Williams, 1993.) This challenge has been expressed in many ways. How can negotiators be both cooperative and assertive? How can they create value and claim value, defend client interests and be creative in joint problem solving, or work to claim their fair share of the pie at the same time as they think about how to expand the pie?

Essentially, these are all versions of the prisoner's dilemma (Axelrod, 1984) in which we are stuck with the choice of risking being taken advantage of in order to promote joint gain or protecting ourselves from exploitation, but in the process setting up a potentially costly power struggle.

Sometimes this comes across to negotiators as a choice between "being a jerk or being a sucker." Often the dilemma surfaces around how much information to share about our real interests, needs, alternatives, and settlement ranges. The most likely way of achieving a creative win-win outcome is for everyone to be open about their most significant interests—but the more open we are, the more easily we can be taken advantage of as well. An effective advocate therefore has to be adept at judging how to balance these two aspects of the negotiation process: an overreliance on either one of these will diminish the effectiveness of the advocate over time in advancing clients' interests.

One of the most interesting studies about what makes for effective advocacy was conducted by Gerald Williams in 1976 and repeated with some variations twenty-five years later by Andrea Schneider (Williams, 1983, 1993; Schneider, 2002). Both studies relied on lawyers' evaluations of the effectiveness of other lawyers as negotiators and their description of the styles of these lawyers. Four categories were identified: effective cooperative, ineffective cooperative, effective adversarial, and ineffective adversarial.

Three essential themes run through both studies. One is that both cooperative and adversarial negotiators can be effective if they are prepared, know the facts and the law, and are prepared for the possibility of the negotiation to fail. The second is that arrogant, aggressive, "obnoxious" behavior is not effective, but neither is overly trusting or obliging behavior. In other words, the reliance on personality to either intimidate or win over others, independent of a direct and relatively transparent effort to discover and address interests and alternatives, is not helpful. Third, over the twenty-five years between these two studies, the amount of aggressive adversarial behavior that was discerned grew in frequency and diminished in effectiveness.

In a very different study on the interaction of different styles of negotiation, this time a structured use of the prisoner's dilemma exercise, Axelrod (1984) identifies the following approaches as being effective:

- *Niceness:* Start out with a cooperative stance that invites a cooperative response.

- *Provocability:* Be ready to respond to an aggressive move with an aggressive response.

- *Forgiveness:* Do not hold grudges. When those with whom we are dealing show signs of moving from an aggressive to a cooperative stance, be willing to become cooperative.

- *Simplicity:* We might also call this transparency. Overly complicated or hard-to-read approaches to negotiation breed suspicion and defensiveness. So whatever approach is used, it should be understandable to others.

Another way of understanding the task of an effective negotiator is to consider the importance of incremental risk taking. Unless we take some risks in negotiation, we cannot be effective because we never open up the possibility for creative exchanges, reciprocal risk taking, or cooperation. Without taking risks, all we can do is take defensive action to limit our potential losses rather than maximize our potential gain.

Taking too great a risk, however, places us in a vulnerable position in negotiation. And what sometimes occurs is that we make an offer or suggestion that feels like a major concession or risk to us and appears or is treated by others as minor or cosmetic. The management of incremental risk taking is essential to effective negotiations.

---

Negotiators have to be effective at many other things as well, such as deciphering implied messages, looking for implied agreements, drafting terms clearly, establishing rapport, sequencing, linking and delinking issues, and drawing the appropriate boundaries around a process. But in the end, underneath almost every negotiation is some version of the integrative-distributive challenge, and this is therefore central to effective advocacy.

## Learning from Advocates

The skills that a good advocate must develop are very similar to the skills that almost all conflict specialists need, although considered from a particular point of view. When we think of the essence of what conflict specialists offer, from a variety of role perspectives, the analytic-strategic, communication, problem-solving, and negotiating skills that advocates have had to hone are key for all of us. This suggests that conflict specialists, particularly those who have primarily operated from a third-party stance, can gain a great deal from the perspective of advocates. Of course, the reverse is true: conflict specialists have a great deal to offer advocates (we will consider this in the next section).

Advocates have something particularly important to offer the conflict field in four broad areas. They know about empowering clients. They know about the distributional aspects of conflict— what it means to struggle over the division of a limited or fixed amount of value. They are familiar with rights- and power-based approaches, and they know about how to cut a deal and when to reject a deal. These are areas of importance to all conflict specialists, and they are areas about which our field has sometimes been ambivalent or confused.

*Empowering Clients.*   As a field, we often promote client empowerment, but we have taken a limited approach to how we understand this. When conflict resolvers talk about client empowerment, they are usually referring to the procedural aspects of empowerment. That is, we empower disputants by trying to give them an effective voice at the table, ensuring that they can be part of the decisions that are affecting their lives, and working on developing and conducting processes that allow for everyone involved to have an important voice. As important as this might be for empowerment, it is only one part of how people can be empowered, and advocates normally have to take a broader view on empowerment, which is one of the reasons disputants so often turn to advocates before neutrals.

Consider some of these approaches to empowerment:

- *Developing alternatives.* Advocates help disputants develop a range of effective alternatives in conflict. They may do this by helping them bolster a legal case, preparing for a job action, working with legislative entities, or developing technical alternatives. However they do this, the better the alternative a disputant has, the more empowered this person is.

- *Building alliances.* Advocates can help disputants form alliances or partnerships or in some other way help them derive power by connecting with the power and influence of others.

- *Articulating their case.* Advocates help disputants make their case in powerful and persuasive terms to those with whom they are disputing, the general public, or third parties.

- *Building on their strengths and probing for others' weaknesses.* Advocates are always considering the strength of their clients' position and the weaknesses of others and how these can be exploited. They are also thinking about what ways they can reward others for cooperating or sanction them for not.

- *Firming up emotional and moral resolve.* When the going gets tough, advocates can help clients contend with their own misgivings, fears, and doubts about the course of action they have chosen.

Of course, there are other ways in which advocates help empower clients, and advocates are not the only ones to try to help disputants in these ways. But these are ways in which advocates are often particularly well situated to empower clients, and they are also ways in which third-party neutrals are often more encumbered. Advocates bring a type of empowerment to clients that third parties cannot provide as effectively.

**Working Along the Distributional Dimension.** In the commercial or labor relations arena, many mediators work primarily along the distributional dimension. They are often dealing with disputes that are essentially about how limited financial resources are going to be distributed between the parties to a conflict when only limited joint gain options are available. These mediators have provided an important perspective to the conflict resolution field. Advocates, however, are particularly well suited to help us understand this dimension—how to work it and how to embrace it. Effective advocates understand this dimension, are realistic about it, and know how to handle it strategically. Disputants often go to advocates specifically because they want help with the distributional aspects of conflict.

Interestingly, advocates may be particularly well suited to increasing our understanding about how to work along the distributional dimension from an interest-based perspective. We tend to equate distributional negotiations with positional bargaining. That is, we see the process of working to claim the most that one can get from a limited set of resources as being characterized by positional negotiation tactics: high opening positions, hiding one's bottom lines, limited exchange of information, gradual and somewhat grudging movement to secondary positions in exchange for concessions from other parties, and so forth. There is a reason for making this connection, but distributional negotiation and positional bargaining are not the same.

Effective advocates, working in a distributional context, generally have had to develop a way of using interest-based approaches: sharing and soliciting statements of concerns, looking for shared principles of decision making and objective criteria, brainstorming different approaches, encouraging creativity, looking for trade-offs among multiple issues, trying to solve the other person's problem, and all the other tactics of an interest-based approach that conflict resolvers often talk about. One particular way in which conflict specialists can learn from advocates is how to take a richer and more rounded view of working in a primarily distributional context.

For example, the offers that experienced real estate agents make for clients are not based solely on positional considerations, such as how to leave room for counteroffers or how to convince the other parties that they are unlikely to get a better deal by waiting. They certainly think about these things, but they also try to assess and address the interests of both their clients and the others. They weigh the relative importance of cash offers versus price maximization.

They take into account timing needs and concerns about the condition of the house, the yard, location, and so forth. In carving offers, they combine a consideration of interests with a presentation of positions. Experienced agents know how to bring interests into what is structured as a positional interchange so as to open up negotiating possibilities and obtain the best price for their clients.

*Using Power and Rights Approaches.* One concept that many of us have used in understanding the dynamics of conflict are the differences among power-, rights-, and interest-based approaches to problem solving (Brett, Goldberg, and Ury, 1988). Power-based approaches involve efforts to attain goals through the use or threat of power tactics (strikes, lockouts, demonstrations, financial incentives or penalties, war, threats, or physical force). Rights-based approaches involve invoking or appealing to some rights-based framework, such as the law, a contract, a set of policies or procedures, or the teachings of an accepted guide to conduct (the Bible, Talmud, Roberts Rules of Order, a group's by-laws). Interest-based efforts involve working toward an outcome on the basis of an understanding of people's needs, concerns, and goals and trying to find ways of satisfying these to the extent necessary to resolve the issue.

For many conflict professionals, an understanding of these three approaches is almost second nature, but we also tend to assume that our job is to promote the use of interest-based approaches and to discourage, or at least to decrease, the reliance on power- and rights-based methods. There are many good reasons for this, but in many conflict situations, an interest-based approach can work only if it is backed up by an adequately developed rights or power approach. This is what is meant by "negotiating (or mediating) in the shadow of the law." In other situations, the possibility of implementing a primarily interest-based approach at all is either limited or not possible.

Effective advocates have to work on helping to develop the power- or rights-based alternatives and to keep an eye on the power- or rights-based alternatives of others as well. They also have to know how to use these alternatives when necessary. Our ability to enhance the potential of interest-based approaches will be limited unless we understand the importance of rights- and power-based avenues and are comfortable using them when necessary and as appropriate.

***Cutting a Deal (or Walking).*** Aren't we all about cutting a deal? Certainly one part of the mediator's job is to help people cut a deal, and we often focus on looking for when a deal is possible, how to discern possible settlement ranges, and how to help people come to closure. But as third parties, we look at it differently than an advocate does. The essential question third parties ask is: How can we help people meet enough of their interests in a negotiation process so that they are willing to reach an agreement? Advocates ask a related but slightly different question: Can I best meet my client's interests if I accept this deal, hold out for more, or walk away from this process? Put differently, what are the costs and benefits of accepting a deal now versus not accepting it?

By inclination in part, but also by role, neutrals are looking at how to arrive at a deal and advocates at how to maximize the achievement of their clients' goals. These are two very rich but different perspectives, and as third parties, we may not fully appreciate the consequences of this difference in explaining the viewpoint and attitude of disputants. They may want an outcome, but they are always wondering if they could do better in a different arena. Advocates work with this all the time, and there are rich insights that they can bring to us as a result.

One challenge for advocates is how to help their clients be realistic when deciding whether to go for a deal. Facing clients with some unpleasant choices ("you don't have a good court case"; "this is the best deal you are likely to get"; "we are not in a strong position to win a strike") is a key responsibility of advocates. It is also an area in which advocates often turn to neutrals for help. Because advocates do not want to be seen as unwilling to carry on the good fight, they often look to a mediator, fact finder, or settlement judge to deliver the bad news to their clients.

This is sometimes a source of tension between third parties, particularly those who do not see their role as primarily evaluative, and advocates who want this kind of help. It is also an area in which advocates sometimes shirk their responsibility by not facing their clients with their alternatives in a realistic way. However, most advocates are experienced with this type of reality testing, and it is a key part of arriving at a deal. Mediators are usually well aware of the importance of reality testing, but they often find it hard to be the agent of reality without losing their neutrality (although this is a key element of the approach of evaluative mediators).

## Lessons from Different Kinds of Advocates

There are many different kinds of advocates, and each brings a unique perspective and view. For example, lawyers are especially able to help with a rights-based framework and with understanding the power of negotiating in the shadow of the law. Union organizers and political activists may be more familiar with developing power-based alternatives. Lobbyists understand how to build power over time, and they also understand the art of cutting a deal. Diplomats work with a broad system orientation, usually in cross-cultural settings, and they understand the larger context within which any particular conflict is played out. Real estate agents work largely along a distributional dimension but use interest-based tactics all the time.

The greater the range of advocates who feel connected to our profession, the more we will be able to be valuable players in significant conflicts. When we speak of advocates, we should be thinking not only of lawyers. Nevertheless, lawyers are perhaps the largest group of trained advocates, and the relationship between the legal profession and the conflict profession is particularly important and sometimes troubled.

Many conflict specialists are lawyers. Many lawyers consider themselves part of the field. We work with lawyer-advocates as third-party neutrals all the time. When we offer our services as advocates, the inevitable question arises: How are we different from lawyers? We will consider this later, but for now let us be clear that lawyer-advocates have something important and specific to offer us about understanding the interplay between a rights-based and an interest-based approach. But they are not the only type of advocates that are relevant to us as we think of embracing advocacy as a conflict resolution function.

## What Conflict Specialists Offer Advocates

If this were a one-way street—that is, if advocates offered something to conflict specialists who come primarily from a third-party neutral perspective, but they did not have to gain from such an association—then we would have reached a dead end. Why should advocates see themselves as part of the conflict engagement field if they did not have something to gain as well? But I think conflict specialists do have a lot to offer to the work of advocates, and that is why I think advocates will relate increasingly to the conflict field.

## Learning from Conflict Specialists

In a general sense, both advocates and conflict specialists are about helping people through conflict, and therefore we are all part of the same system. Inevitably, we all have to work with each other. We have a different perspective on the same set of circumstances, and the more we can work with each other to share these perspectives and learn from them, the better. This is true for all of us, no matter what our particular role in conflict is. But there are some particular aspects to what conflict specialists in general have to offer to advocates and as advocates, and there is a significant potential synergy that will be created if we see advocacy as one element of a conflict specialist's services. In some respects, these are just the flip side of what advocates offer us. So let's look at the four parallel categories to those we considered previously but from a different perspective.

*Empowering Disputants.* Conflict specialists must come to appreciate deeply that genuine empowerment of disputants in conflict can rarely be attained at the expense of others. Building alternatives and being effective at the distributional elements of conflict are important to being empowered, but in the end, they are not the most important source of power. The people who can best empower disputants are those they are in conflict with. In the end, the Israelis will have to empower the Palestinians, and vice versa, if either is to obtain their objectives. In a divorce, only the parting spouses have the power to give each other what they most need. In this sense, fundamental empowerment is truly an integrative dynamic. In their work to empower their clients or constituents in the midst of difficult conflicts, advocates can lose sight of this. But to be genuinely effective in empowerment, advocates need to be able to see the mutual aspect of empowerment, and that is a perspective that conflict specialists may be particularly well equipped to bring to advocacy.

Also, advocates often do not focus on the procedural elements of empowerment. Giving their clients a direct voice at a negotiating or decision-making table is something many advocates do not think of, and in fact they are often very much against it. Therefore, they often overlook this element of empowerment. But this is the element of empowerment, of giving voice to people in conflict, that conflict specialists think about and work toward all the time.

*Finding the Integrative Potential.* No matter how attuned an advocate may be to both the integrative and distributive potential of a conflict, it is genuinely hard to pay attention equally and simultaneously to both aspects. Yet that is what has to occur in most conflicts. As we work along both dimensions, we have to stay attuned to the system we are working in, the full range of interests and needs in play, and all the dimensions of conflict that are operative (behavioral, attitudinal, emotional). It's hard to do this, and from any given role or orientation, we can easily fall into a distorted or skewed approach.

Although conflict specialists may sometimes rely too much on the potential of integrative approaches and therefore need the corrective that advocates bring by their realism concerning the distributional aspects, advocates can easily fail to take seriously or adequately explore the integrative potential, particularly when the going gets rough. Conflict specialists always have to keep some focus on the integrative potential because that is often the way through what appear to be intractable situations. The real art to dealing with conflict is being able to hold both elements of conflict in our consciousness simultaneously and to work effectively on both aspects. If traditional advocates are more oriented toward one dimension and third parties to another, then conflict specialists have to develop the ability to bring both perspectives to the table, no matter what their particular role.

The union and management of a company are meeting to consider how to deal with the financial crisis the company is facing. The union wants to make sure that the management does not use the financial downturn as a means of disempowering the local and unnecessarily rolling back benefits. Management wants to make sure that it cuts the workforce enough to stabilize the company's financial position rather than going through a series of small reductions that are never adequate to help the company turn its situation around. They also want to make sure that the union does not intrude on management prerogatives.

An overly distributional approach would limit consideration to how many jobs would be reduced—and from where (supervisory or unionized positions), how much management salaries would be cut back, how much workers' benefits would reduced—in other words, how the pain would be distributed. An overly integrative approach might focus solely on the ways in which union and management could work together to increase productivity, share information, create and apply joint criteria for reductions or reemployment, and look for creative ways to trade off immediate cutbacks against long-term benefit improvements.

The problem with focusing only on the distributional elements is that it is likely to exacerbate relationships and ignore the ways in which the two groups could work together in the company's interest. The problem with focusing exclusively on the integrative approach is that the need to make some very hard choices that pit the interests of the company against the union might easily be avoided or ignored until the situation deteriorated further.

It's hard to consider both aspects simultaneously, particularly under duress, but that is exactly what situations such as this call for and what conflict specialists need to assist with.

*Focusing on Needs.* Conflict exists because of the interplay of human needs, and effective conflict engagement requires working with those needs at an appropriate level of depth and breadth. The challenge of working at the appropriate level of depth is to get beyond the immediate interests in terms of which a conflict may be framed and to consider the most significant needs that can be driving a dispute.

Sometimes there is no difference, but at other times, what is motivating people to stay with a conflict is not the direct interests they have in the issue but the underlying needs that may be driving their engagement. This is particularly true of deeply rooted, long-standing conflicts, but to some extent, it is present in almost every dispute. These needs can include what we normally refer to as interests, but they can also include identity needs and survival needs. To deal with conflict at an effective level of depth means to reach that level in the motivational structure of disputants at which the conflict really "lives," that is, the level at which the conflict is most meaningful and perhaps most painful to them.

To work appropriately across the breadth of conflict means to consider the full range of interests and concerns that people have and not just the presenting needs. In particular, it means being aware of the psychological, procedural, and substantive elements of the interests people have (Moore, 1991). Substantive interests refer to the particular and tangible outcomes people are looking for, procedural interests to the way in which a process is conducted, and psychological interests to how we feel we have been treated (in particular, issues about saving face, maintaining dignity, wanting an apology, or needing an apology to be accepted).

Often the key to understanding conflict is to become aware of the linkages among these different types of interests and to grasp the full range of interests involved. When we do this, we are better able to identify the integrative potential of a conflict and to understand when difficult distributive decisions must be made. In understanding the constellation of interests and how these will affect a conflict interaction, we are looking for three different relationships among the interests of different parties. We are looking for mutual interests on which to build a cooperative framework. We are looking for separate but compatible interests that can lead us to creative trade-offs. (Sebenius, 2001, identifies these as a particularly overlooked resource in negotiations and suggests that we may often be too focused on looking for common ground.) And we are looking for incompatible interests that suggest the need to deal with the distributional dimension of conflict. Conflict specialists work with this rich variety of interests all the time. Our ability to discern the different types of interests and their varying relationship to each other is key to our effectiveness.

If most advocates appreciate the role of power- and rights-based approaches as they interact with interest-based approaches, conflict specialists understand the richness and potential of working with the full range of human needs, of appreciating how deep we need to go to reach the place where conflict lives and of how to work with the interplay of substantive, procedural, and psychological needs. Our grasp of the breadth and depth of human needs is one of the specific tools and insights that conflict specialists can bring to their work as advocates.

**Reaching Closure.** The problem with viewing deal making as equivalent to resolution is that deals, agreements, or settlements are really just way stations along the road to resolution. Closure does not occur simply because some agreement may have been reached (or a solution ordered), although this is sometimes a necessary condition or at least an important aid to resolution. Closure occurs when parties are genuinely ready to move on—emotionally, behaviorally, and attitudinally. Both advocates and third parties can fall prey to equating agreement with resolution and therefore become too fixed on the search for a good deal. Disputants do this all the time as well.

Advocates may be oriented to getting the most advantageous deal and may be less likely to view a mutually agreed-on solution as an end in itself. And third parties are often more oriented to understanding how a deal must reflect the broad range of interests of all the parties involved if it has a hope of resulting in genuine resolution of significant conflicts. These perspectives, taken together, can help refocus conflict specialists from a narrower search for an agreement to a broader search for resolution. Sometimes a deal is essential to help parties take the next step. When this is the case, the perspective of conflict specialists on how to reach a deal through addressing all parties' concerns is an important addition to the natural emphasis of most advocates to how to maximize their clients' interests.

## Conflict Specialists as Advocates

I am not just proposing that conflict specialists learn from advocates or invite advocates into our field but that we act as advocates on behalf of clients. As I discussed in the previous chapter, I believe that the role of advocate is one that conflict specialists should add to their range of services. We cannot be an advocate for a particular party and at the same time act as a neutral in a conflict that involves this party. But we can offer ourselves as advocates when this appears to be the most beneficial and powerful role we can play in a conflict. We can do this because of the particular skills we have as conflict specialists. When we offer ourselves as advocates from the vantage point of being conflict specialists, we are asserting that the knowledge we have about conflict provides us with a special set of skills that makes us effective advocates. We may also bring substantive knowledge to our advocacy if, for example, we are trained as lawyers, therapists, scientists, accountants, financial managers, or planners, but our knowledge of conflict is what particularly enables conflict specialists to act as advocates.

As advocates are drawn into the conflict engagement field and begin to see themselves as conflict specialists and as those of us who come from a conflict resolution background assume the advocacy role, clients will be able to benefit from a richer and more powerful approach to advocacy. This approach will be informed by the skills, experience, and outlook of both traditional advocates and conflict resolution practitioners. The more that advocates and conflict specialists are around each other and share work, insights, and questions, the richer will be our understanding of conflict and the broader our ability to work effectively across many situations to help people engage in conflict in a powerful and constructive way.

## Bringing Advocates into the Conflict Field

If advocates have something of particular value to offer to others in the conflict field and if other specialist roles offer something of particular value to advocates, should it not be easy to envision ourselves as part of the same field and act accordingly? As we all know, this is not so easy. There are some significant obstacles, but there are some important trends that might help as well. Let's consider some of these obstacles and trends, and how specifically we might embrace advocacy in the conflict field.

### Obstacles to Embracing Advocates

Perhaps the most significant obstacle is that advocates may not feel the need for the perspectives we offer. Furthermore, there could be considerable concern that we are moving into areas where we do not belong and might even be dangerous. Foreign service officers have not exactly rushed to conflict resolution programs to learn what we have to teach (and I am not sure how many conflict resolvers with an interest in international conflict have engaged in a disciplined study of international relations). Union activists and labor relations officers may occasionally come to a course on interest-based negotiation but have been mostly interested in coming to us to learn how to use mediation effectively.

By far the largest group of professional advocates to consider is the legal community. Our field's ability to work with the legal profession as we consider whether, when, and how to take on the advocate role will be critical to our ventures in this area. Lawyers will naturally be concerned that our efforts to offer ourselves as advocates may constitute a move into their turf, particularly when non-lawyers offer to fulfill an advocacy role. Bar associations and law societies are likely to be watching to make sure we do not engage in the unauthorized practice of law or that lawyers in our field do not fail to fulfill their ethical obligations as lawyers. The discussions we have about this in the years to come will no doubt be difficult at times, but I suspect that in the end, they will be very helpful to us as we work to define exactly what it is we have to offer and how we can do it in an ethical way.

Nothing we do as conflict specialists will obviate the need for strong legal advocacy. Legal advocates need to know the legal side of their business very well, and those of us who are not legally trained need to be well aware of our limitations in this respect. But legal advocates are also conflict specialists, and for that reason our field has something of value to offer them as well. Furthermore, lawyers do not own advocacy in conflict. They are a significant force in this arena, but not the only one.

The best way to counter these concerns is for us to remain clearly focused on who we are, what we can do, and what we cannot do. Unless we are lawyers, we cannot represent people in legal tribunals or advise them on their legal obligations, rights, or alternatives. But we can act as an advocate and an ally in many circumstances without taking on the responsibility or offering the particular services of legal representation. If we are offering services that the public wants and finds of value, and if we are clear on what we can offer and what we can't, then ultimately the various different advocate groups will accept us, teach us, learn from us, and even join us.

Another significant obstacle has to do with the practicalities of embracing advocacy. What does it really mean? Are we talking about an advocacy section to our professional organizations? (Ultimately I think we are.) If so, why would people come to this given all the other places they could go and ways in which they could expend their time and financial resources? People will come if and as they find the connection and the identification worthwhile to them. It will have to happen based on demand, not on a sales effort. Our challenge will be to find ways of providing something of tangible value to advocates.

A third obstacle is a definitional one. What do we mean by *advocates*? We can define this broadly or narrowly, with a conflict focus or without, with clear criteria for participation or very loosely. We know whether we are litigators, mediators, arbitrators, trainers, facilitators, or system designers, but in some way, don't we all think we are advocates for something? And where exactly does advocacy stop and a third-party perspective take over?

We cannot force the answers to these questions. As we become clear about the potential to take on new and expanded roles in conflict, the definitions will develop, and the answers will emerge. Whether or not *advocacy* is the term we use, I think it is very clear that we will be in the position of taking on more ally functions, including representational ones. As we do this, we will develop an ever clearer understanding of what we do and who we are in this area.

Our attitude as conflict specialists toward advocacy may prove to be the most difficult of all obstacles to overcome. If we view advocacy as a destructive and coercive approach to conflict and if we view the work of third-party neutrals as somehow morally superior to that of advocates, then we will not be able to embrace advocacy or advocates in our field. Most of us do not overtly express the view that advocates are generally part of the problem rather than an important and necessary component of effective conflict engagement.

But this view is probably held by many conflict resolution practitioners. To be sure, there are advocates who do not play a constructive role in conflict, but the advocacy function is essential to people in conflict. For us to embrace advocacy, we need to examine our own tendencies to denigrate this approach to conflict, and we need to develop a healthy respect for the work of advocates and their contributions to constructive conflict engagement.

## Contributing Trends

A number of interesting trends suggest that advocates themselves understand the need for incorporating the insights and skills of conflict professionals into their work and that they occasionally do see themselves as having a professional home alongside conflict specialists.

A number of organizations incorporate advocates and neutrals quite successfully. The Association of Family Conciliation Courts has a history of providing an important home for judges, family lawyers, child custody evaluators, mediators, and family therapists. In Colorado (and other states with similar groups). the Interdisciplinary Committee on Child Custody has provided important opportunities for lawyers, therapists, evaluators, and mediators to meet as well. The Alternative Dispute Resolution Committee of the American Bar Association is a flourishing source for lawyers and nonlawyers alike to come together under the auspices of an advocacy organization. The National Conference of Peacemaking and Conflict Resolution (now PeaceWeb) originated with the idea that peace activists, who are essentially advocates, and conflict resolution practitioners naturally belong in the same organization. So the idea that advocates and conflict specialists belong in the same professional home is not a new one.

Several professional trends have suggested that the strong lines between advocacy and conflict resolution are breaking down as well. The growth of restorative justice and victim-offender programs suggests that the best way to advocate for victims may often be through a process that is more traditionally associated with the conflict resolution field. This is one of the fastest-growing elements of our field, which reflects a growing realization that victims need the kind of resolution that is not wholly available through normal approaches to justice or traditional mediation processes (Strang and Braithwaite, 2001; Bazemore and Schilff, 2001).

In the legal arena, one interesting recent trend is the collaborative law movement (Macfarlane, forthcoming; Tessler, 2001). In this development, which has taken root in many Canadian and American locations and has spawned its own professional organization, advocates, who are primarily in the area of family law, have developed a new approach to handling the distributive pressures while keeping sight of the integrative potential in settlement efforts.

Collaborative lawyers enter into a formal contract with their clients and those on the other side of the dispute that they will represent their clients only in settlement efforts, not in litigation. If settlement efforts fail, all clients will have to contract with new attorneys to represent them in litigation. Collaborative lawyers often work with teams of mental health divorce coaches and sometimes financial professionals as well. Occasionally they work with mediators, although many of them see their efforts as a substitute for and sometimes superior to mediation (Macfarlane, forthcoming).

Collaborative lawyers view their work in terms of the creation of a settlement process in which the lawyers for each side, the other professionals, and all the disputants are part of a team whose goal it is to find a good solution to the problems posed in the dispute. They draw on much of the work and experience of family mediators and are trying to integrate the approach of mediators with that of traditional advocates.

Numerous other trends challenge some of the boundaries between advocacy and conflict resolution. The holistic law movement, therapeutic jurisprudence movement, and nonviolent communication movements are other examples. How any of these will develop and the extent to which they will take root is hard to predict, but it is clear that many efforts are being made to break down what is essentially an artificial boundary between advocacy and conflict specialization.

## How to Embrace Advocacy

What specific steps will help us as a field provide a home for advocates and a path for conflict specialists to embrace advocacy? As with any other fundamentally new development in the field, only a very small part of what happens will be due to intentional planning. Professions too are complex adaptive systems, and any specific steps we take can help encourage a certain adaptation but will not in any causal way produce it. If the time is right and the need significant, we will find a way of reaching out to advocates, and they will find it useful and appropriate to connect with the conflict field. Several things might help encourage this—for example:

- *Changing our self-concept*. The more we see advocacy as an appropriate role for conflict specialists to play, the clearer we are about what conflict specialists as a group have to offer to and to gain from the advocate's perspective, the better able we will be to include advocacy in our field.
- *Acting as advocates with a conflict specialist's perspective*. Many of us have worked as advocates and still do. Taking advantage of appropriate advocacy opportunities and seeing these as part of our conflict work, not as separate from it, will begin to change everyone's thinking about this, including our own.
- *Presenting, participating, writing*. The more we have a presence at conferences that advocates attend, in journals they read, and as part of organizations they relate to (many of us already do), the more we will create important connections and linkages. Just as advocates are unlikely to participate in conflict organizations unless they find it worth their while, so too the only way conflict specialists will participate over time in the professional organizations of advocates is if we feel it worth our while. But often we don't do this because of assumptions about what it may be like. We can at least

try this out. We should also encourage presentations about advocacy and by advocates at our conferences and in our journals.

• *Studies, research, case analysis, dialogue*. The more we write up our experiences as advocates, using the analytic tools of conflict specialists, the more we engage in ongoing case dialogue with colleagues who function in advocacy roles, the more we research the effectiveness of different approaches to advocacy, the more engaged we will be with advocates.

• *Practice guidelines*. As we learn how to incorporate advocacy into our field, we will need to develop best practice documents and ethical guidelines (more on this next chapter). These will help clarify how to handle multiple roles, the boundaries between roles, and approaches to advocacy that are consistent with the most important values of our field. There are existing models for this that we can build on, such as the guidelines that help lawyers establish the boundaries among the different roles they might play.

What much of this amounts to is taking some chances. The sign of a vibrant field is that it is open to change, can adapt to circumstances, and has an adventurous spirit. This implies some risk taking. We can do this, and I believe we will, because the alternative will be to overlook opportunities to play an important and constructive role in significant conflicts that will present themselves to us regularly.

When I studied for my master's degree in social work at Columbia University in the late 1960s, there was an interesting and productive debate among the faculty about the appropriate role for social work practitioners. One school, led by George Brager, argued that social workers' essential function was to act as advocates for their clients with regard to the various systems they were involved with. Another viewpoint, put forward by William Schwartz, described the social worker's role as that of a mediator between clients and systems. From my perspective thirty years later, they were both right. The issue was then, and is today, one of judging the particular needs and circumstances of the client and the systems they are engaged with, our connection to these, and how we can help accomplish the essential task of helping them engage with each other productively—and that sometimes means conflictually.

Many of us moved on from an advocacy orientation because we did not like the effect that our approach was having on our clients, the system as a whole, or us. But advocacy is an essential need people have in engaging in conflict, and if the impact was unproductive, the answer is not to reject advocacy but to reclaim it. The importance of other conflict engagement roles is not diminished if we also pay heed to the critical role of advocacy. Third-party roles, system roles, and other ally roles are essential to an effective overall approach to conflict, as are advocacy roles. If our field embraces and supports only one set of roles, it will not provide a comprehensive service to people dealing with conflict.

Third parties and advocates are much more kindred spirits than we might suppose. We can support each other, learn from each other, share insights and perspectives, and expand our roles as appropriate to incorporate the best insights, approaches, and interventions of each approach. In this way, we can offer a much more complete and meaningful service to people in conflict.

---

Much of what I have written here is based on my understanding of the challenges and opportunities that we face as a field. I do not pretend to know what is going to happen or how all this will play out. How practical is it to consider ourselves to be conflict specialists and to approach conflict from an engagement rather than a resolution perspective? Will there be work, how will this translate into practical action, and what trends can we expect? Although these are impossible questions to answer, they are very important ones to consider. In the final chapter, I will consider the future of the conflict field.

# 9

## Redefining Conflict Resolution

The signs are everywhere that our field is changing. Professional organizations are merging, changing, re-forming, and redefining themselves. The need for effective approaches to conflict is as great as ever before, but the call for our services is becoming more focused and often more limited. Major sponsors of the field (such as the Hewlett Foundation, the Pew Charitable Trust, and the Mott Foundation) have been reconsidering their commitment. Significant institutional consumers (for example, some major governmental agencies and large corporations) are either questioning their use of alternative dispute resolution or changing the way in which they use these services. We have explored these trends in this book, and I have suggested some of the ways in which we can confront and respond to what I think is a crisis in our field.

We have a choice about how to respond to this crisis. We can deny or avoid the challenges confronting us, or we can adapt to them and emerge as a stronger field. I think we can be confident that many of the basic services we have developed over the past twenty-five years are well accepted and will continue to be used. But there are significant ways in which we have not made inroads into the way conflict is conducted, and some of our operating assumptions are either wrong or at least limited. This is a time to face the changing responses and the limits we have encountered or to accept a very encapsulated role for our field. Which will it be?

I suspect that we will not settle for a secondary and circum-scribed role. Our roots are too heavily connected to social change objectives for a strategic retreat to work for us. Therefore, I think we can anticipate that our field will change dramatically during the next twenty-five years. I think we will redefine our task to include a greater emphasis on assisting people in engaging in conflict. I think we will take on a much broader definition of our role. In order to do this, however, we will have to address several important questions. We will have to revisit what our purpose is, what our knowledge base is, what our defining values are, and what is at the heart of what we have to offer. Perhaps the hardest and most immediate question, however, will be a practical one. Can we make a new concept of service into a viable business?

## The Business of Being a Conflict Specialist

All of these ideas about focusing on conflict engagement and be-coming conflict specialists may be well and good in theory, but will they fly in the real world? Can we sell this to clients, government agencies, foundations, courts—to the people who pay for our services? And can we imagine ourselves handing out a card that says "conflict specialist" (or "conflict engagement specialist") with a straight face? What kind of training will be offered to aspiring conflict specialists? What practice standards and codes of ethics will govern our activities? How will we actually carry out our work in a businesslike manner?

I want to address these issues as best as I can at this stage of our field's development—but first a very strong caveat. The ideas in this book represent an emerging trend that is hard to predict or control. In fact, it is impossible. But we can think about how a change might come about and what general initiatives and specific actions might need to occur. We can also think about different ways we might present ourselves to potential clients and to the communities we serve and work with. In this way, we can imagine the route we might follow and prepare to take the first steps along this path.

The first step is to change our consciousness about what we do—about how we can help people in conflict and about what our fundamental role ought to be. The next step is to push the limits on the set of roles we are now playing and see where this takes us and what kind of responses we get. As we become better able to help disputants be effective throughout the life cycle of a conflict process, the more we will grow into this new concept and these new role definitions.

In the early days of the mediation movement, when it was not so clear how this field would evolve, if it would be accepted, and what kind of market there would be, a number of efforts were made to force the development of the field into certain set patterns. These were attempts to make the nascent field predictable, acceptable, and marketable. By and large, they were failures.

One notable effort in this respect was the work of O. J. Coogler (1978), one of the originators of the family mediation movement. Coogler outlined a mediation process that he thought would be appealing to family lawyers. His approach prescribed the number of sessions, the issues that would be dealt with in each session, and how each session would unfold. The process never worked that way at all, although his contribution to the launching of family mediation as a recognized field of practice was significant.

Coogler failed in his attempt to superimpose a strict methodology. What mediators in that era had to do instead, and what I am sure we will have to do with the broader concept of conflict engagement, was to let the market work. In the early years of the mediation field, we had to address the needs that we saw in a clear and flexible way, and let our customers respond and shape our work. This response helped us define our approach, our standards of practice, how we presented ourselves to the public, and the kind of cases we focused on. We'll have to take the same path with any new approach to conflict, and the concept of conflict specialist is no exception. Our key task will be to adapt to the changing conditions we are facing with creativity and flexibility.

Having said this, let's consider some specific issues concerning whether we can make this a business. In particular, how shall we describe our practice, how can we market this new service, and to what standards will we hold ourselves accountable?

## Describing Our Practice

When I started working at CDR Associates in 1980, we were called the Center for Dispute Resolution. We had also flirted with the name Denver Conciliation Services. In the mid-1980s, we changed our name (after a year of discussion) to CDR Associates because we wanted to deemphasize the word *dispute* since some organizations had a difficult time reaching out to an organization with that in its name ("Conflict? Of course not, we are just having a discussion").

We have had several different taglines under the name over the years ("Cooperation, Decisions, Results" and "Collaborative Decision Resources"—although I have always thought "Can't Decide Really" would do quite well), but the basic lesson seems to be that a slightly unclear role delineation makes sense. This allows clients to use us in a variety of ways and allows for role flexibility as appropriate. Under this general name, we can give all sorts of specific descriptions of our work and our mission. Nonetheless, we have to have a way of characterizing what we do if we want to be able to describe ourselves to the world. How can we do this if we take on the self-concept of conflict specialists?

Let me suggest an imaginary organization called MAD ("Making a Difference in a Mad World"). MAD subscribes to the conflict engagement approach and is structured as a partnership of a variety of conflict specialists: some focus on mediation and facilitation, some on coaching, some work as advisers and advocates to groups in conflict, some as systems designers, and almost everyone takes on a variety of these functions. MAD's mission statement might read something like this:

> MAD is committed to helping individuals, groups, and organizations to accept conflict as a normal and potentially healthy part of our lives and to deal with conflict in an effective, courageous,

and productive manner. MAD provides services that assist others in engaging in conflict with a full understanding of its challenges, its dangers, and its creative potential.

In a brochure, MAD might describe what it does and who it is as follows:

MAD is a group of conflict specialists with experience in conflict resolution, mediation, negotiation, coaching, facilitation, advocacy, and dispute systems design. All of us have worked to help individuals and organizations deal with the conflicts that they encounter in their work, their community, and their organizations, so that they can face, discuss, and handle these disputes in a way that accomplishes their goals and is in keeping with their values.

We work with people on understanding the nature of their conflict, raising the conflict to the level required to ensure that it is dealt with effectively, engaging with those with whom they are in conflict, and, when appropriate, finding a constructive path towards resolving the conflict.

Specific services we offer include:

- *Assessment:* Working with disputants to evaluate the nature of a conflict or conflict procedure and to consider the alternatives they have in dealing with the conflict.
- *Coaching and Consultation:* Providing advice, strategic consultation, and personal coaching to individuals or groups engaged in a conflict process.
- *Advocacy:* Working with disputants as advocates in conflict processes. We do not offer legal representation or advice, but we will work as negotiators or representatives to help advocate for disputants in a constructive and powerful way.
- *Mediation and Facilitation:* Acting as third parties to bring people together to discuss the issues that are of concern to

them and, where appropriate, to consider means of resolving these issues.

- *System Design:* Helping groups and organizations to design conflict systems that allow people to raise the issues they have clearly, safely, and effectively and that provide constructive mechanisms for dealing with these issues.

- *Evaluation:* Providing systematic research and evaluation about the effectiveness of conflict systems and programs in dealing with disputes.

If MAD's experience in writing brochures is anything like any organization I have ever been part of, these description will have to be vetted by many people, rewritten at least ten times, and revised periodically. This is not just an academic exercise; it is how we develop our presentation of ourselves based on the response we are getting from our clients and the general public we deal with.

This is just my take on how we might present ourselves in a practical way. I believe it is a useful exercise for any of us who think we want to expand our view of what we do and how we do it to try writing a mission statement and service description in order to see how consonant it is with our view of ourselves and to see how others react to it as well. After writing something like the description above, I think we might feel comfortable with cards that read "MAD, Inc., Conflict Specialists."

## Marketing Our Services

In *Making Mediation Work* (2001), Mosten provides a comprehensive approach to organizing and marketing our services with many specific suggestions and ideas. He starts with a very simple principle: we all have to establish what he calls our "mediation signature"— what it is that distinguishes and identifies what we do—and each of us has to do this for ourselves. But we also have to do this as a field.

I am suggesting that the field expand or alter its signature so that it is less focused on resolution and third-party neutral roles. Within the altered signature of the field, each of us as individuals and organizations will have to develop our own signature that will be an amalgam of the purposes and roles that I have been describing—and no doubt other roles as well. How we do this will depend on our individual interests, strengths, background, connections, and reputation. I believe that effective marketing of our work as conflict specialists will be characterized in the following ways:

• *Changing incrementally.* For the most part, we won't go out and announce a whole new service to the world or a major recast of our identity. We will gradually change our descriptions and add to our offerings.

• *Building on our successes.* As we are asked to serve as advisers, coaches, or strategists, for example, we will refine our approach to these roles and expand our offerings based on our experience and success in these roles. For example, the more we have been asked to serve as system designers, the easier it has been to market our services in this arena.

• *Focusing on needs.* We should always market to the needs of our potential clients. To the extent that clients are focused on the need for resolution, then that is what we will continue to market to. I think we have sometimes misunderstood clients' needs. When they want help in contending with a conflict that they see no likelihood of being resolved to their satisfaction, that is what we should market to.

• *Taking risks.* We will never innovate or recast our practice without taking some risks. The first time we substitute engagement in conflict for resolution of conflict or add advocacy to our list of services, we will experience all the uncertainty and anxiety many of us did when we first added mediation to our service package. The first time we say to a potential client that we can help, but not by offering an immediate path toward resolution, particularly if this is a potentially big contract, we will be taking a risk. We may occasionally lose clients this way. But on other occasions this will allow us to tap into exactly what a potential client is experiencing and needing and will become the path to getting the business that we need.

At CDR, we have sometimes said that we are always marketing and we are never marketing. By that, we mean that everything we do creates our signature, our reputation, and our standing and is therefore marketing, but when we specifically focus on trying to market, we can be less effective. I don't think this is exactly true: some activities are just about marketing, and others do not really assist with marketing at all (and are confidential anyway). But the general idea is that the most important marketing we can do is to create a clear message for ourselves and our client base about who we are, how we think of ourselves, and what we do, and that we do this whenever we present ourselves to the public in any way. Effective marketing will come from a clear self-concept, from being creative in adapting to new opportunities, from continually refining our offerings, and from being willing to present new services and approaches assertively and with confidence.

## Holding Ourselves Accountable

We need clear standards of accountability as we move forward for ethical and practical reasons. If we are going to deconstruct and reconstruct our role, we can easily slip into practices that can end up being dangerous or misleading for our clients. For example, we can loosen the boundaries between neutrality and advocacy in a dangerous way if we are not careful. Or we can use inside information we have received in one role to advance the particular interests of one party to a dispute in another role. We have an ethical obligation to address these concerns.

But there are very practical reasons as well. By developing clear standards of practice and consequences for violating them, we diminish the chances of the kind of horror stories that can inhibit acceptance of a new field. We have all encountered resistance to conflict resolution services based on some terrible individual experience that someone has heard about or been through. We can't prevent these in our work any more than doctors, lawyers, or psychotherapists can prevent them in theirs, but we can take steps to diminish their likelihood, and we can have standards we can point to that articulate what we believe to be appropriate practice.

There is another practical reason as well. By developing wise standards, we further the important process of self-identification. In a sense, all practice standards make the same statement. They proclaim, "This is who we are; this is what we will do." As mediators, for example, we say that we are third-party neutrals who conduct confidential discussions to address issues in a constructive manner. Our practice standards then go on to specify what we mean by *third party*, *neutrality*, *confidential*, and *constructive*. There are many variations on this theme, but they all more or less address the same question.

The danger will be in moving too rapidly to establish standards— in trying to force the development of a practice in a certain direction through standards or ethical guidelines as opposed to having the guidelines reflect the best practices that have developed more organically over time. But as these best practices emerge, standards will be essential. Many of the existing standards will continue to be valid for an expanded role, including standards about the boundaries between different roles that we might play in our work and about disclosure and confidentiality. We are not inventing an entirely new field, but recognizing changes that need to occur in an existing profession. We can build on what we have and add incrementally and cautiously to these standards.

There are several key questions that conflict engagement standards will have to address. They will have to address role clarity versus role flexibility (how clear do we have to be about the role we are playing, and what is required to change that role?). They will have to address the issue of acceptable or constructive approaches to conflict (are we committed to nonviolence, to honesty, to creating a fair process for all, no matter what our role?). They will have to revisit the issue of confidentiality since not all of the roles we play will allow the same kind of confidentiality that mediators or arbitrators can offer. They will have to address the issue of qualifications, making sure that these are not done in a way that is mainly intended to create a market for trainers.

Ethical standards often evolve from how we have handled ethical dilemmas. The first time mediators faced information about child abuse or criminal activity, they had to start thinking about the principles that ought to govern their actions in these areas (and their legal obligations as well). I believe that ethical dilemmas, troubling though they may be, are healthy—if we face the challenges they pose. The more dilemmas we face, the clearer we are about who we are and what we do, and the better able we are to present ourselves in a coherent way. I look forward to the dilemmas a new self-concept will present and the opportunity to use them to define ourselves, refine our standards, improve our practice, and protect the public.

## Our Purpose and Values

At the heart of what I am suggesting about redefining our field is actually a continuity of purpose and values—but a broadening conception of how we think about implementing these. We have always been about helping people, groups, and organizations handle conflict in a productive, constructive way. We have always expressed the belief that the issue was not whether we were in conflict but how we conducted ourselves as disputants. We have always advocated a belief that avoiding conflict could be as big a problem as escalating it. Nothing I am suggesting changes that.

Our values about conflict, although articulated in many different ways, have generally included certain common principles:

- *Being hard on the problem, easy on the people.* We may articulate this as "separate the people from the problem," "respect our adversaries," or "love the sinner, hate the sin," and for many of us, this has translated into a commitment to nonviolence. The underlying goal is to ensure that conflict is carried out in a way that does minimal damage to the basic well-being of any of the participants.

• *Empowering disputants.* Underneath many of our activities and approaches is the belief that if disputants can be empowered to engage in conflict, they will do so productively. Rather than take over decision making for people in conflict, we try to find ways of enabling disputants to handle their own conflict. When they can't, we work to minimize the degree to which they must cede power to others to deal with their issues. Implied here is the belief that people know what is best for them, and in the end they have the right to make what we might consider to be bad decisions.

• *Respecting diversity.* We may not always actualize this the way we would like, but as a field, we have made a commitment to ensuring that our services are accessible to people from a diversity of backgrounds. This has meant working to increase the diversity of our field and being sensitive to the diversity of approaches people take to conflict based on their cultural experience and background.

• *Believing in communication.* Much of what we do in almost every approach we take is to try to establish and nurture effective communication. Communication itself cannot solve all problems, but it is a sine qua non for people who want to handle conflicts effectively.

• *Promoting social justice.* Conflict is a necessary part of social change, and if we are committed to a more just world—more peaceful, democratic, and egalitarian—then we must not suppress conflict. Part of a commitment to social justice (and to empowerment) is a belief that those who are vulnerable to exploitation and oppression need special forms of protection when they are in conflict, but they do not need to be shielded from conflict itself.

• *Valuing creativity.* Much of our approach to conflict is about how to help people discover ways through what appears to be an intractable problem, and this means helping people be creative. When we talk about exploring interests, reframing problems, and paying attention to the integrative potential, we are mostly talking about ways in which we can help people stay creative in the face of conflict, fear, anger, and stress.

- *Maintaining optimism*. We might not state this as a value, but it is embedded in much of what do. Conflict professionals often work in dismal situations, but we do so in the belief that good can come out of bad circumstances, that people can grow, organizations can learn, bitter hatred and animosities can change. It is this optimism that fuels this book. There is a crisis. We can face it, and in the end we will be stronger because we have.

Nothing that I am suggesting implies abandoning or even changing any of these values in a significant way. If anything, I am simply suggesting that we face the implications of our values and recommit to them. If we are going to empower people, give meaning to our social justice concerns, honor diversity, value the creative potential of conflict, and promote authentic communication, we have to do more than focus on resolution. We have to be more than third-party neutrals. I am suggesting that there is a continuity of purpose and beliefs inherent in what we have to do to confront the current challenges to our field. The deeper we commit ourselves to our purpose and values, the more flexible we will be about how to implement them.

## The Knowledge Base of the Conflict Field

Broadening our role definition and purpose raises the question, Why us? Why should we be the ones to take on this broader approach to conflict? What is relevant about what we know and what we have done? I have addressed this question throughout the book, but I think it gets to the heart of both our identity and our potential.

Intertwined with these questions are all the doubts we have about what it is that we really have to offer to people in conflict. These doubts, which we all experience at some level, can limit our thinking and willingness to take risks. If what we feel confident about is how to act as third-party neutrals or how to conduct a mediation or facilitation process, then those are the roles that we will naturally limit our practice to. But we know much more than that. To be effective as third-party neutrals, we have to have knowledge and skills that are also relevant to the broader roles I have proposed. Just as the background many of us have had as advocates or activists has helped prepare us for our third-party roles, the experience we have had as third parties has honed skills that we can apply in other ways as well.

The foundation on which we have built our work goes well beyond understanding the process and role of mediation or facilitation. It includes the following dimensions:

- *Understanding the dynamics of conflict*. We have had to develop ways of making sense of conflict. Some of us use fairly broad theories of conflict and others very concrete and tangible models, but all effective conflict professionals need some way of understanding the nature of the conflicts that we encounter.

- *Understanding communication*. Working to alter unproductive patterns of communication is built into almost everything we do. Sometimes we do this by inserting ourselves in the middle of a communication, sometimes by coaching people how to communicate differently, sometimes by helping people look at their own communication pattern. Attention to listening, framing, nonverbal communication, cultural differences in communication, structures of communications, and other aspects of communication is key to our ability to be effective.

- *Dealing with power dynamics*. One aspect of all conflict is the application of some form of power. Although we never really balance power or create a level playing field, we do look at the power dynamics and work with these. As neutrals, we often reinforce the use of certain types of power (for example, persuasion or rewards) and discourage other forms (coercion or punishment). We look at what people's real choices are, how these can be expanded, and how these can be put on the table in a useful way. In this and many other ways, we work with the currency of power in conflict.

- *Looking at the interplay between the interpersonal and the systemic aspects of conflict.* Most conflict has both an interpersonal and a systemic component. A conflict between an employer and a worker may involve both interpersonal animosity and the structural setup of labor-management relations in an organization. We are used to helping people sort out these differences and work with them.
- *Understanding the relationship between power, rights, and interests.* We work with the range of human needs and interests people bring to conflict. That is a key part of our training and experience. But we also work with the interplay among these and the rights people are asserting and the power they are employing.
- *Working with both the integrative and distributive aspects of conflict.* In the end, no person working with conflict can avoid or ignore the complex interaction between these two aspects—the problem of the prisoner's dilemma. Some of us may try to emphasize one element or another, but in the end, we always have to work in some way with both, as do all people in conflict.
- *Understanding the negotiation and problem-solving process.* We may not work as negotiators, but we do work with negotiation and problem solving in almost any role we take. If we are going to work directly as negotiators, we will have to develop new skills to be sure, but the experience and perspective we have from our work as third parties will be very relevant.
- *Being culturally aware.* Unless we are functioning in a monocultural context, we have had to deal with the interaction of different cultural approaches to conflict or decision making.

These areas of knowledge and skill are relevant not just to mediation or facilitation, but to everything that we can do as conflict specialists. How well we have developed our understanding or skill in any of these areas is of course varied, and how well we are able to generalize their application from one context to another and one role to another will also vary. But we have much broader skills and knowledge about conflict than simply how to function in one role.

Our challenge is to take a broad enough view so that we are not locked into the particular framework we have practiced in. Instead, we have to look beyond our specific context to our values and knowledge base in order to maximize what we have to offer people in conflict. How we do this as individuals may be less to the point than how our field as a whole faces this challenge. The key for us as individuals and as a field is to trust that we have a set of valuable skills that we can offer to people in conflict from a greater diversity of roles and with a broader purpose than we have traditionally embraced.

Our new self-concept will have to be reflected in the educational programs and avenues by which people enter conflict resolution. Some of this is already happening. Many negotiation and alternative dispute resolution courses in law schools reflect the experience, knowledge, and values of the conflict resolution field but are geared to preparing people to be effective advocates. There are also courses and seminars preparing advocates to represent their clients in conflict resolution processes. This is just the beginning. As we rethink our role as conflict practitioners, the courses we teach, seminars we present, conference sessions we offer, and degree programs we contribute to will all have to be retooled to reflect our new self-definition. Instead of degrees in conflict resolution, we will have more programs in conflict engagement. There are already programs in conflict transformation (for example, at Eastern Mennonite University) that reflect a realization that our job is not necessarily to resolve all conflict but to change the way it is conducted. We should look to these as models for where we need to go and build on them as we create more opportunities for teaching a broader approach to our work.

## Reaching Our Potential

The underlying reasons for the work of conflict resolution practitioners have not diminished. Our services are needed. But we have not realized our full potential, and this is something we have to face if we are going to continue to grow and thrive as a professional field. What is that potential?

The conflict field has the potential to make a much bigger difference than we have made in how conflicts are handled in almost all arenas. We can play a role in international, interpersonal, communal, organizational, and societal conflicts. We can't take away the social forces that produce conflict. We can't get rid of violence, exploitation, oppression, racism, inequality, or hatred—certainly not by ourselves. But we can offer people in conflict better choices, more productive alternatives, a far more extensive range of services, and in the end more optimism and hope than we have been able to do so far. In this way, we can have a constructive impact on the most important conflicts of our time.

I believe conflict professionals have something important to offer to the people of the Middle East and the Persian Gulf. We have a great deal to contribute to the most strident and challenging conflicts of our time, whether we are talking about abortion, oil drilling, religious conflicts, or labor wars. We have something to offer because these conflicts are crying out for a transformation. But they are not likely to see our services as valuable unless we are ready to work with the people, communities, and systems involved on their terms and in pursuit of their goals. We can do this if we focus on our most essential purpose: to help people pursue conflict effectively and constructively.

This is not a simple or easy change. But it is the challenge that our field as a whole has to undertake in the next twenty-five years if we want to continue to reach for our potential, to offer the most and the best we have to give to people in conflict. It is how we can build on the experience of the previous twenty-five years and continue to grow as both a field of practitioners and a service to society. As with almost all of the most significant changes we make in our lives, the hardest challenge is also the simplest. Our greatest challenge will be to think of ourselves and the work we do in a different way. As we do this, we will be able to project our role more broadly and creatively, and I believe we will find many new opportunities and a whole new range of eager clients. But changing the way we think of ourselves is not so easy. Our self-view is at the core of how we function and what we do. When we see ourselves differently, people and communities engaged in conflict will also see us in a new way, and they will be more attracted to seeking out our services. Our changing view of ourselves will both reflect the market for our services and shape it.

The actual change in how we think of ourselves is not even that great, but its implications are. When we think of ourselves as conflict specialists, we don't give up anything about our identity; we add to it. When we focus on helping people engage in conflict, we don't abandon a commitment to effective conflict resolution or conflict management; we put it in a broader context. At times, this will mean challenging ourselves greatly as we look at what we actually do in a conflict. For example, the first time we work with people to escalate a conflict may be very difficult. But we know that raising the level of conflict is sometimes a necessary prelude to settling it.

Many of us have been struggling with these issues and will continue to do so. As time goes on, we will develop the conceptual tools, the educational system, the organizational structures, the professional skills, and the track record that will allow us to help people engage in conflict and resolve it, to find their own voice and respect others, to mobilize their own resources and power and work with others, to raise their most important issues and concerns, and to appreciate the concerns of those with whom they are in conflict.

As exciting and rewarding as it has been to be part of our profession's development for the past twenty-five years and to see the way in which we have grown from an idea and offering to a large and diverse field of practice, the next twenty-five years will be even more exciting. I believe we will experience a dramatic and rich expansion in our thinking, our services, our acceptance, and our impact on conflict. It won't be easy or smooth, but it will be important and energizing. We can look forward to interesting, challenging, and rewarding times.

# References

Alfini, J. J. "Trashing, Bashing, and Hashing It Out: Is This the End of Good Mediation?" *Florida State University Law Review*, 1991, *19*, 47–66.

Alinsky, S. *Reveille for Radicals*. Chicago: University of Chicago Press, 1946.

Auerbach, J. E. *Personal and Executive Coaching: The Complete Guide for Mental Health Professionals*. Ventura, Calif.: Executive College Press, 2001.

Axelrod, R. *The Evolution of Cooperation*. New York: Basic Books, 1984.

Barris, M. A., and others. *Working with High Conflict Families of Divorce: A Guide for Professionals*. Northvale, N.J.: Jason Aronson, 2001.

Bazemore, G., and Schiff, M. (eds.). *Restorative Community Justice: Repairing Harm and Transforming Communities*. Cincinnati, Ohio: Anderson Publishing, 2001.

Bingham, L. B. "Why Suppose? Let's Find Out: A Public Policy Research Program on Dispute Resolution." *Journal of Dispute Resolution*, 2002, *2002*(1), 101–126.

Bingham, L., Chesmore, G., Moon, Y., and Napoli, L. M. "Mediating Employment Disputes at the United States Postal Service: A Comparison of In-House and Outside Neutral Mediators." *Review of Public Personnel Administration*, 2000, *20*(1), 5–19.

Brett, J. M., Goldberg, S. B., and Ury, W. L. *Getting Disputes Resolved: Designing Systems to Cut the Costs of Conflicts*. San Francisco: Jossey-Bass, 1988.

Britell, J. "Can Consensus Processes Resolve Environmental Conflicts?"

Aug. 12, 1997. [http://www.harborside.com/home/j/britell/use/use10.html].

Bush, R. A., and Folger, J. P. *The Promise of Mediation: Responding to Conflict Through Empowerment and Recognition*. San Francisco: Jossey-Bass, 1994.

Bush, R. A., and Folger, J. P. "Transformative Mediation and Third Party Interventions: Ten Hallmarks of a Transformative Approach to Practice." *Mediation Quarterly*, 1996, *13*(4), 263–278.

Cloke, K. *Mediating Dangerously*. San Francisco: Jossey-Bass, 2000.

Coogler, O. J. *Structured Mediation in Divorce Settlement*. San Francisco: New Lexington Press, 1978.

Coser, L. A. *The Functions of Social Conflict*. New York: Free Press, 1956.

Curle, A. *Making Peace*. London: Tavistock, 1971.

Engle Merry, S., and Silbey, S. S. "What Do Plaintiffs Want? Reexamining the Concept of Dispute." *Justice System Journal*, 1984, 9(2), 151–178.

Fisher, R., and Ury, W. *Getting to Yes*. Boston: Houghton Mifflin, 1981.

Fiss, O. M. "Against Settlement." *Yale Law Journal*, 1984, 93, 1073–1090.

Goldsmith, M. (ed.). *Coaching for Leadership: How the World's Greatest Coaches Help Leaders Learn*. San Francisco: Jossey-Bass, 2000.

Golten, M. M., Smith, M., and Woodrow, P. "Hammers in Search of Nails: Responding to Critics of Collaborative Processes." 2002. [http://Consensus.fsu.edu/ epp/hammers.html].

Grillo, T. "The Mediation Alternative: Process Dangers for Women." *Yale Law Journal*, 1991, *100*, 1545–1593.

Hann, R., Barr, C., and Associates. *Evaluation of the Ontario Mandatory Mediation Program: Final Report—The First 23 Months*. Ontario: Queens Printer, 2001.

Haynes, J. *Divorce Mediation: A Practical Guide for Therapists and Counselors*. New York: Springer, 1981.

Hensler, D. R. "Suppose It's Not True: Challenging Mediation Ideology." *Journal of Dispute Resolution*, 2002, 2002(1), 81–99.

Hudson, F. M. *The Handbook of Coaching: A Comprehensive Guide for Managers, Executives, Consultants, and Human Resource Professionals*. San Francisco: Jossey-Bass, 1999.

Innes, J. E., and Booher, D. E. "Consensus Building and Complex Adaptive Systems: A Framework for Evaluating Collaborative Planning." *Journal of the American Planning Association*, 1999, 65(4), 412–424.

Jones, W., and Hughes, S. "Complexity, Conflict Resolution, and How the Mind Works." *Conflict Resolution Quarterly*, Summer, 2003, 20(4), 485–484.

Kakalik, J., and others. *Just, Speedy and Inexpensive?* Santa Monica, Calif.: Rand Institute, 1997.

Kelly, J. B. "Is Mediation Less Expensive? Comparison of Mediated and Adversarial Divorce Costs." *Mediation Quarterly*, 1990, 8(2), 15–26.

Kressel, K., and Pruitt, D. (eds.). *Mediation Research*. San Francisco: Jossey-Bass, 1989.

Kriesberg, L., Northrup, T., and Thorson, S. (eds.). *Intractable Conflicts and Their Transformation*. Syracuse, N.Y.: Syracuse University Press, 1989.

Kristol, I. "Conflicts That Can't Be Resolved." AEI Online, Sept. 5, 1997. [http://www.aei.org/publications/pubID.8011/pub_detail.asp].

Kronman, A. T. *The Lost Lawyer: Failing Ideals of the Legal Profession*. Cambridge, Mass.: Harvard University Press, 1993.

Kruk, E. (ed.). *Mediation and Conflict Resolution in Social Work and the Human Services*. Chicago: Nelson-Hall, 1997.

Landre, B. K., and Knuth, B. A. "Success of Citizen Advisory Committees in Consensus-Based Water Resources Planning in the Great Lakes Basin." *Society and Natural Resources*, 1993, 6(3), 229–257.

Lang, M., and Taylor, A. *The Making of a Mediator*. San Francisco: Jossey-Bass, 2000.

Laue, J., and Cormick, C. "The Ethics of Intervention in Community Disputes." In G. Bermant, H. Kelman, and D. Warwick (eds.), *The Ethics of Social Intervention*. Washington, D.C.: Halstead Press, 1978.

Lax, D., and Sebenius, J. *The Manager as Negotiator*. New York: Free Press, 1986.

Leach, W. D., and Sabatier, P. A. "Facilitators, Coordinators, and Outcomes." In R. O'Leary and L. Bingham (eds.), *The Promise and Performance of Environmental Conflict Resolution*. Washington, D.C.: Resources for the Future Press, 2003.

Lederach, J. P. *Preparing for Peace: Conflict Transformation Across Cultures*. Syracuse, N.Y.: Syracuse University Press, 1995.

Lederach, J. P. *The Little Book of Conflict Transformation*. Intercourse, Pa.: Good Books, 2003.

Lipsky, D. B., Seeber, R. L., and Fincher, R. *Emerging Systems for Managing Workplace Conflict: Lessons from American Corporations for Managers and Dispute Resolution Professionals*. San Francisco: Jossey-Bass, 2003.

Luban, D. "Settlements and the Erosion of the Public Realm." *Georgetown Law Journal*, 1995, 83, 2619–2662.

Macfarlane, J. *Court-Based Mediation in Civil Cases: An Evaluation of the Toronto General Division ADR Centre*. Toronto: Ontario Ministry of the Attorney-General, 1995.

Macfarlane, J. "Why Do People Settle?" *McGill Law Journal*, 2001, 45, 663–711.

Macfarlane, J. "Culture Change? A Tale of Two Cities and Mandatory Court-Connected Mediation." *Journal of Dispute Resolution*, 2002, 2002(2), 241–345.

Macfarlane, J. "Experiences of Collaborative Law: Preliminary Results from the Collaborative Lawyering Research Project." *Journal of Dispute Resolution*, forthcoming.

Mayer, B. "The Dynamics of Power in Mediation and Conflict Resolution." *Mediation Quarterly*, Summer 1987, no. 16, 75–86.

Mayer, B. "Conflict Resolution." In R. Edward and others (eds.), *Social Work Encyclopedia*. (19th ed.) Washington, D.C.: NASW Press, 1995.

Mayer, B. *The Dynamics of Conflict Resolution: A Practitioner's Guide*. San Francisco: Jossey-Bass, 2000.

Mayer, B. "Who Pays? Money Matters from a Practitioner's Perspective." In J. P. Lederach and J. M. Jenner (eds.), *Into the Eye of the Storm: A Handbook of International Peacebuilding*. San Francisco: Jossey-Bass, 2002.

Mayer, B. "Facilitative Mediation." In J. Folberg, A. Milne, and T. Salen (eds.), *Divorce Mediation*. (2nd ed.) New York: Guilford Press, forthcoming.

Mayer, B., Ghais, S., and McKay, J. A. *Constructive Engagement Resource Guide: Practical Advice for Dialogue Among Facilities, Workers, Communities and Regulators*. Washington, D.C.: U.S. Environmental Protection Agency, 1999.

Mayer, B., Wildau, S., and Valchev, R. "Promoting Multi-Cultural Consensus Building in Bulgaria." *Cultural Survival*, 1995, 19(3), 64–68.

McAdoo, B., and Hinshaw, A. "The Challenge of Institutionalizing Alternative Dispute Resolution: Attorney Perspectives on the Effect of Rule 187 on Civil Litigation in Missouri." *Missouri Law Review*, 2002, 67, 473–572.

McCloskey, M. "Concerns over the Push to Do Business Collaboratively." *High Country News*, May 13, 1996.

McEwen, C. A. "Toward a Program-Based ADR Research Agenda." *Negotiation Journal*, 1999, *15*(4), 325–334.

McEwen, C. A., and Maiman, R. J. "Mediation in Small Claims Court: Achieving Compliance Though Consent." *Law and Society Review*, 1984, *18*, 11–49.

McEwen, C., and Milburn, T. W. "Explaining a Paradox of Mediation." *Negotiation Journal*, Jan. 1993, pp. 23–35.

McEwen, C. A., and Wissler, R. L. "Finding Out If It Is True: Comparing Mediation and Negotiation Through Research." *Journal of Dispute Resolution*, 2002, *2002*(1), 131–142.

Mnooken, R. H., Peppet, S. R., and Tulumello, A. S. *Beyond Winning: Negotiation to Create Value in Deals and Disputes*. Cambridge, Mass.: Harvard University Press, 2000.

Moore, C. W. *The Mediation Process: Practical Strategies for Resolving Conflict*. San Francisco: Jossey-Bass, 1991.

Mosten, F. *Mediation Career Guide: A Strategic Approach to Building a Successful Practice*. San Francisco: Jossey-Bass, 2001.

Nader, L. "The ADR Explosion—The Implications of Rhetoric in Legal Reform." *Windsor Yearbook of Access to Justice*, 1988, *8*, 269–291.

Nader, L. "Controlling Processes in the Practice of Law: Hierarchy and Pacification in the Movement to Re-Form Dispute Ideology." *Ohio State Journal on Dispute Resolution*, 1993, *9*(1), 1–25.

Noble, C. "Coaching Conflict Management." Unpublished paper, 2001. [www.cinergycoaching.com].

O'Neal, M. N. *Executive Coaching with Backbone and Heart: A Systems Approach to Engaging Leaders with Their Challenges*. San Francisco: Jossey-Bass, 2000.

Osterman, P. *Gathering Power: The Future of Progressive Politics in America*. Boston: Beacon Press, 2003.

Pearson, J. "An Evaluation of Alternatives to Court Adjudication." *Justice System Journal*, 1982, *7*, 420–444.

Pearson, J., and Thoennes, N. "The Mediation and Adjudication of Divorce Disputes: Some Costs and Benefits." *Family Advocate*, 1982, *3*, 4.

Pearson, J., and Thoennes, N. "Divorce Mediation: A Decade of Research." In K. Kressel and D. Pruitt (eds.), *Mediation Research*. San Francisco: Jossey-Bass, 1989.

Pearson, J., Thoennes, N., and Vanderkooi, L. "The Decision to Mediate: Profiles of Individuals Who Accept and Reject the Opportunity to Mediate Contested Child Custody and Visitation Issues." *Journal of Divorce*, 1982, 6(1).

Raiffa, H. *The Art and Science of Negotiation*. Cambridge, Mass.: Harvard University Press, 1982.

Rifkin, J. "Mediation from a Feminist Perspective: Promise and Problems." *Law and Inequality*, 1984, 2, 21–31.

Robson, M. *Quality Circles: A Practical Guide*. Brookfield, Vt.: Gower Publishing Co., 1982.

Ross, M. G. *Community Organization: Theory, Principles, Practices*. (2nd ed.) New York: HarperCollins, 1967.

Rothman, J. *Resolving Identity-Based Conflict in Nations, Organizations, and Communities*. San Francisco: Jossey-Bass, 1997.

Schneider, A. K. "Shattering Negotiation Myths: Empirical Evidence on the Effectiveness of Negotiation Style." *Harvard Negotiation Law Review*, 2002, 7, 143–233.

Sebenius, J. K. "Six Habits of Merely Effective Negotiators." *Harvard Business Review*, Apr. 2001, 87–95.

Senge, P. M. *The Fifth Discipline: The Art and Practice of the Learning Organization*. New York: Doubleday, 1990.

Shaffer, M. "Divorce Mediation: A Feminist Perspective." *University of Toronto Faculty of Law Review*, 1998, 46(1), 162–200.

Sherman, L. W., Strang, H., and Woods, D. J. "Recidivism Patterns in the Canberra Reintegrate Shaming Experiments (RISE)." Camberra: Centre for Restorative Justice, Australian National University, 2003. [http://www.aic.gov.au/RestorativeJustice/rise/recidivism/index.html].

Silbey, S. S. "The Emperor's New Clothes: Mediation Mythology and Markets." *Journal of Dispute Resolution*, 2002, 2002(1), 171–178.

Strang, H., and Braithwaite, J. (eds.). *Restorative Justice and Civil Society*. Cambridge: Cambridge University Press, 2001.

Tessler, P. H. *Collaborative Law: Achieving Effective Resolution in Divorce Without Litigation*. Chicago: American Bar Association, 2001.

*Thirteen Days*. New Line Studios, 2000.

Thomas, K. W. "Conflict and Conflict Management." In M. D. Dunnette (ed.), *Handbook of Industrial and Organizational Psychology*. Skokie, Ill.: Rand McNally, 1983.

Ury, W. L. *The Third Side: Why We Fight and How We Can Stop*. New York: Penguin Putnam, 2000.

Walton, R. W., and McKersie, R. B. *A Behavioral Theory of Negotiations*. New York: McGraw-Hill, 1980.

Welsh, N. A. "Making Deals in Court-Connected Mediation: What's Justice Got to Do with It?" *Washington University Law Quarterly*, 2001a, 79(3), 787–861.

Welsh, N. A. "The Thinning Vision of Self-Determination in Court-Connected Mediation: The Inevitable Price of Institutionalization?" *Harvard Negotiation Law Review*, 2001b, 6(1), 25–96.

Welsh, N. A. "Disputants' Decision Control in Court-Connected Mediation: A Hollow Promise Without Procedural Justice." *Journal of Dispute Resolution*, 2002, 2002(1), 179–192.

Wheeler, L. "Mandatory Family Mediation and Domestic Violence." *Southern Illinois University Law Journal*, 2002, 2002(26), 559–574.

Williams, G. R. *Legal Negotiations and Settlement*. St. Paul, Minn.: West, 1983.

Williams, G. R. "Style and Effectiveness in Negotiation." In L. Hall (ed.), *Negotiation: Strategies for Mutual Gain*. Thousand Oaks, Calif.: Sage, 1993.

Wissler, R. L. "Court-Connected Mediation in General Civil Cases: What We Know from Empirical Research." *Ohio State Journal on Dispute Resolution*, 2002, 17(3), 642–704.

Zehr, H. *Changing Lenses: A New Focus for Crime and Justice*. Scottsdale, Pa.: Herald Press, 1990.

Zylstra, A. "Mediation and Domestic Violence: A Practical Screening Method for Mediators and Mediation Program Administrators." *Journal of Dispute Resolution*, 2001, pp. 253–300.

# About the Author

*Bernard S. Mayer,* Ph.D., is a partner at CDR Associates in Boulder, Colorado. He has worked since the late 1970s in the conflict resolution field as a mediator, facilitator, trainer, researcher, program administrator, and dispute systems designer. He has mediated or facilitated the resolution of many different types of conflicts, ranging from labor-management, public policy, and ethnic conflicts, to business, family, community, housing, and intergovernmental conflicts. He has worked with corporations; labor unions; Native American governments and associations; federal, state, and local agencies; public interest groups; professional associations; public schools; child welfare programs; mental health services; and universities. He has consulted on conflict management procedures and trained mediators, negotiators, and conflict intervenors throughout the United State and internationally. He has been internationally recognized as a trainer and an innovative leader in applying mediation and conflict resolution to new arenas such as child welfare, mental health, and disputes between public agencies and involuntary clients. Mayer is the author of *The Dynamics of Conflict Resolution: A Practitioner's Guide* (Jossey-Bass, 2000) as well as many other writings about conflict and conflict resolution.

# Index

## A

Academy of Family Mediators, 153
Accountability, 287–289
Adaptation, 199–205
ADR. *See* Alternative dispute resolution
Advocacy: constructive criticism *versus*, 129–133; embracing, 277–279; neutrality and, 118–119. *See also* Advocates
Advocates: bringing, into conflict resolution field, 272–279; as conflict analysts and strategists, 253; as conflict specialists, 250–260; as counselors, 256–257; definition of, 250–259; learning from, 259–265; lessons from different kinds of, 265–266; as negotiators, 257–259; obstacles to embracing, 272–275; as problem solvers, 256; and working along distributional dimension, 261–263
African Americans, 172, 173
Alaska Wolf Summit, 15–17, 239
Alfini, J. J., 113
Alinsky, S., 225
Alternative dispute resolution (ADR), 43, 74, 159, 162
Alternative Dispute Resolution Committee (American Bar Association), 153, 275
American Bar Association, 7, 153, 275
Anger, respect *versus*, 133–135

Annan, K., 108
Aria Institute (Yellow Springs, Ohio), 76
Arctic National Wilderness Reserve, 12
Association for Conflict Resolution (ACR), 7, 10, 11, 67, 153, 154, 244
Association of Family Conciliation Courts, 7, 67, 153, 275
Assumptions, 170–171
Auerback, J. E., 231
Australia, 67, 172
*Avocat*, 250
Avoidance: and deciding to engage, 206–210; from, to engagement, 205–206
Axelrod, R., 257, 258

## B

Barr, C., 68
Barris, M. A., 216
BATNA (best alternative to a negotiated agreement), 197
Bazemore, G., 276
Begin, M., 84
Bible, 263
Bingham, L. B., 56, 57, 73
Black Panthers, 196, 197
Booher, D. E., 202
Bosnia, 92
Brager, G., 278
Braithwaite, J., 276
Brett, J. M., 35, 48, 263

Britell, J., 43, 63
Bush administration, 65
Bush, G. H., 92
Bush, G. W., 92
Bush, R. A., 146, 190–192

C

California, 58, 59
Camp David negotiations, 84
Canadian Industrial Relations Board, 92
Carter Center, 4
Carter, J., 10, 84, 92, 108
CDR Associates, 4, 283, 287
Chesmore, G., 57, 73
Cincinnati, Ohio, 76, 77
Civil Rights Act (1964), 159
Civil rights movement, 196
Clients: demand of, for new roles of conflict specialists, 217–220; empowering, 260–261
Clinton administration, 65, 110, 199
Cloke, K., 184, 239
Closure, 270–271
Coaching, 230–237
Collaboration, 31
Colorado, 275
Columbia University, 278
Common Sense Initiative (EPA), 50
Communication: and advocate as communicator, 253–255; constructive, *versus* passionate advocacy, 129–133
Community conflict, 75–77
Community Relations Service (Department of Justice), 159
Competition: constructive, 122–123; *versus* cooperation, 120–123
Complexity, value of, 202–205
Conditional realization, 93–94
Conference on Racial Equality, 197
Conflict: community, 75–77; as complex adaptive system, 199–205; efficiency and effectiveness of, 48–52; essential value of social, 175; family, 66–72; formal and informal approaches to, 156–158; integrative potential of, 35; organizational, 72–75; understanding developmental tasks of, 187–190; what people want in, 23–29
Conflict resolution: critiques of, 41–55; efficiency and effectiveness of critiques

of, 48–52; experiential and personal critiques of, 48–52; facing resistance to, 78–81; nature of crisis in, 49; as process, 144–147; responding to crisis in, 79
Conflict resolution field: birth of, 158–160; bringing advocates into, 272–279; essence of, 34–38; four problematic assumptions of, 29–33; knowledge base of, 291–294; values, 106
Conflict resolution, redefined: and accountability, 287–289; and business of being conflict specialist, 281–289; describing practice of, 283–285; and marketing services, 285–287; purpose and values of, 289–291; and reaching potential, 294–296
Conflict resolution, societal dimension of: and birth of conflict resolution as field, 158–160; brief history of, 155–156; and diversity, 170–176; and formal and informal approaches to conflict, 156–158; and individualizing societal problem, 174–175; and limit of resolution and power of engagement, 176–178; as profession, 152–155; as social control, 160–167; as social movement, 150–152
Conflict specialist: as advocate, 223–224, 271–272; advocates as, 250–266; client demand for new roles of, 217–220; as coach, 230–237; expanding role of, 217–222; as organizer, 225–229; roles and skills, 220–222; as strategist, 229–230; and third party, 237–243; what, offer advocates, 266–272
Consensus Building Institute, 4
Consensus-based processes, 63; and decision-making authority, 64–66
Coogler, O. J., 67, 282
Cooperation, competition *versus*, 120–123
Cormick, C., 224
Coser, L. A., 175
Counseling, 256–257
CPR Institute for Dispute Resolution, 74
Cuba, 35, 102, 103
Cuban American community, 102, 103
Curle, A., 184

## D

Deal, cutting, 264–265
Democracy, preserving, 167–168
Disputants: commitment to empowering, 37; empowering, 267. *See also* Clients
Diversity: assumptions about, 170–171; and essential value of social conflict, 175; and talking about racism, sexism, ethnocentrism, and homophobia, 171–174

## E

Elian Gonzales case, use of mediation in, 102–103
Employment Tribunal (New Zealand), 92
Energy, displacing, 164–165
Engagement, conflict: from avoidance to, 205–206; constructiveness of, 193–196; definition of, 184–193; field, 178; from, to resolution, 212–214; incorporating, in system roles, 244–246; as ongoing activity, 211–212; power of, 38–39, 176–178; from resolution to, 119–120; and third party, 238–240; *versus* transformation, 190–193
Engle Merry, S., 76
Environmental policy, 60–66
Environmental Protection Agency (EPA), 5
Equal employment opportunity (EEO), 57, 73
Ethnocentrism, 171–174

## F

Family conflicts, 66–72
Family Mediation Canada, 67
Federal Mediation and Conciliation Service (FMCS), 159
Feinberg, K., 109
Fighting: and helping people fight, 196–199; how to assist in, 198–199; value of, 197–198
Fincher, R., 73
Fisher, R., 4, 10, 35, 125
Fiss, O. M., 46
Folger, J. P., 146, 190–192
Ford Foundation, 159

*Foundation for Negotiation and Conflict Resolution*, 227
*Functions of Social Conflict, The* (Coser), 175
Furbearers Roundtable, 60

## G

Gandhi, M., 120, 132, 143
*Getting Disputes Resolved* (Brett, Goldberg, and Ury), 48
*Getting to Yes* (Fisher and Ury), 125
Ghais, S., 64
Goldberg, S. B., 35, 48, 263
Goldsmith, M., 231
Golten, M. M., 58
Gonzales, E., 99, 102, 103
Great Lakes region, 64
Grillo, T., 52, 67

## H

Haiti, 92
Hann, R., 58, 68
Haynes, J., 67
Hensler, D. R., 52
Hewlett Foundation, 159, 280
Hidden agenda, 105–108
Hierarchical institutions, confronting, 168–69
Hinshaw, A., 58
Holbrook, R., 92
Homophobia, 171–174
Hopi nation, 159
Hudson, F. M., 231
Hughes, S., 38, 201

## I

Impact, 27–28
India, 10
Individualization, 174–175
Inequality, reinforcing, 162–163
Innes, J. E., 202
Integrating roles, 246–247
Integrative potential, 267–269
Integrative trap, 123–125
Interdisciplinary Committee on Child Custody (Colorado), 275
Interests, *versus* positions, 125–129
Iraq, 11
Ireland, 67

Israel, 133
Issues: defining, 165–166; privatizing, 161–162

**J**

Jones, W., 38, 201
Justice, procedural, 24–25

**K**

Kakalik, J., 52, 88
Kelly, J. B., 58
Kennedy, J. F., 36
Khrushchev, N. S., 36
Knuth, B. A., 64
Kressel, K., 41
Kriesberg, L., 191
Kristol, I., 44
Kronman, A. T., 224, 251
Kruk, E., 66

**L**

Landre, B. K., 64
Lang, M., 232
Laue, J., 224
Law Enforcement Assistance Act, 159
Lax, D., 35, 198, 257
Leach, W. D., 58–59, 64
Lederach, J. P., 191
Level playing field, 141–144
Lipsky, D. B., 73
Local interests, 63
Luban, D., 46

**M**

Macfarlane, J., 53, 56, 68, 97, 98, 113, 276
Maiman, R. J., 56
Major conflicts, 88–89; role of conflict resolution in, 9–21
Making Mediation Work (Mosten), 285
Manager as Negotiator (Lax and Sebenius), 198
Mandela, N., 108
Marginalization, 91–95
Marketing, 285–287
Mayer, B., 32, 35, 53, 64, 66, 105, 135, 143, 150, 166, 227, 233
McAdoo, B., 58

McCloskey, M., 43
McEwen, C. A., 23, 56, 57, 112
McKay, J. A., 64
McKersie, R. B., 35, 195
McNamara, R., 35
Mediation: acceptance of, 99–102; beyond, 113–114; and conditional realization, 93–94; defining, 85–86; and direct resistance, 90–91; and fear of impact, 94–95; and hidden ideological agenda, 105–108; hostile dependence of, on mandatory programs, 111–113; and indirect resistance, 89–90; marginalization of, 91–95; misuse of, 95–99; problem of neutrality in, 83–86; reasons for rejection of, 86–91; as supply-driven practice, 56; when, works, 103–105; and working on major conflicts, 88–89
Mennonite Central Committee, 15
Middle East, 10, 92, 110, 191, 199, 295
Milburn, T. W., 23, 112
Mitchell, G., 92, 108, 110
Mnooken, R. H., 257
Moon, Y., 57, 73
Moore, C. W., 35, 239, 269
Mosten, F., 285
Mott Foundation, 159, 280

**N**

NAACP, 197
Nader, L., 43, 46
Napoli, L. M., 57, 73
National Association for Community Mediation, 7, 153
National Association for Mediation in Education, 153
National Conference of Peacemaking and Conflict Resolution (PeaceWeb), 7, 153, 275
National Mediation Board, 159
Navajo nation, 159
Needs, focusing on, 269–271
Needs-based approach, 35–36
Negotiating, 257–259
Neutrality: and advocacy, 118–119; problem of, 83–86, 116–120; suspicion about, 17
Neutrals, 63–64
Noble, C., 232
North Korea, 10, 199–200

Northern Ireland, 15, 92, 138, 214
Northrup, T., 191

O

O'Laughlin, J., 102
Ombudsperson, 216
O'Neal, M. N., 231
Optimism, 169–170
Organizational conflict, 72–75
Osterman, P., 225
Ottawa, 97

P

Pakistan, 10
Palestine, 133
Papua, New Guinea, 22, 172
Pareto optimality, 124
Partners for Democratic Change, 15
PeaceWeb, 7
Pearson, J., 51, 57, 58
Peppet, S. R., 257
Persian Gulf, 295
Pew Charitable Trust, 159, 280
Policy critiques, 43–48
Political critiques, 43–48
Positions, interests versus, 125–129
Powell, C., 92, 108
Power: mediators with, 108–111; using,
   263–264
Practitioner, conflict resolution: definition
   of, 9–21; expanded role for, 15–17;
   role of, in major conflicts, 13–15;
   what, offers, 21
Process, focus on, 37
Professional identity, 109–110
Promise of Mediation (Bush and Folger), 190
Public: resistance to what practitioner
   offers, 22–23; six needs of, that cannot
   be met by mediation or consensus-
   building processes, 23–29; what,
   wants, 21–29
Public policy, 60–66

Q

Quakers, 151

R

Rabin, Y., 143
Racism, 171–174

Raiffa, H., 257
Rand Corporation, 52
Relationships, 138–141
Research, lukewarm results of, 55–59
Resistance: direct, 90–91; indirect, 89–90
Resolution: from engagement to,
   212–214; from, to engagement,
   119–120; limit of, 176–178; trap,
   182–184
Respect, versus anger, 133–135
Rifkin, J., 52
Right approaches, 263–264
Roberts Rules of Order, 54, 263
Robson, M., 73
Roman Catholic Church, 162
Ross, D., 110
Ross, M. G., 225
Rothman, J., 76, 182

S

Sabatier, P. A., 58–59, 64
Sadat, A., 84, 143
Safety, 28
Saunders, H., 4
Schiff, M., 276
Schneider, A. K., 257, 258
Schwartz, W., 278
Search for Common Ground, 15
Sebenius, J., 35, 198, 224, 257, 270
Seeber, R. L., 73
Senge, P. M., 72–73
September 11 terrorist attacks, 109
Sexism, 171–174
Shaffer, M., 52
Sherman, L., 57
Sierra Club, 43
Silbey, S. S., 24, 76
Smith, M., 58
Social change: and confronting hierarchi-
   cal institutions, 168–169; and preserv-
   ing democracy, 167–168; and
   providing optimism, 169–170
Social conflict, essential value of, 175
Social control: and defining of issue,
   165–166; and displacing energy,
   164–165; and mediator as part of prob-
   lem, 166–167; and privatization of
   issue, 161–162; and reinforcing
   inequality, 162–163
Social movement, conflict resolution as,
   150–155

Society of Professionals in Dispute Resolution, 153
Solomon, King, 156
Southern Christian Leadership Conference, 197
Strang, H., 57, 276
Strategist, advocate as, 253
Student Nonviolent Coordinating Committee, 197
Substantive influence, 135–138
System: adaptive, 200–202; conflict as, 200; focus on, 37; roles, 243–247

T

Talmud, 263
Taylor, A., 232
Tessler, P. H., 276
Third party, 83–84, 116–118; and being ally, 240–243; conflict engagement and, 238–240. *See also* Neutrality
*Third Side, The* (Ury), 116, 172
*Thirteen Days* (New Line Cinema), 35
Thoennes, N., 51, 57
Thomas, K. W., 35, 195
Thorson, S., 191
Toronto, 97
Total Quality Management (TQM), 73
Track II initiatives, 14
Transformation, 190–193
Tulumello, A. S., 257
Twain, M., 156

U

Uniform Mediation Act, 141
United Kingdom, 67
United Nations, 88, 208
United States Army Corps of Engineers, 74
United States Department of Agriculture, 61, 72

United States Department of Fish and Game, 61
United States Department of Justice, 159
United States Department of the Interior, 5, 72
United States Environmental Protection Agency, 50
United States Postal Service (USPS), 57, 72
United States Rules of Engagement, 36
Ury, W. L., 4, 10, 22, 35, 48, 116, 117, 125, 172, 173, 263
U.S. Conciliation Service, 159
User perspectives, 59–77

V

Valchev, R., 227
Validation, 26
Vindication, 25–26
Voice, 23–24

W

Walton, R. W., 35, 195
Welsh, N. A., 24, 53, 56, 70, 113
Wheeler, L., 52, 53
Wildau, S., 227
Williams, G. R., 257, 258
Win-win solutions, 123–125
Wissler, R. L., 21, 41, 56–58
Woodrow, P., 58
Woods, D. J., 57

Y

Yellowstone National Park, 65

Z

Zylstra, A., 71